IMAGES
of America

GARZA COUNTY

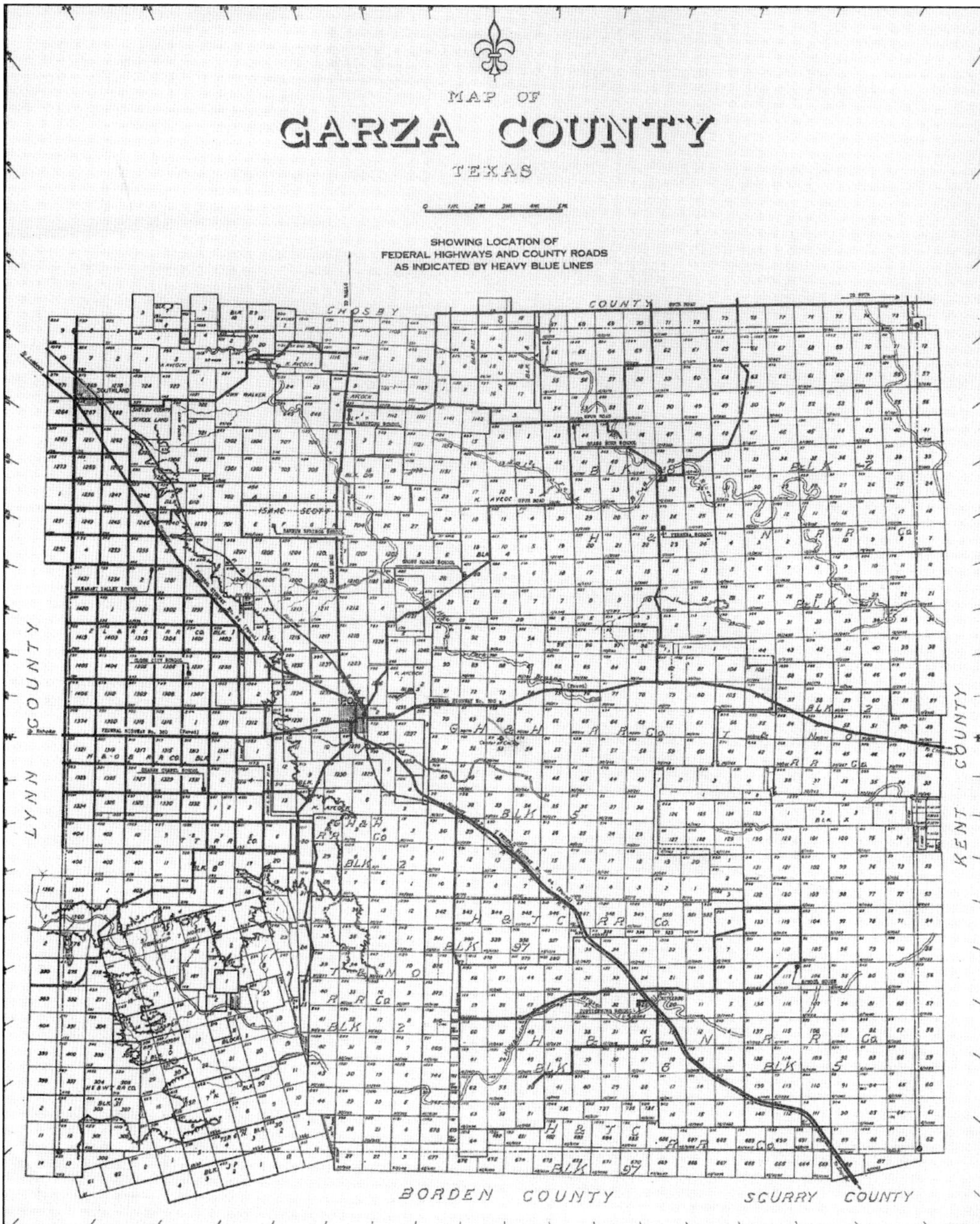

This map of Garza County, Texas, provides a visual concept of the locations of the Caprock Escarpment, Brazos River, and the junction of U.S. Highways 84 and 380. (Courtesy Garza County Historical Museum archives.)

On the Cover: OS cowboys make a striking pose near the old ranch headquarters in 1898. The cowboys are, from left to right, O. B. Kelley, Joe Smith, Bud Boren, Hal McCarty, Will Williams, and Bud Marable. (Courtesy Garza County Historical Museum archives.)

IMAGES
of America

GARZA COUNTY

Linda Puckett and the
Garza County Historical Museum

ARCADIA
PUBLISHING

ISBN 978-0-7385-7909-2

Published by Arcadia Publishing
Charleston SC, Chicago IL, Portsmouth NH, San Francisco CA

Printed in the United States of America

Library of Congress Control Number: 2009943764

For all general information contact Arcadia Publishing at:
Telephone 843-853-2070
Fax 843-853-0044
E-mail sales@arcadiapublishing.com
For customer service and orders:
Toll-Free 1-888-313-2665

Visit us on the Internet at www.arcadiapublishing.com

To the early pioneer families who settled Garza County,
and to the brave men and women of the United States armed services
who serve, protect, and make the ultimate sacrifice for our freedom.

Contents

Acknowledgments

The Garza County Historical Museum has existed since 1972, when a group of wonderful people known as the Garza County Historical Survey Committee put together the meager beginnings of a museum. They also placed historical markers all over the county. Their early research on historic places and events has become a valuable tool for me. Most committee members are gone now, but their dedication is well remembered.

In 1995, my friend JoAnn Mock hired me as director of the museum. And for 16 years, I have been on a mission to preserve a massive 8,500-square-foot historic building while attempting to make the Garza County Historical Museum into a conservatory of the history of Garza County. I am having the greatest time of my life. By museum standards, we are classified as a small museum, but we know we are a large museum in a small town. So thank you, JoAnn, for believing I could do it. Special thanks to Garza County Commissioners Court for supporting us all through the years. Thank you Post-Montgomery and all the donors who make this all possible. All photographs in this publication are from the archives of the Garza County Historical Museum unless otherwise noted.

Thanks to my trusted sidekick, Pat Cruse, who has assisted me in every aspect of this book. I think my dreams have rubbed off on her, for she is as energized as I am and is always ready to go that extra mile to succeed.

I especially want to thank our history makers, who have left us both a wealth of knowledge that sustained them through the tough times and the joy they found along the way. We are honored that their descendants trust us with family heirlooms, photographs, and with written and oral histories that allow us to experience some of their journeys.

Sincere thanks to Arcadia Publishing for allowing us to tell the story of Garza County, Texas. I only hope we have told it well. Remember, today becomes history tomorrow, and Garza County is collectively working on its 103rd year.

INTRODUCTION

For two centuries, the Native American people roamed the South Plains amid herds of buffalo and grasslands. History shows that as the white settlers came to the area they provoked the rage of the Comanche and Kiowa tribes, resulting in fierce retaliation and loss of life. Treaties between the whites and the natives failed, prompting the U.S. army to begin a merciless campaign against all Native Americans who defied confinement on reservations. The vast herds of buffalo were the life source for all Native Americans on the plains, providing food, clothing, and lodging. Then along came the white buffalo hunters, who slaughtered the buffalo, selling their hides and tongues for a price and leaving their carcasses to rot on the prairie. Gen. Philip Sheridan stated, "Let them kill, skin and sell until the buffalo is exterminated, as it is the only way to bring lasting peace and allow civilization to advance." It depends on which side of the fence you stand on whether the process of the natives' demise was right or wrong. Surely we have learned that it is the nature of man to fight against those who take away one's land and livelihood. This was a tragic end for one era but just the beginning of another.

Garza County, Texas, is as unique as it is beautiful. The county consists of 914 square miles with portions in the north reaching the Llano Estacado and partly into the breaks of the lower plains. The Cap Rock Escarpment weaves its way from north to south on the west side of the county and the Brazos River on the east, each creating phenomenal landscapes that only nature could provide. Garza County was formed from Bexar County in 1876, just one year after Quanah Parker led his Quahadi clan to Fort Sill, Oklahoma, surrendering on June 2, 1875.

The Texas legislators named Garza County in honor of the de la Garza family of San Antonio, Texas. Jose Antonio de la Garza, son of Leonardo de la Garza, became one of the wealthiest landowners in Bexar County, with holdings that lay near the San Antonio and Medina Rivers. Garza was the first person to mint money in Texas, a coin with his initials JAG–1818 on one side and a lone star on the flip side. Some say this may have inspired the use of the lone star symbol of Texas.

During the period of open range in the 1880s, the census recorded a population of only 36 people in the county, mostly cowhands and landowners of the ranches operated in the area, many owned by cattle companies from Missouri and Kansas. The first ranch of record was owned by the Lexington Cattle Company of Lexington, Missouri, located in the southeast part of the county. By 1900, the population had grown to 180, with only 534 acres in cultivation.

The county was created in 1876, but 30 years would pass before it became organized. All judicial matters were handled in the adjoining county of Borden. In 1906, area ranchers, including cereal magnate C. W. Post, cowboys, and early settlers gathered for a picnic at the OS Ranch. A petition was created and signed by those in attendance to put in motion the organization of the county. A Texas historical marker stands at the OS Ranch commemorating this event. Legend has it that 65 names were needed to charter the county and that even the horses voted. The reality is, according to Borden County court documents, the petition was presented to the court on May 13, 1907, with 181 signatures and no hoof prints. C. W. Post had a vested interest in organizing the county, for he planned to build a town that would become the county seat. The date of June 15, 1907, was set by the court for an election to be held in four locations: precinct no. 1 at Graham Chapel, precinct no. 2 at Davies School, precinct no. 3 at residence of J. B. Faulkner, and precinct no. 4 at the LeForest School. Garza County was finally organized, and the voters elected the first county officials to be sworn into office.

In the spring of 1906, C. W. Post, accompanied by his wife, Leila, and daughter, Marjorie, made a trip to Garza County to visit the Curry-Comb ranchland, traveling by train to Colorado City. They set out in hacks to make the 70-mile trip, stopping in Gail one night and arriving in the evening of the next day at the OS Ranch, where they were to stay. The Post family and associates were guests of honor at the infamous OS Picnic. Post gave a speech outlining his plans of colonizing, building a model town, bringing the railroad, and creating industries. Little did the attendees know they would be part of the shaping of progress for the next 100 years.

Post purchased the Curry-Comb Ranch, consisting of 112,577 acres, from the Llano Cattle Company; another 47,749 acres from Slaughter Ranch; 27,175 acres from the OS Ranch; and other smaller parcels of land. By January 1907, Post had acquired 189,101 acres in Garza and Lynn Counties and additional lands in Hockley for a total of 231,324 acres.

One

Landscapes to Latigos

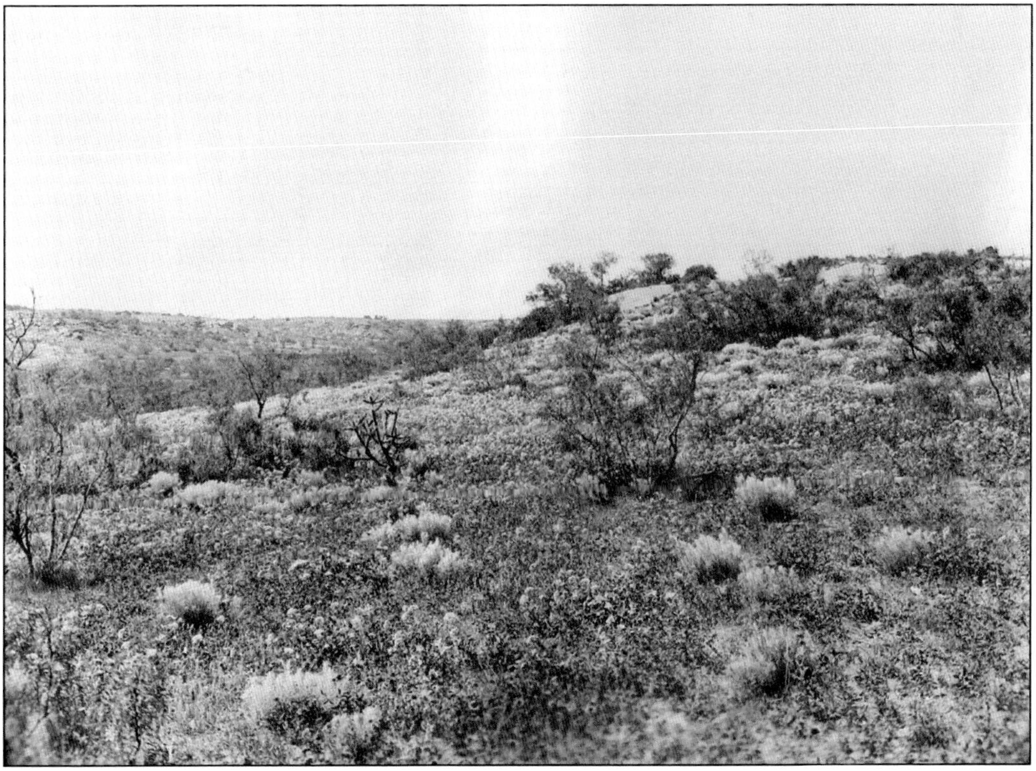

This beautiful landscape is called Lavender Hill. Springtime in Garza County is a sight to behold. Wildflowers line the roadways and pastures, and even grow out of rock formations, luring photographers to capture the scene. A stroll through the rocky terrain discloses intoxicating flower fragrances—some smell like grape Kool-Aid—but caution is necessary to not miss that rattlesnake sunning on a rock.

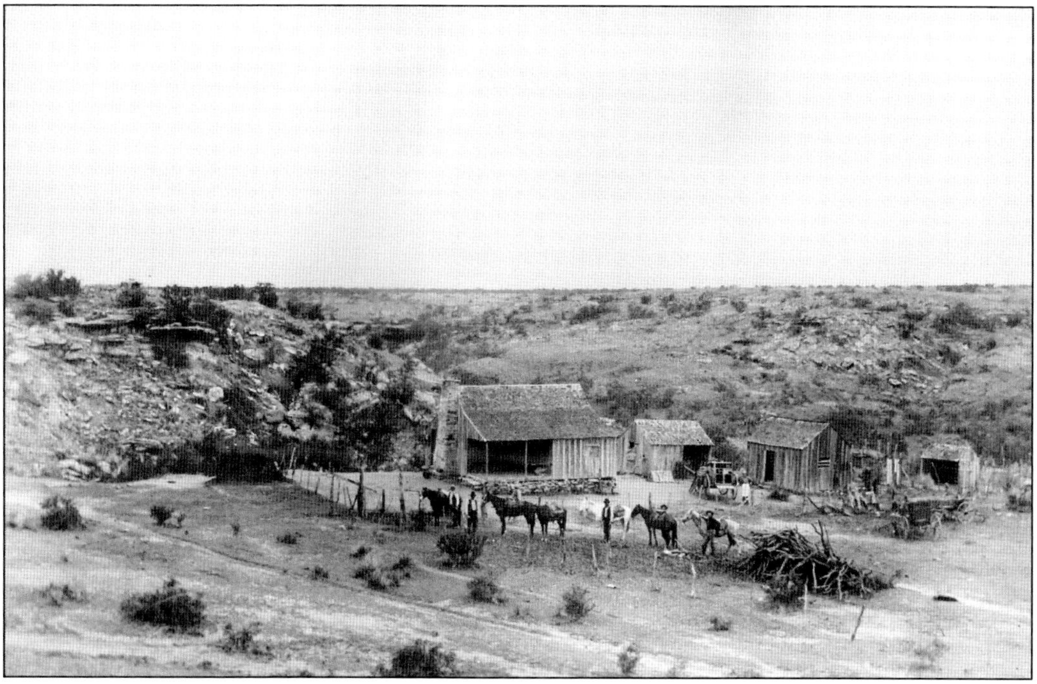

In the c. 1898 image above is the old OS Ranch headquarters, the former 202. It is now the Cross H Ranch, owned by Giles W. Dalby, great-grandson of W. E. Connell. The first cattle ranch of record operated in the southeast portion of Garza County and was known as the Lexington Cattle Company. In June 1901, partners W. E. Connell, John Scarborough, and E. W. Clark purchased the holdings of the Long brothers, consisting of 26,411 acres, for $40,000. They also bought 9,500 head of cattle, 312 bulls, 118 head of horses, and all wagons, tack, and camp gear at an additional cost of $200,239.25. The new owners continued buying land until their holdings reached 100,000 acres. The photograph below shows the OS Ranch house, built in 1901.

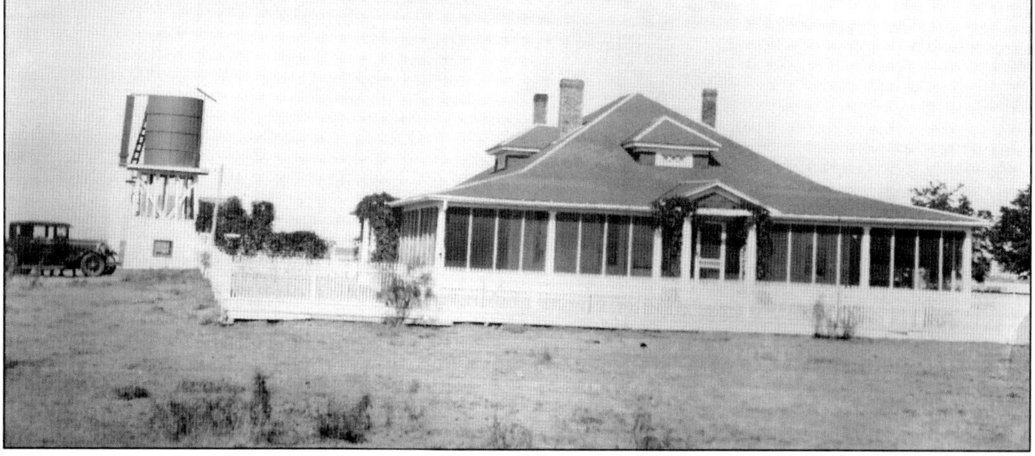

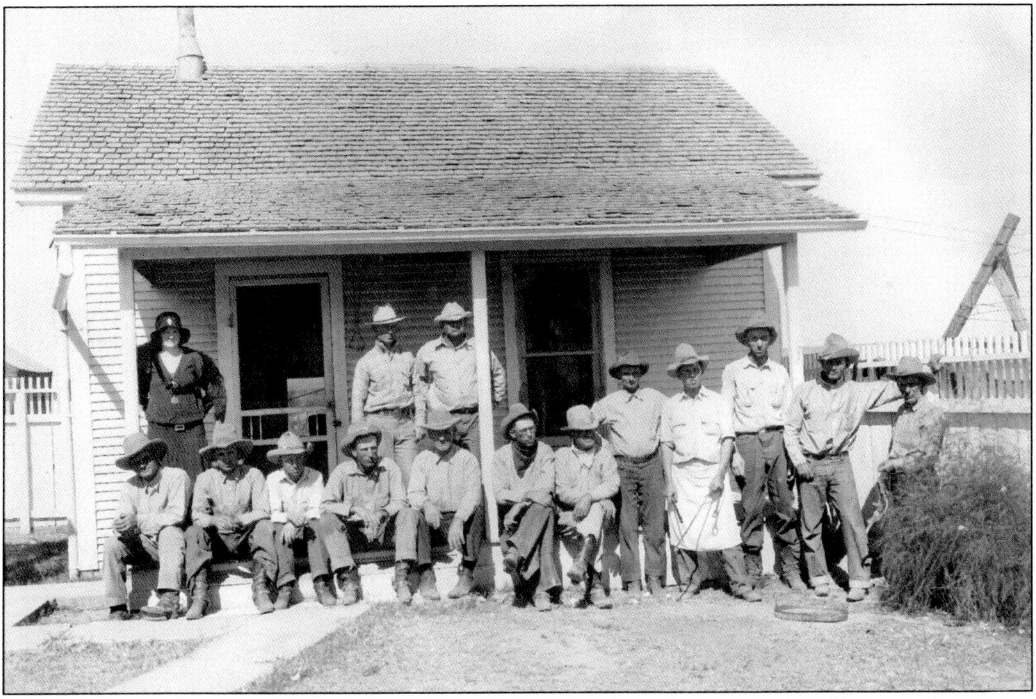

In front of the OS Ranch bunkhouse in 1928 are, from left to right, (first row) George Duckworth, Pete Kennedy, Blondy Awalt, Cecil Smith, Cap Roy, Add Jones, G. W. Connell, Jimmy Miller, L. P. Kennedy, Bob Callis, Morris Neff, and Ed Scott; (standing on porch) Gussie Connell, Lewis Coleman, and Wilson Connell.

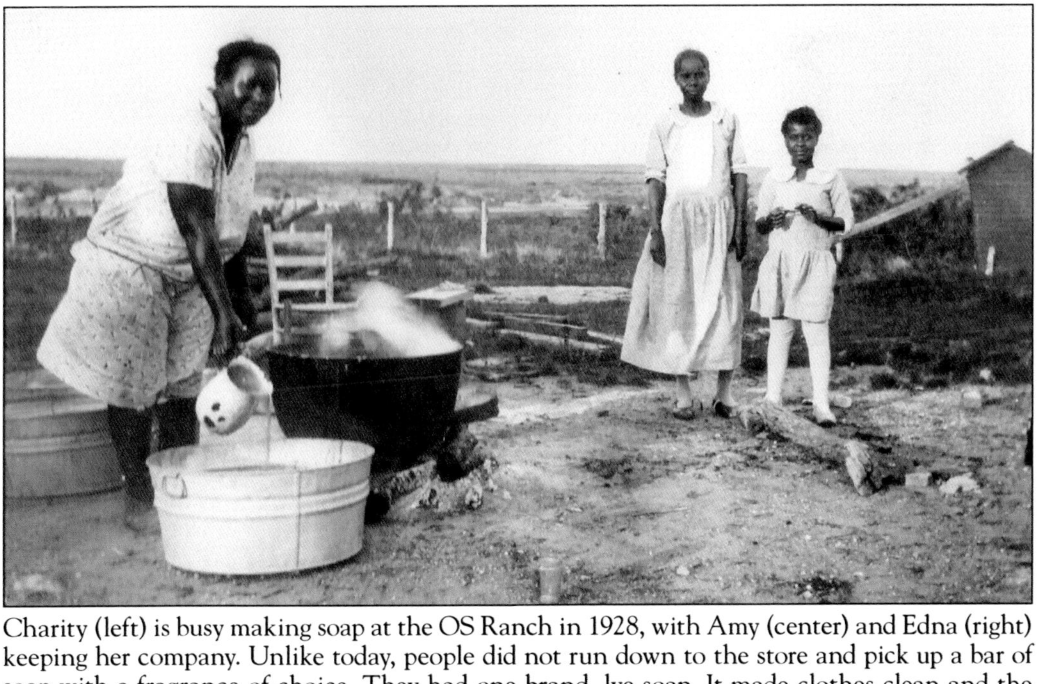

Charity (left) is busy making soap at the OS Ranch in 1928, with Amy (center) and Edna (right) keeping her company. Unlike today, people did not run down to the store and pick up a bar of soap with a fragrance of choice. They had one brand, lye soap. It made clothes clean and the whites a bright white. (Courtesy Giles Dalby.)

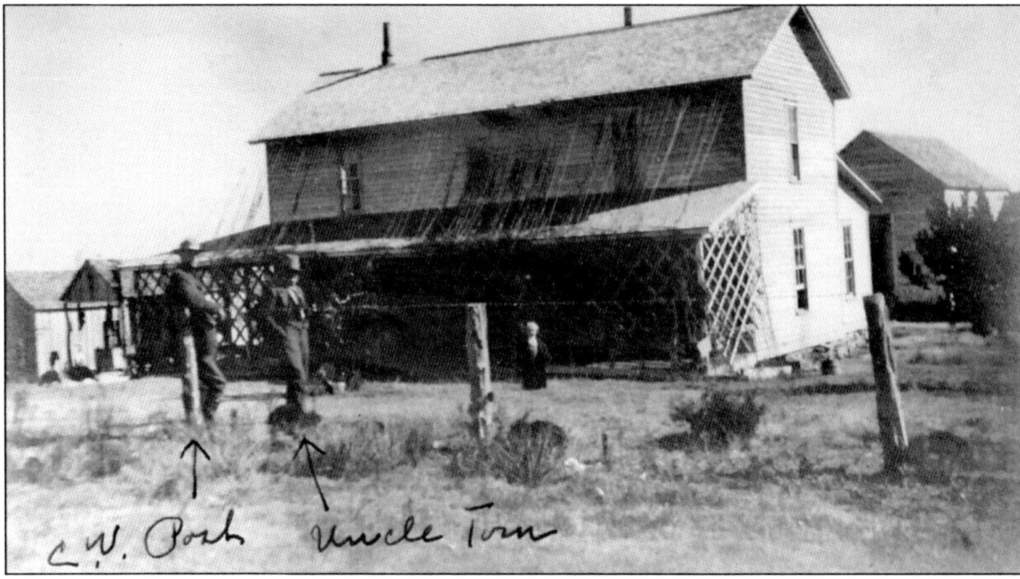

The Llano Ranch, later named the Curry-Comb Ranch, was the site of the last Native American raid in 1883. In the 1906 photograph above, C. W. Post (left) and Uncle Tom Stevens are seen standing at the fence, along with an unidentified child. Post purchased the Curry-Comb Ranch on June 9, 1906. Below is an old photograph of cowboys enjoying chuck at the wagon, probably taken after 1884, as the barbwire fence visible in the background would indicate. A cowboy's clothing has seen little change over time: a good hat, a pair of rugged jeans worn with a long sleeved shirt, a tough pair of boots, spurs, and chaps. A bandana is a must to wipe sweat, clean a wound, or just to keep from breathing trail dust. From left to right, the cowboys are ? McGraw of New York, Dennis Jones, three unidentified, Olen Hendrix, Perry Graham, Russell Wilks Sr., and Walter Jolley.

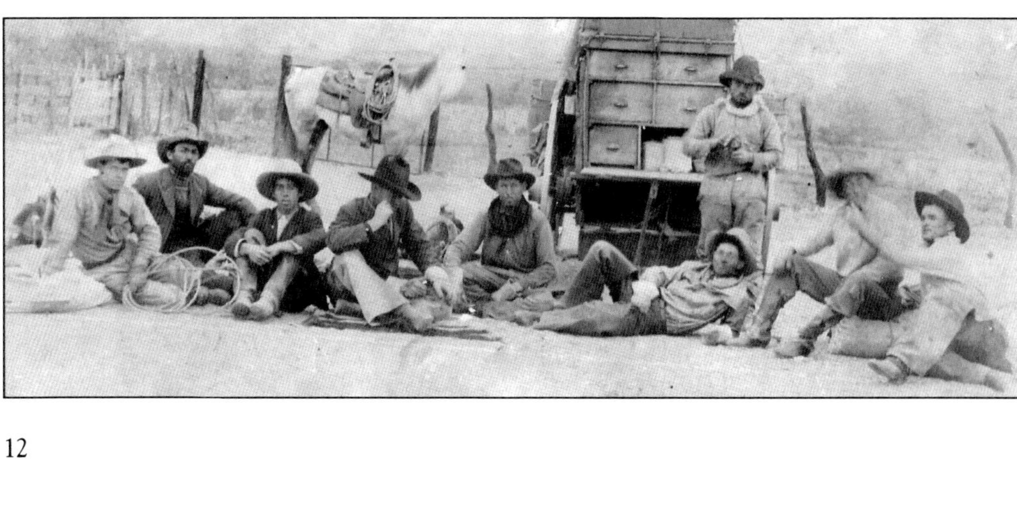

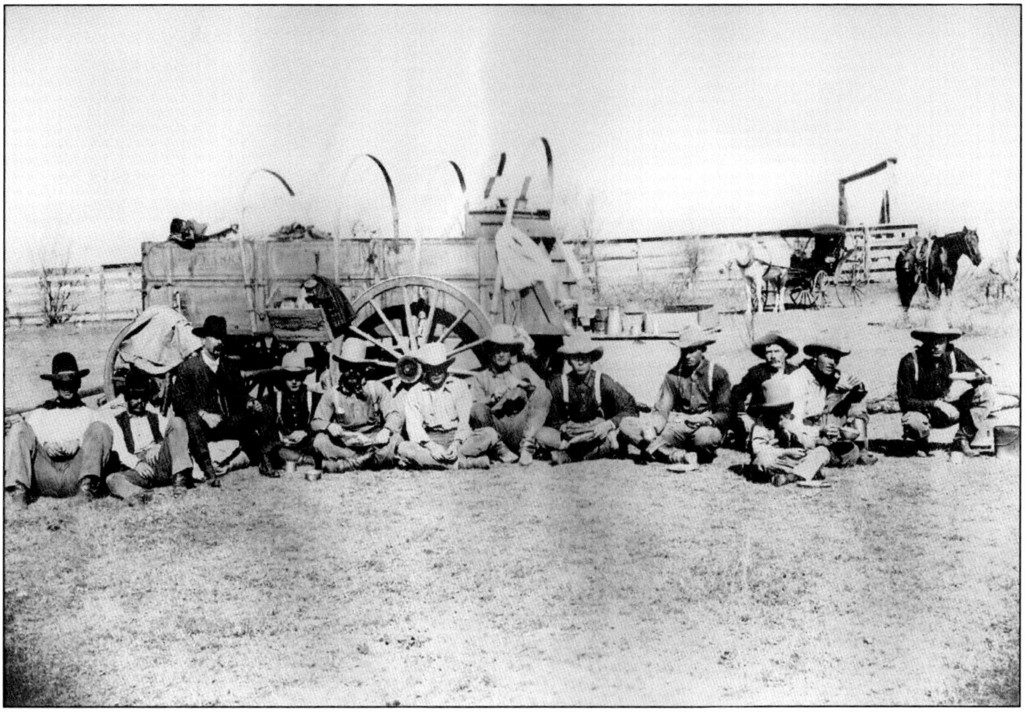

The group in the photograph above has just finished shipping OS cattle. They are having a little chuck and taking a rest before heading back to the ranch. From left to right, the cowboys are Cap Roy, Ed Scott, E. W. Clark, Elmore McCormick, Jim Chin, Russ Wilks, Joe Smith, Charley Callis, Lon Holloman, unidentified, William Wilks, Sam Wilks, and the lad seated in front is Ira Lee Duckworth. Pictured below is G. W. Connell on his horse, Smith.

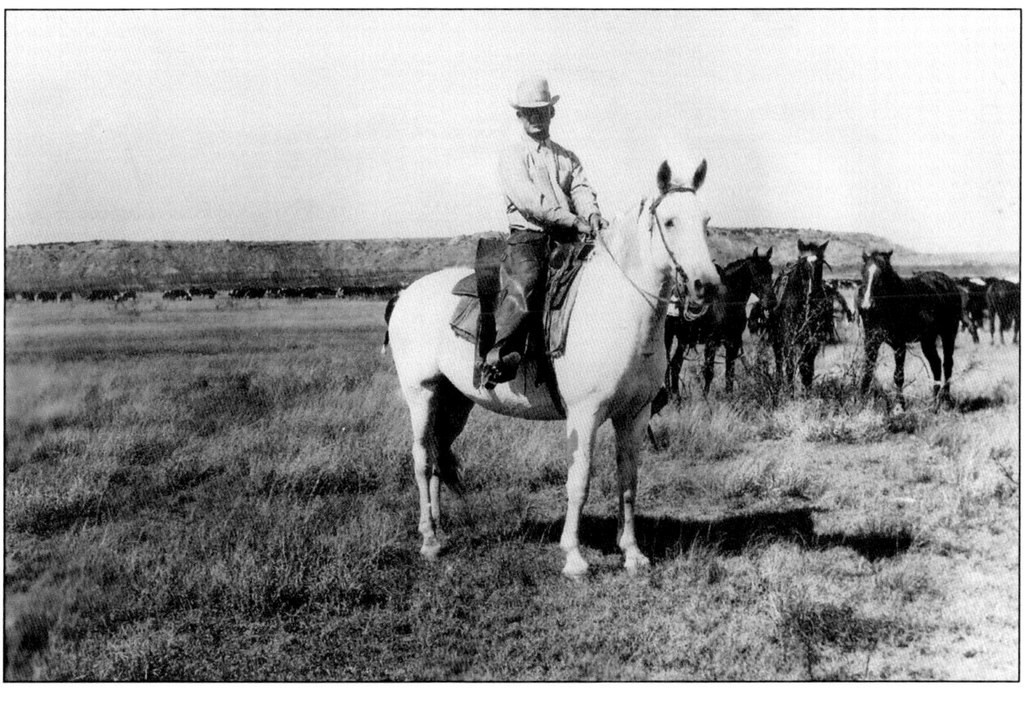

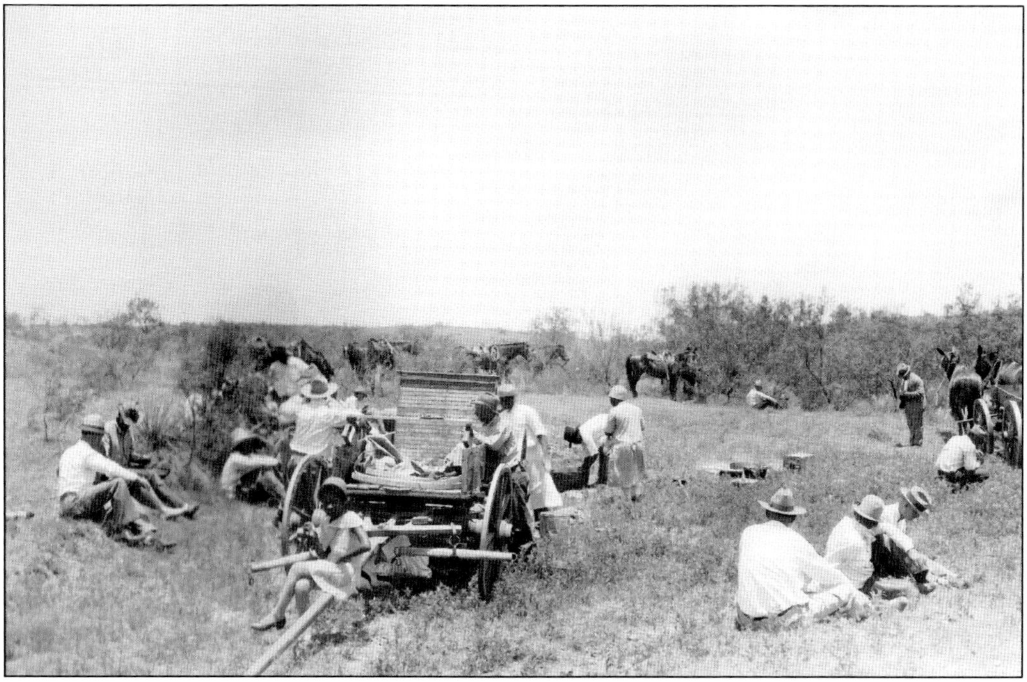

It appears to be visitors' day at the Green Tank roundup grounds. Guests seem well dressed for the occasion. Edna is posed on the wagon tongue, as her parents prepare a fine meal for all to enjoy.

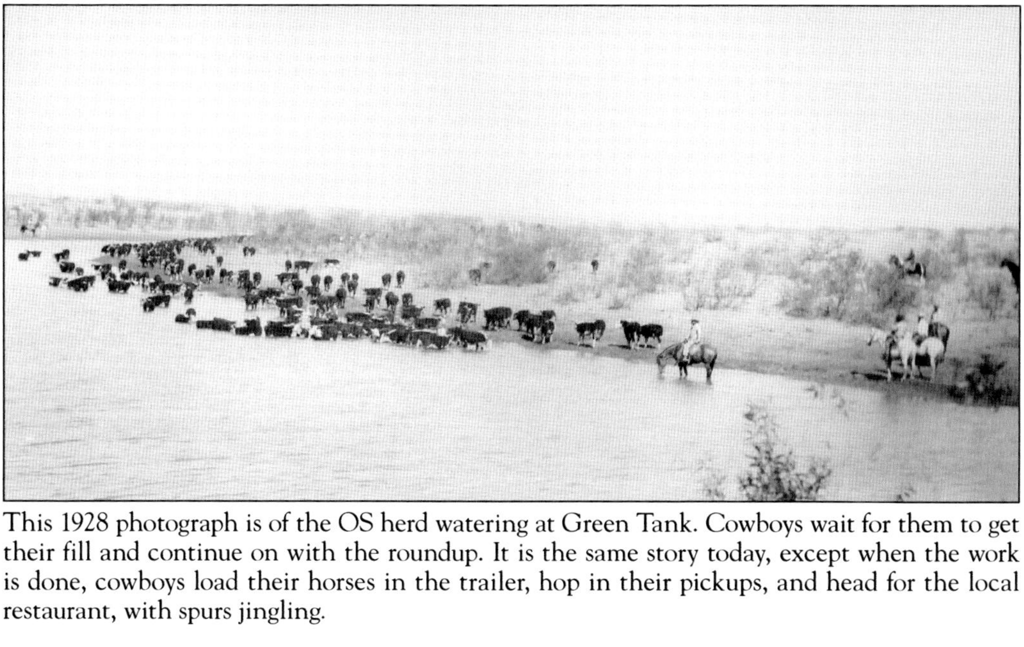

This 1928 photograph is of the OS herd watering at Green Tank. Cowboys wait for them to get their fill and continue on with the roundup. It is the same story today, except when the work is done, cowboys load their horses in the trailer, hop in their pickups, and head for the local restaurant, with spurs jingling.

This young man is Giles C. McCrary, grandson of W. E. Connell, owner of the OS Ranch. Giles lived in Fort Worth and would come by train during the summer to visit the ranch. In this photograph, he seems to be standing his ground at the ranch house. Giles is now the owner of this portion of the OS Ranch. (Courtesy Giles Dalby.)

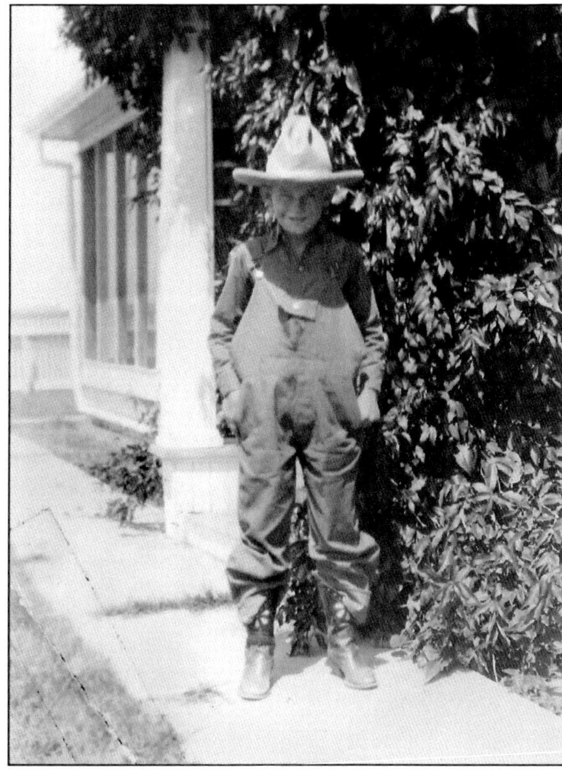

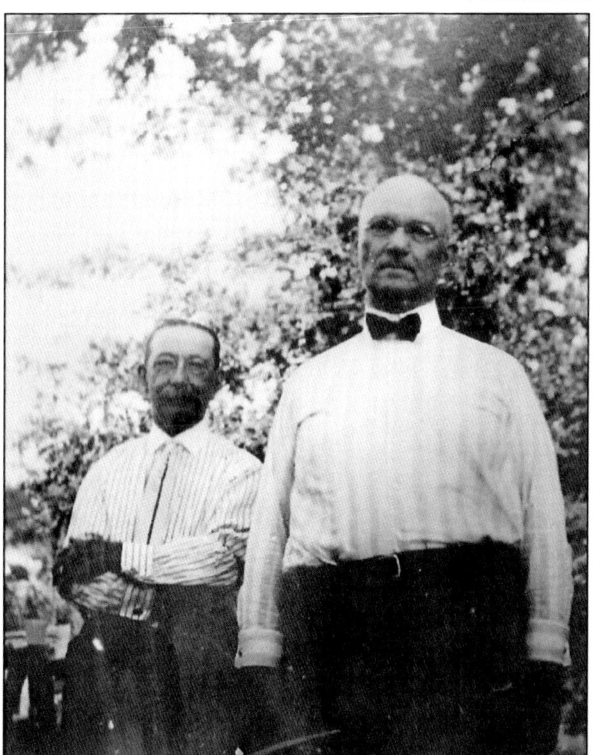

E. W. Clark (left) and W. E. Connell (right) were partners in the OS Ranch from 1901 until 1913, when Connell bought Clark's shares and became sole owner. W. E. Connell was a banker in Fort Worth but a rancher at heart. He once stated, "I'd rather have them [ranches] than all the rest of the things I own."

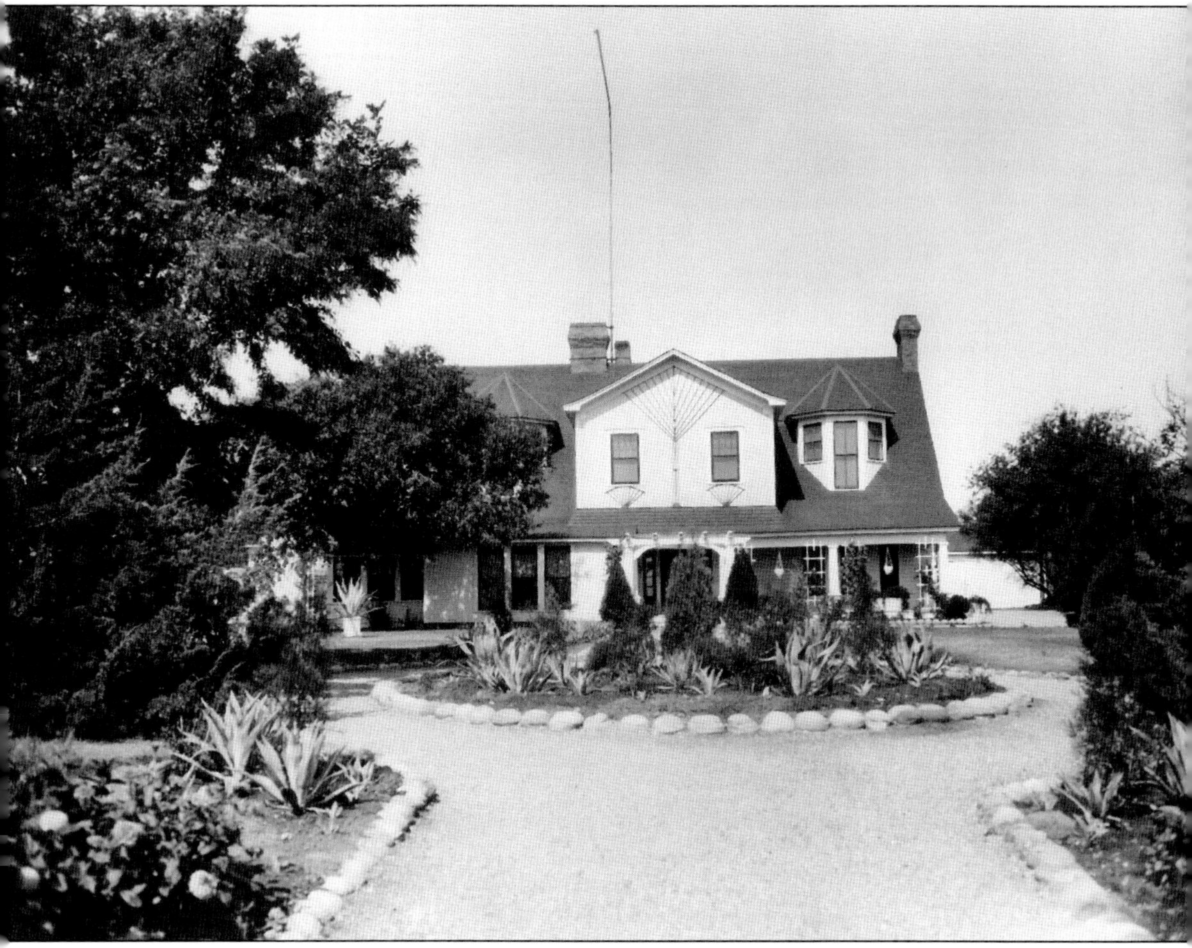

The Slaughter ranch house, a 20-room structure, was built in 1902. It was said to be the most beautiful residence in the West. John B. Slaughter came from a family of legendary cattlemen in Texas, who shaped his life from an early age; he earned that same status. Slaughter moved his brand, the U Lazy S, to Garza County in 1898. By 1901, he had purchased the Square and Compass Ranch—totaling 99,188 acres at a selling price of $1.60 per acre, including 5,000 head of cattle— from the Nave-McCord Cattle Company. By 1905, he had increased his holdings to 126,227 acres. In 1902, he moved his family to the ranch. Sadly, in 1937, a fire destroyed the ranch house. It was a tremendous loss of literature, art, furnishings, and family history.

John B. "Jay" Slaughter Jr. was born on July 18, 1891. He would go on to graduate from Yale University and take the reins of running the U Lazy S Ranch in 1928, following the passing of his father. Jay was active in the community, serving as president of the school board, organizing the Post Rotary Club, and was an active Mason. (Courtesy Southwest Collections.)

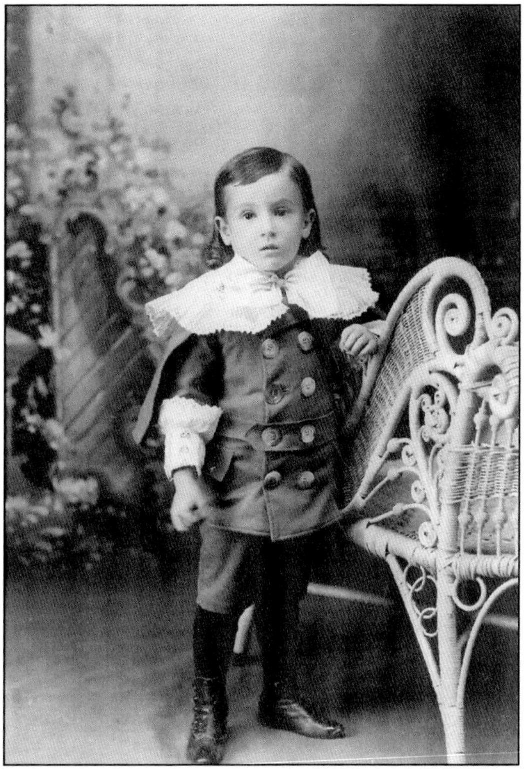

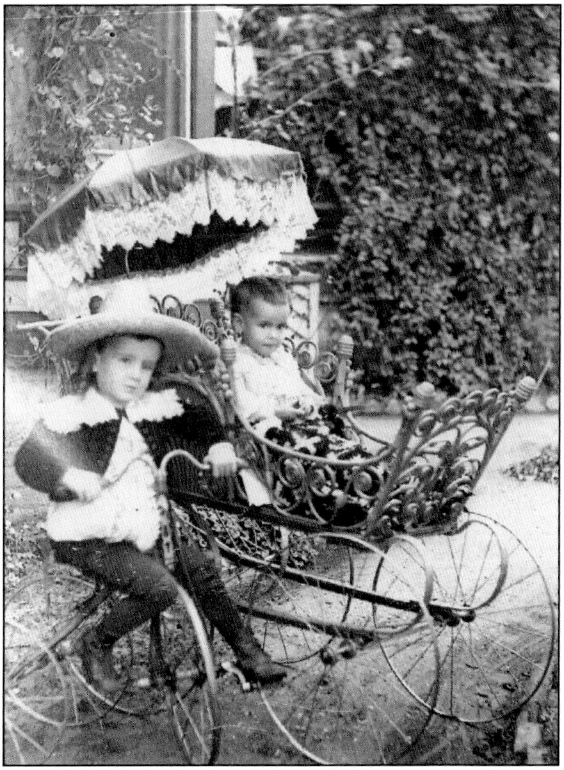

Jay Slaughter (left) and little sister Louie Antoinette Slaughter, born on July 21, 1894, appear to be ready for a stroll aboard their great-looking tricycle and carriage. (Courtesy Southwest Collections.)

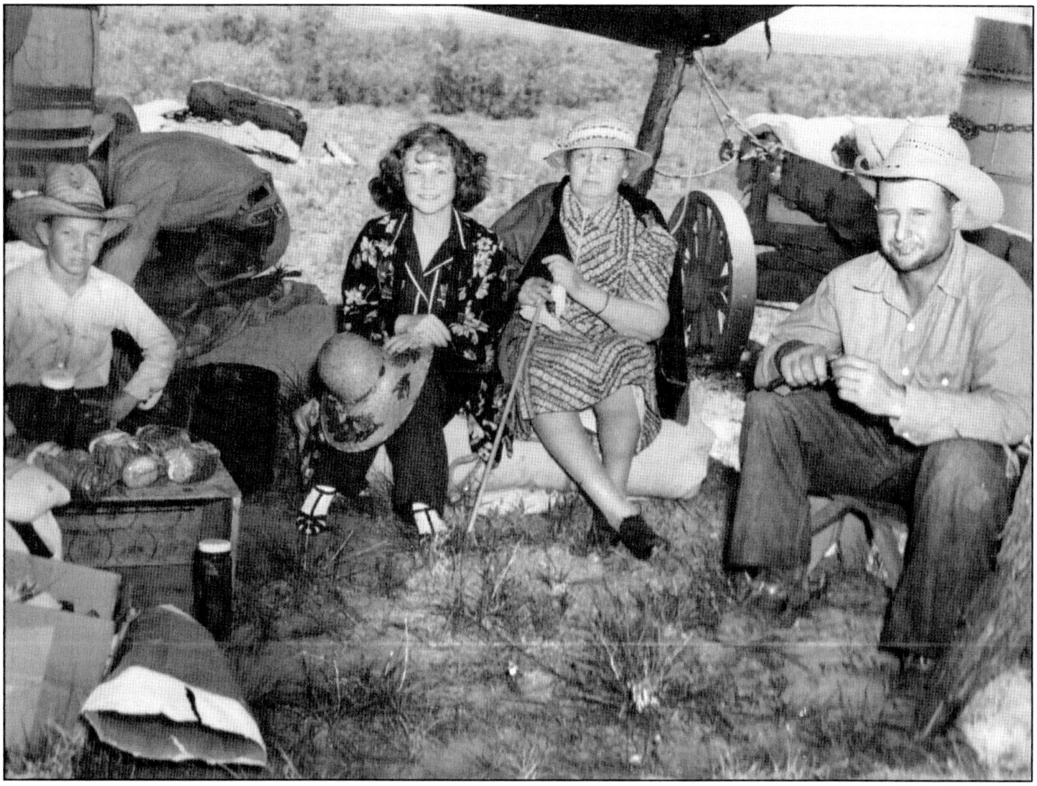

The Slaughter ladies pay a visit to the U Lazy S cowboys at the branding pens. Seeking a little shade at the chuck wagon are, from left to right, two unidentified, Skeeter Slaughter, Isabella Slaughter, and Henton Fluitt. (Courtesy Southwest Collections.)

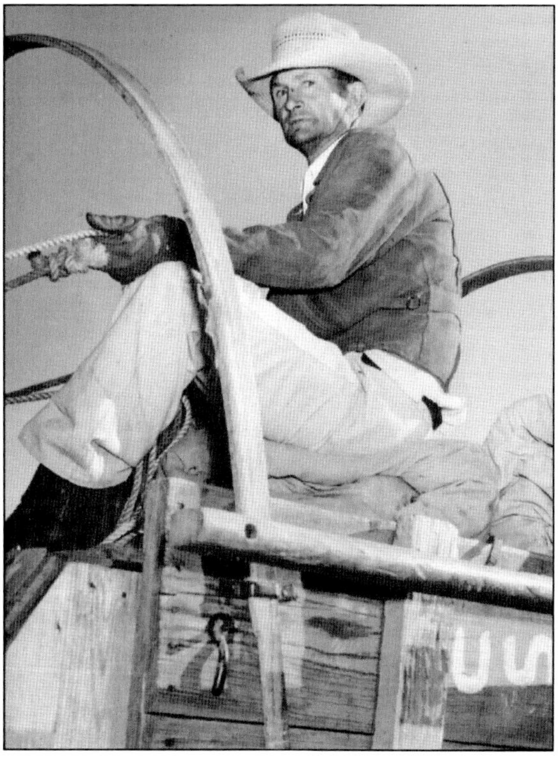

This 1940s photograph is of the Slaughter ranch chuck wagon, with the U Lazy S brand. The gentleman in charge of the wagon is unidentified. (Courtesy Southwest Collections.)

J. W. "Sally" Satterwhite came to Garza County the first time in 1897. He apparently relocated but returned in the fall of 1915, with his wife and three daughters to take on the job of foreman of the U Lazy S Ranch. The young man on the right is unidentified, but he is undoubtedly learning from Sally. (Courtesy Southwest Collections.)

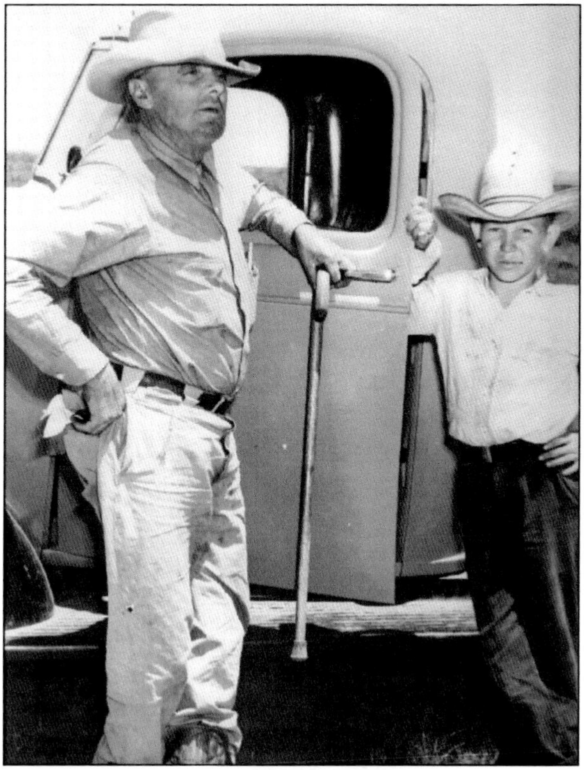

This 1900 photograph features cowboys from the Square and Compass Ranch. The two men wearing ties may well be the ranch's two owners, Abraham Nave and James McCord. The two were also wholesale grocers headquartered in St. Joseph, Missouri. Nave was a Master Mason, which may have influenced his decision to use the Masonic emblem as the ranch brand.

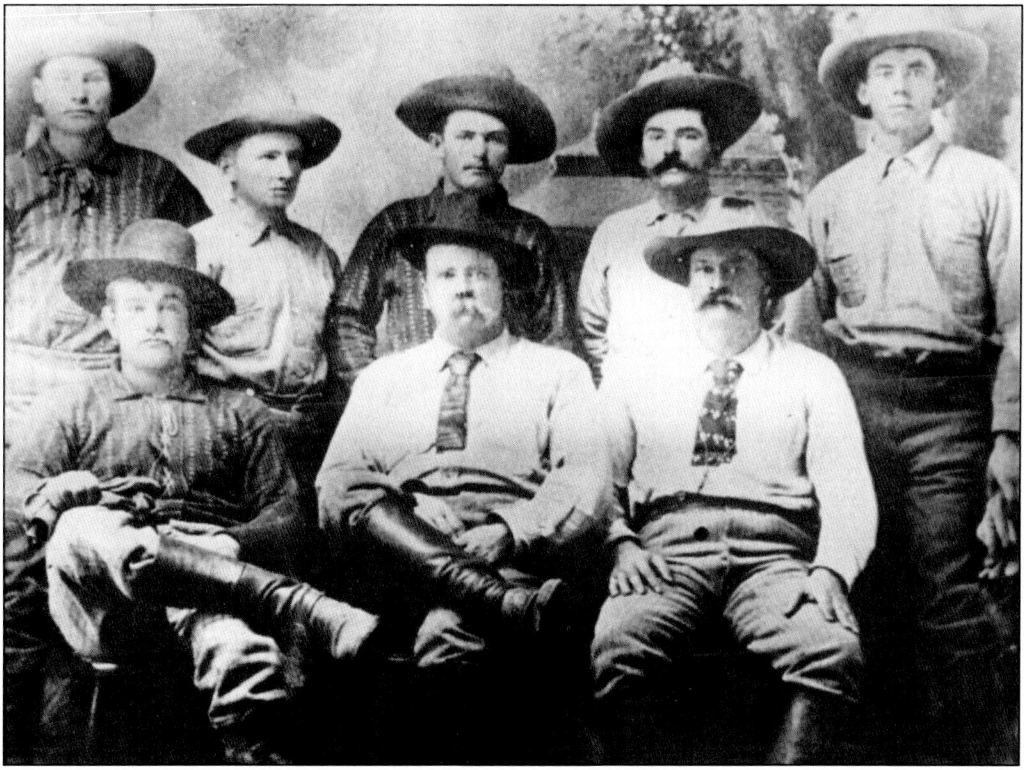

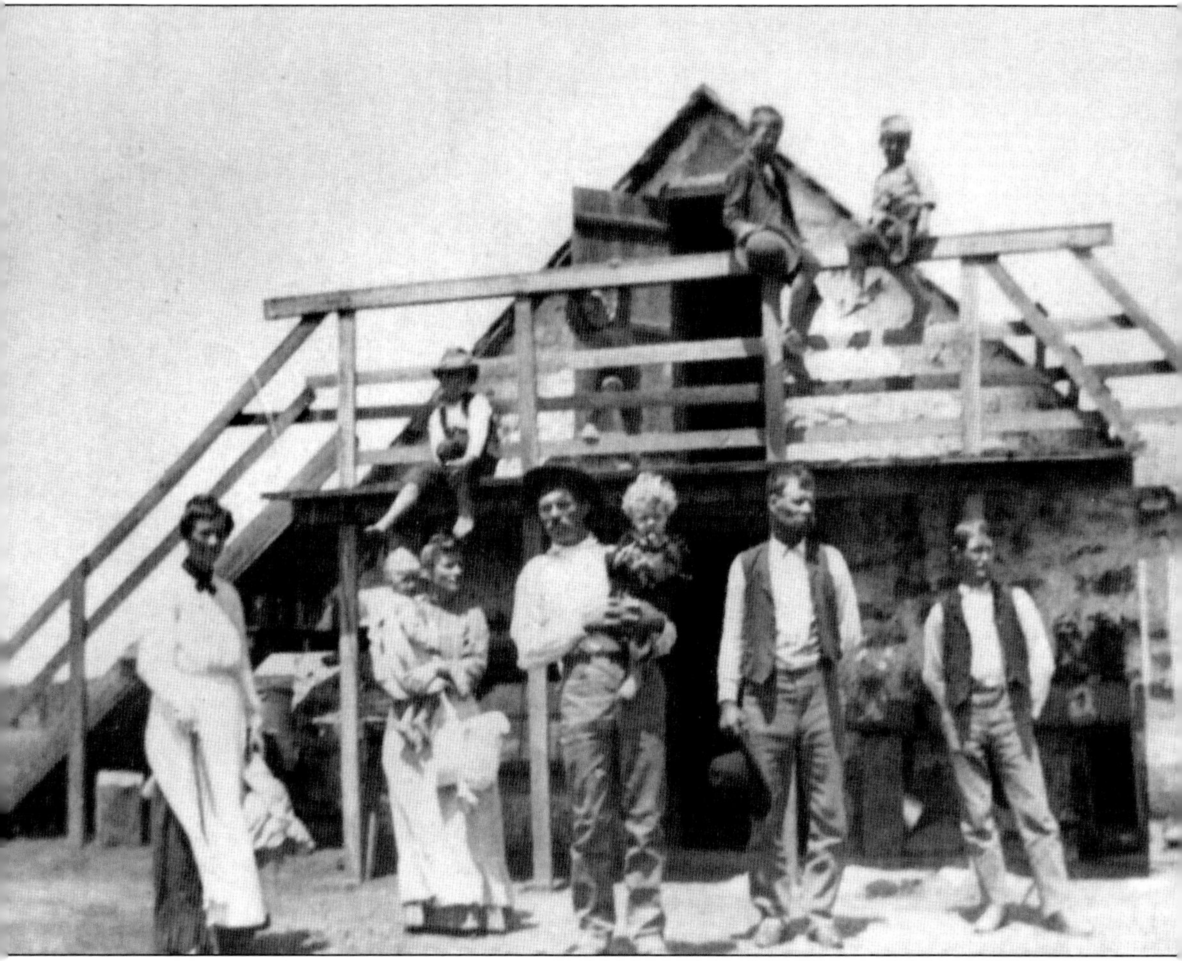

This is an early-1900s photograph of the Bird farm and ranch. Buelah Bird (second from left) told the story of how the family came to Garza County in a mule-drawn wagon and lived in a dugout with a dirt floor. The lumber to build the half-dugout had to be hauled from Colorado City. The upstairs attic had a bed, and the lower floor was used as a bedroom, living room, and kitchen, with a fireplace in the north end. Her story is amazing. When she was 86 years old, she lived alone on her little ranch 13 miles east of Post. She had a telephone, a good dog for company, and drove her car anywhere she wanted to go. When the old sanitarium was given to the county for a museum, she said," I hope I live to see this building as a museum with all the valuable antiques of this county put there, so the younger generation can see and relive the old days of their pioneer ancestors."

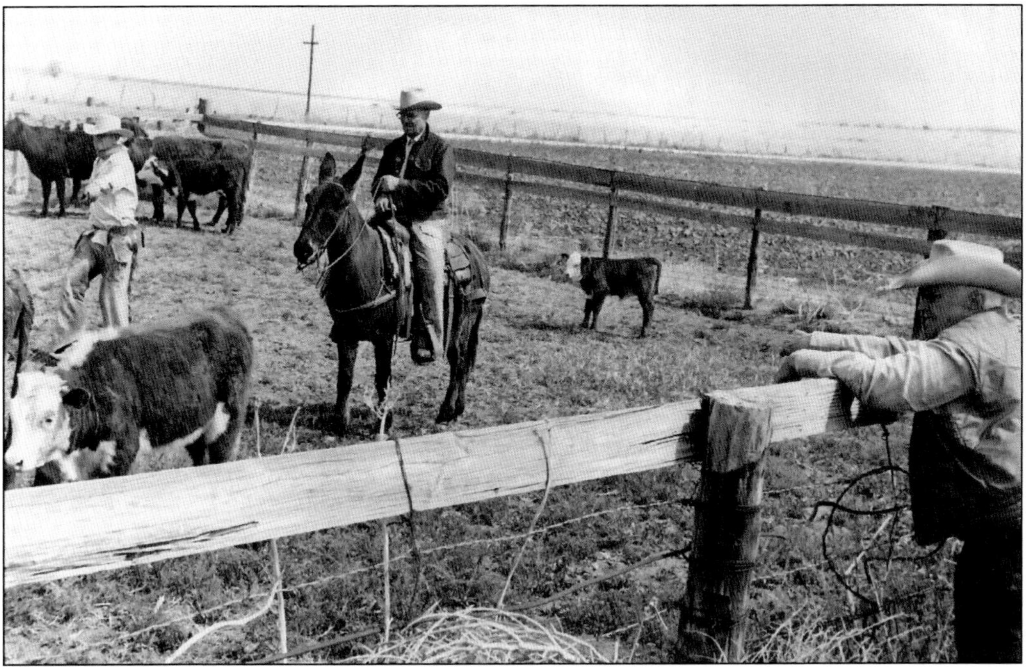

Working cattle at the Pearl and Ott Nance ranch at Justiceburg are Henry Key (left) and an unidentified man on a mule. Pearl Nance is leaning on the fence. She was as known to be as tough as the men and most certainly dressed the part. A family member once said that every morning Pearl went to the lot to feed the stock while Ott made breakfast.

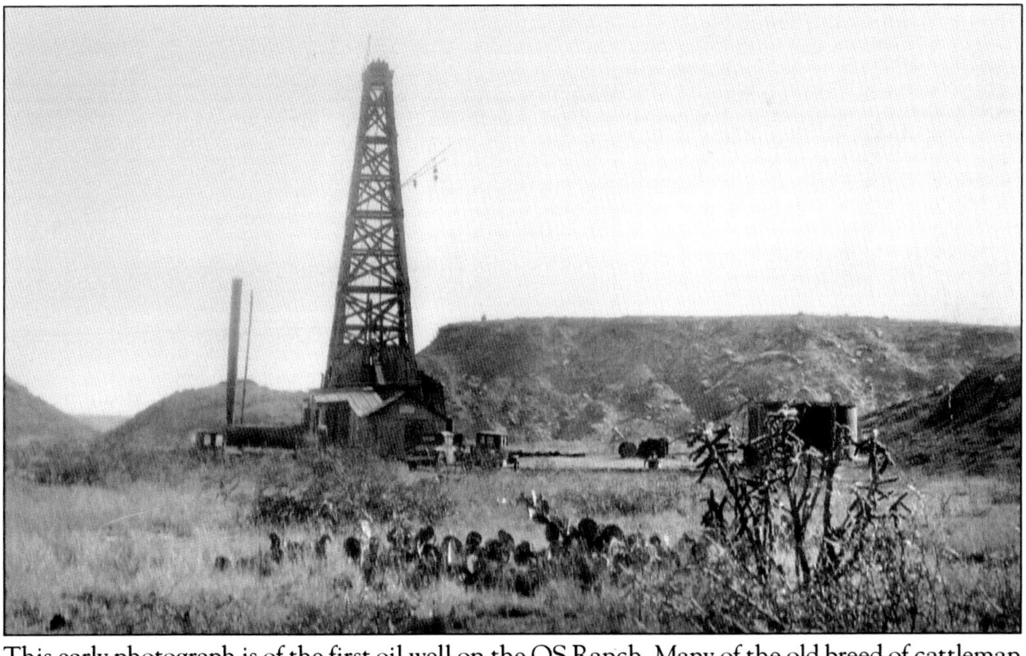

This early photograph is of the first oil well on the OS Ranch. Many of the old breed of cattleman were reluctant to have rigs drilling on their land and driving heavy loads across their pastureland. Oil would become a major industry in Garza County, a real godsend that would repair the damages left over by the Depression.

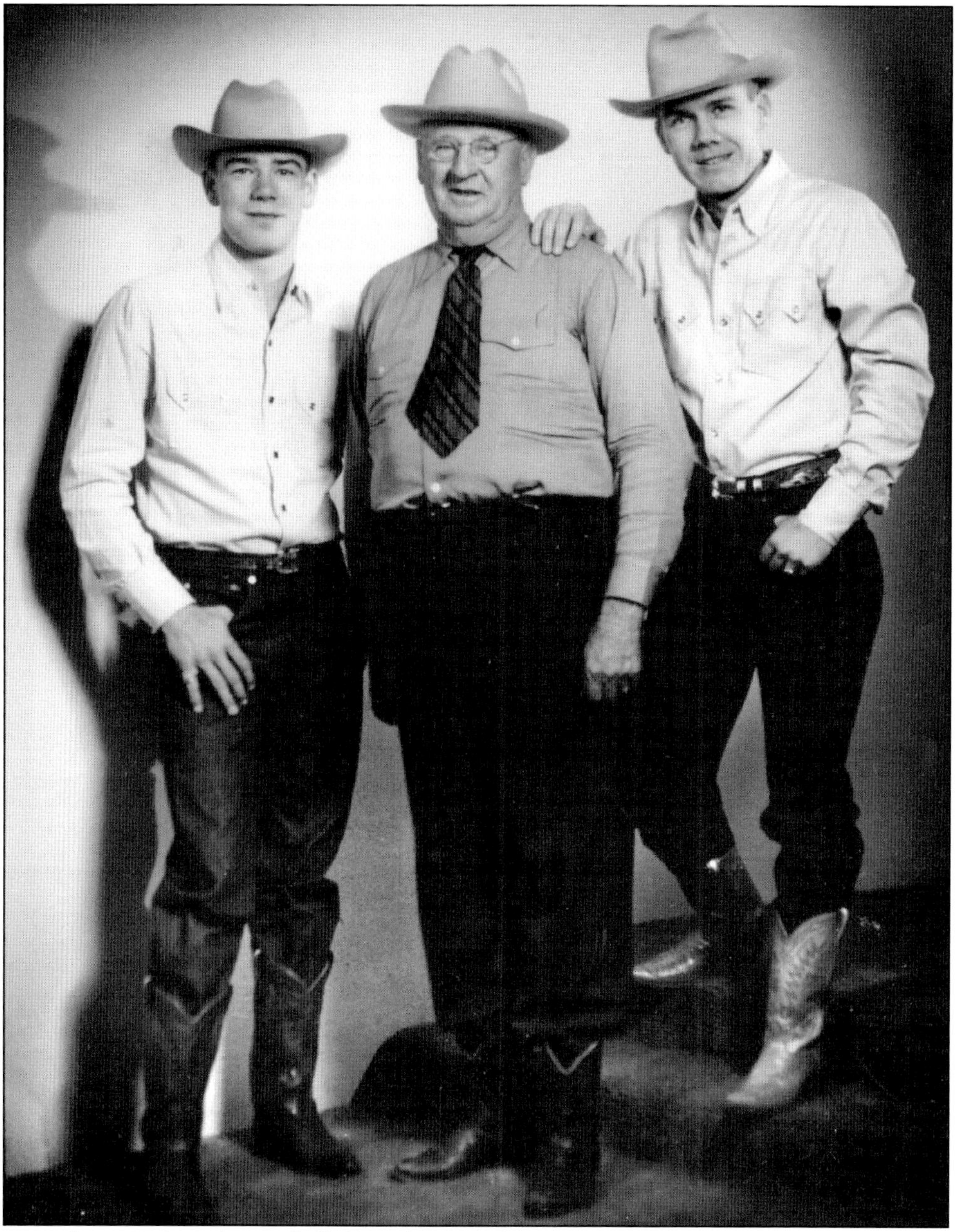

His grandsons Jack Kirkpatrick (left) and Kay Kirkpatrick (right) flank K. Stoker. The Stoker-Kirkpatrick ranch saga began in 1921, when brothers K. and J. B. Stoker found the West Texas ranch that they had been looking for. Both brothers married ladies from the same pioneer family in Breckenridge, Texas. In time, K. Stoker bought his brother's share of the ranch and continued acquiring more land. The family also maintained a home in Pomona, California. In 1927, their only daughter, Ruby Belle, married Willard Kirkpatrick. The newlyweds spent their honeymoon traveling to Garza County to reside in the new family ranch house 5 miles southeast of Post. Ruby said her father lived each day as though he would live forever, a man of determination and vision until his death at age 83. Lottie Stoker was a homemaker and ranch woman who could shoot a gun and ride a horse, when the occasion called for it.

Two

Gateway to the Plains

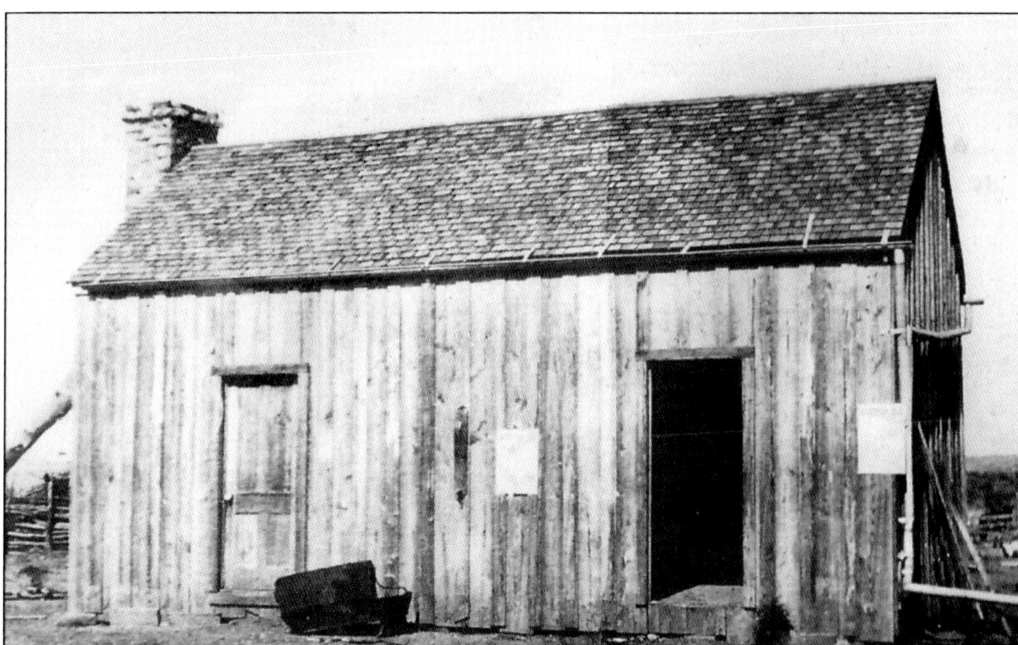

This 1906 photograph shows the OS bunkhouse, located at the old headquarters. It is rumored to be the site where the organizers' picnic occurred. Garza County was created in 1876, but 30 years would pass before it was organized. Until then, all judicial matters were handled in Gail, the seat of Borden County.

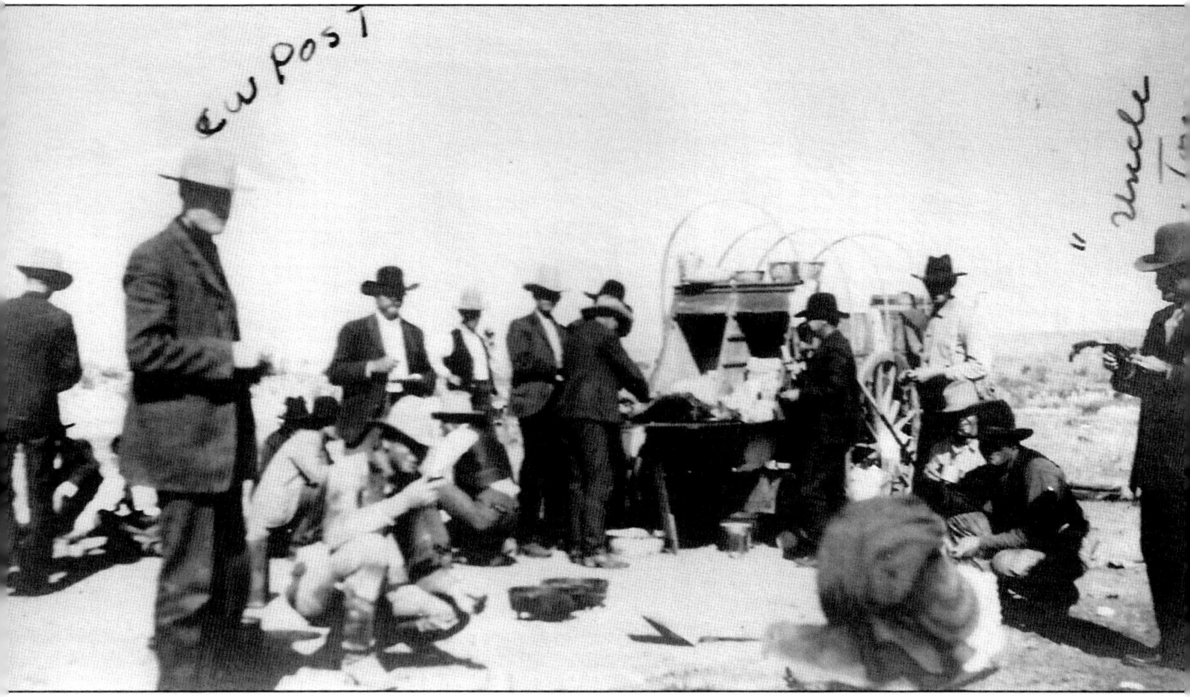

In 1906, area ranchers (including cereal magnate C. W. Post), cowboys, and early settlers all gathered at the OS Ranch. After the meal, Post was asked to speak. He wore black boots, silver spurs, and black corduroy trousers, with a maroon shirt and held a white Stetson hat in his hand. A Litwalton correspondent for the *Lynn County News* took notes. Post spoke to the crowd about his plans to build a town to be the county seat, as well as homes and a waterworks, and to bring electricity and industry. He also spoke of his endeavor to get the railroad to build through the new county. As a result, a petition was created and signed by those in attendance to put in motion the organization of the county. Interesting to note, there were many women present for the occasion, yet none of them signed the petition, only the men.

James M. Boren came to Garza County in 1898 and was elected county judge in 1907. The date of June 15, 1907, was set by the Borden County Court to organize Garza County by holding an election of county officials. The election was held, and the first officials of the newly organized county were sworn into office.

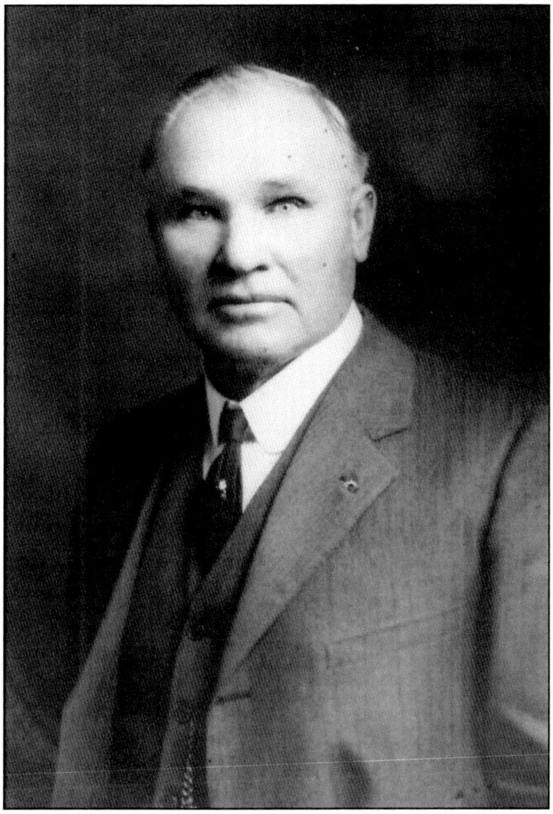

The county's first court was held July 15, 1907, somewhere out on the prairie; note the tent in the background. The old tent has survived more than 100 years and is now in the permanent collection of the museum. The commissioners' court voted to designate the northwest corner of the Double U building as the temporary location to conduct the county's business, with a rental fee of $5 per month.

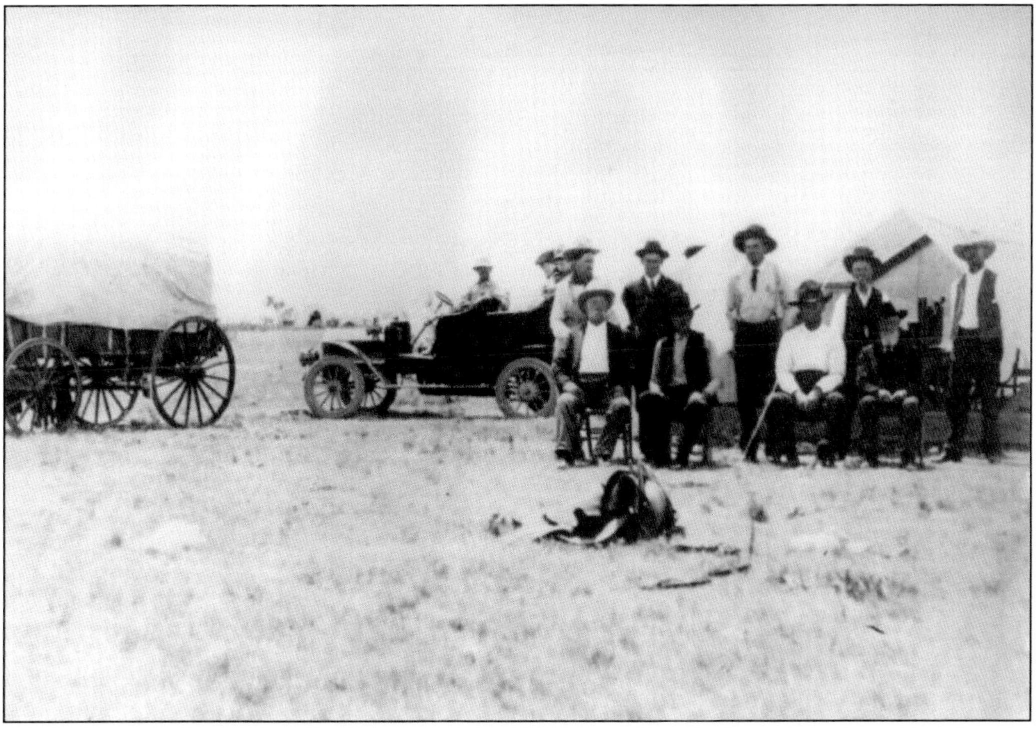

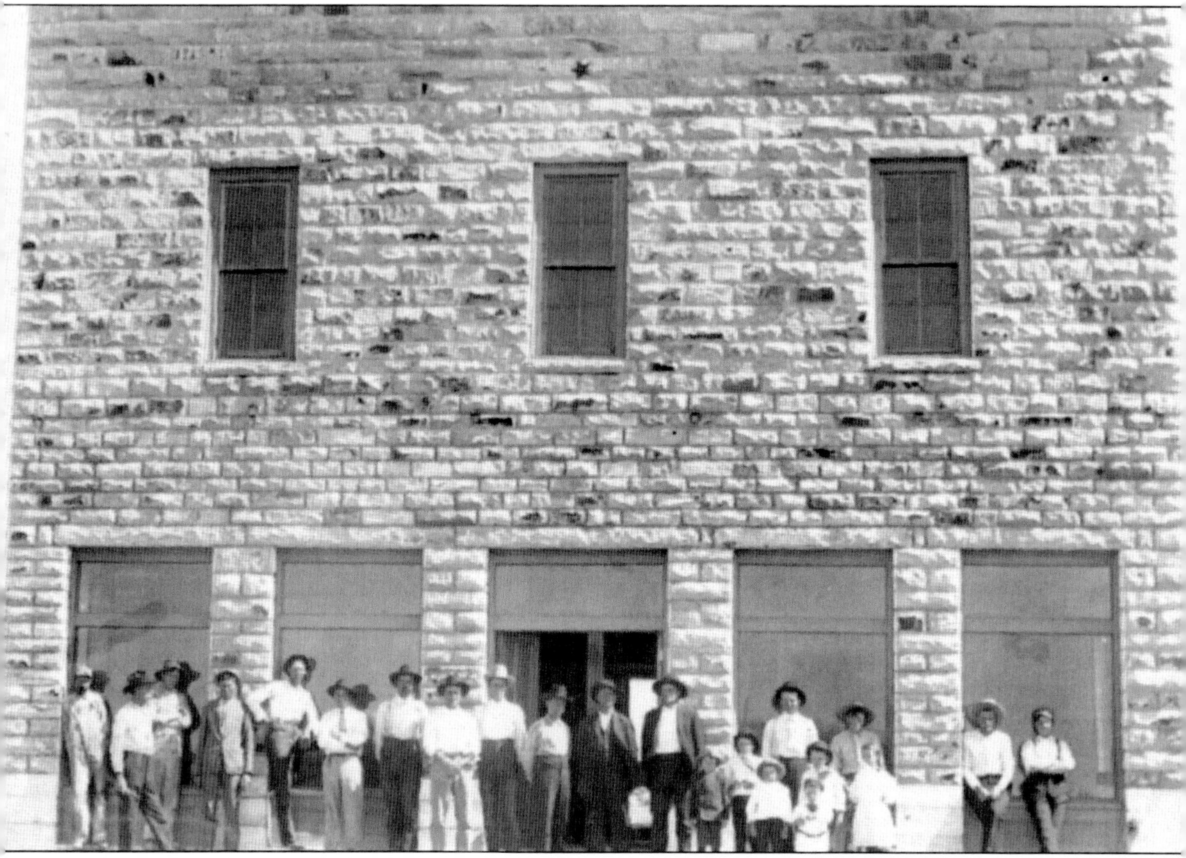

In a special session held on January 6, 1908, county commissioners approved plans to build a temporary courthouse. The court awarded a contract of $5,044 to F. L. Maupin for the construction of the two-story stone building. The project was completed and ready to be occupied by July of that year. The temporary courthouse served the county for 15 years.

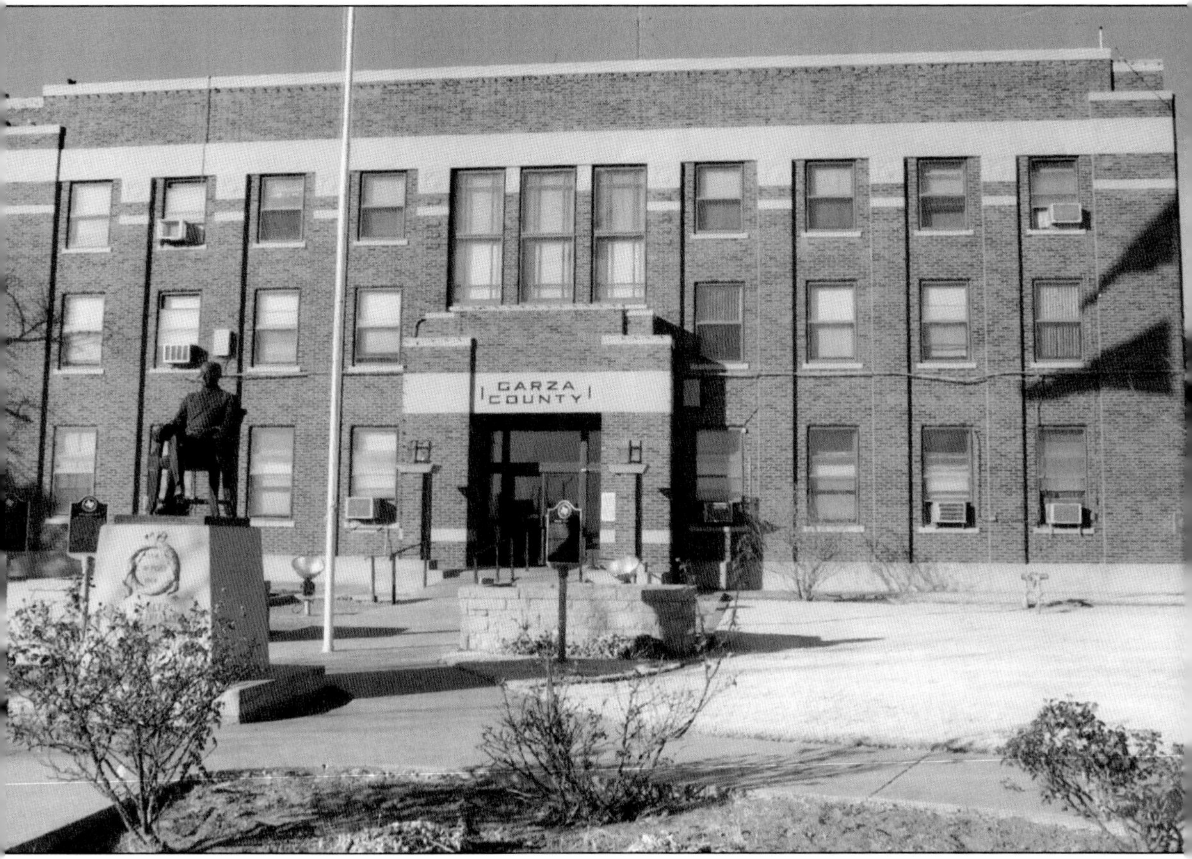

The prosperity of the 1920s led to the growth of Garza County government. As the population grew, so did tax revenues, prompting commissioners to pursue the building of a new courthouse. An election was held on July 22, 1922, with voter results of 579 for and 355 against. A new courthouse was built on the courthouse square reserved by C. W. Post in the original town plat. The total cost for the courthouse and jail was $81,026, and it was occupied by September 1923. The old courthouse was finally sold in 1924 to the Odd Fellows Lodge for $4,000.

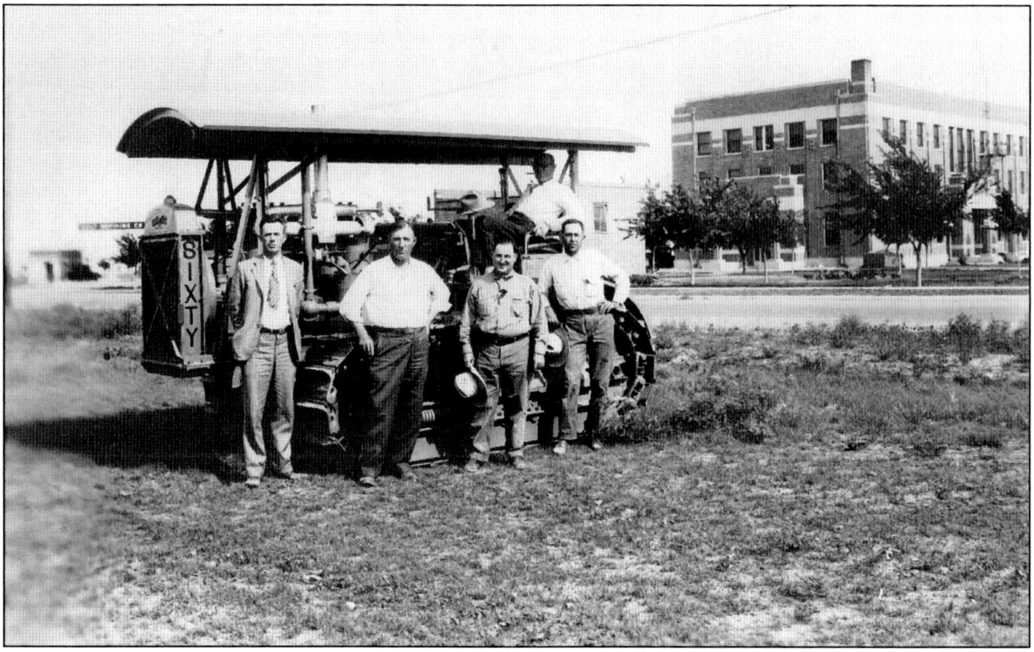

This 1928 photograph shows the new Caterpillar Sixty purchased by Garza County. The salesman is seated in the cab. In front of the tractor, from left to right, are Judge H. D. Smith and commissioners W. L. Cross, Jay Slaughter, and H. M. Ford. The old jail is behind the tractor, and the new courthouse is on the right.

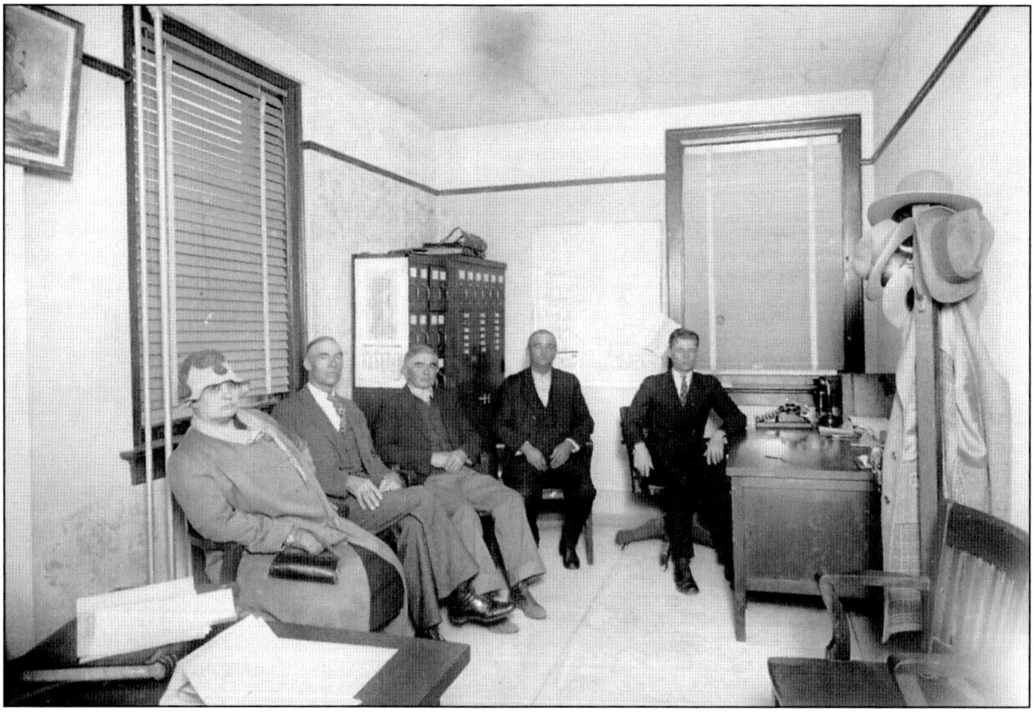

C. W. Tinney (seated at desk) was the first county superintendant. He is seen here with unidentified members of the Garza County School Board.

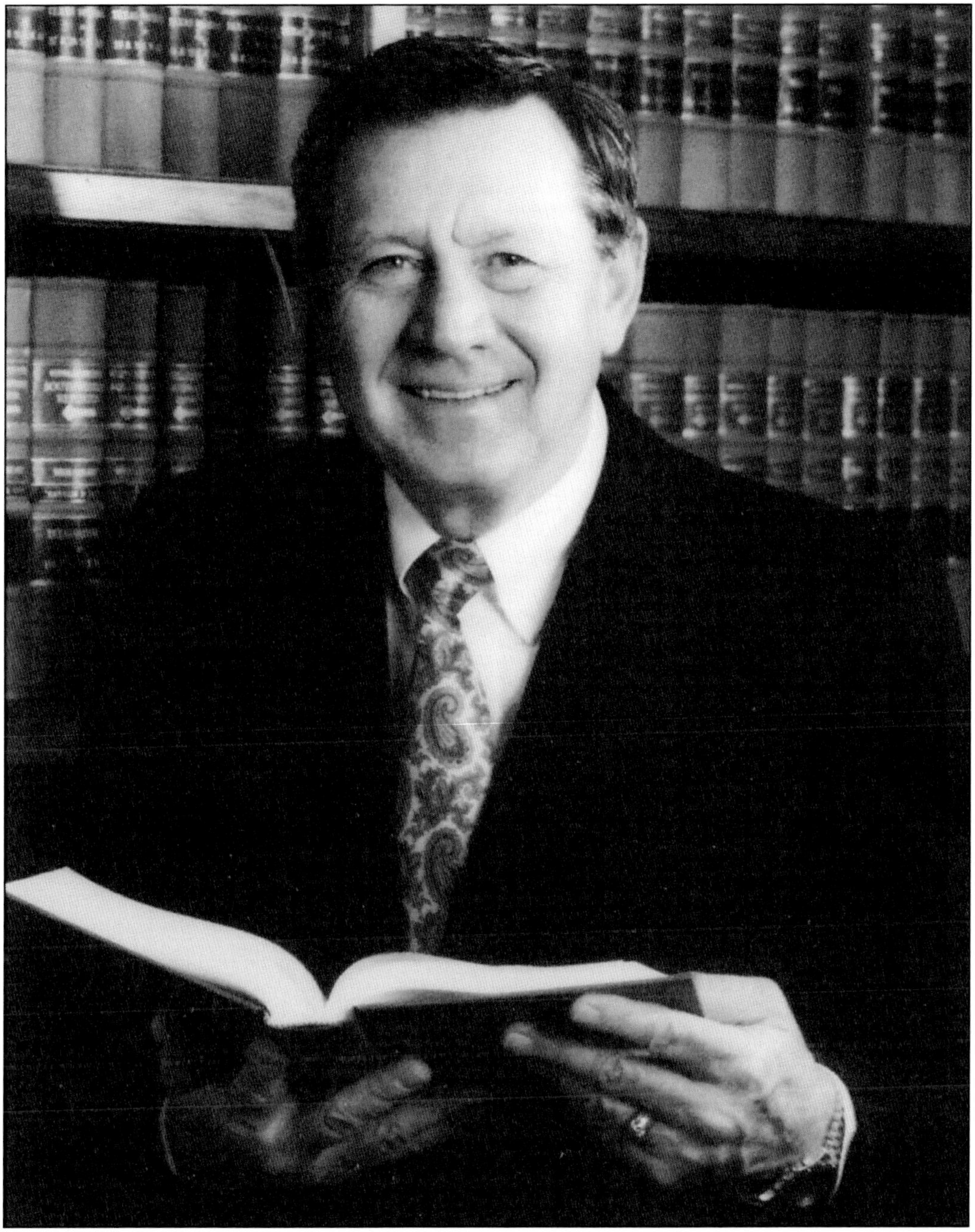

Giles W. Dalby, a Garza County judge for 34 years, is the longest-tenured judge in the State of Texas and the first recipient of the Giles W. Dalby Award for Judicial Leadership. The award was established to recognize Dalby's character, integrity, and service to the judiciary, county government, and community. For more than three decades he has held numerous leadership roles, including past president of the West Texas County Judges and Commissioners Association and the Texas Association of Counties, as well as the chair of the Texas County and District Retirement System and the Judicial Education Committee. Even in retirement, he continues to serve various organizations around the state of Texas and at home in Garza County.

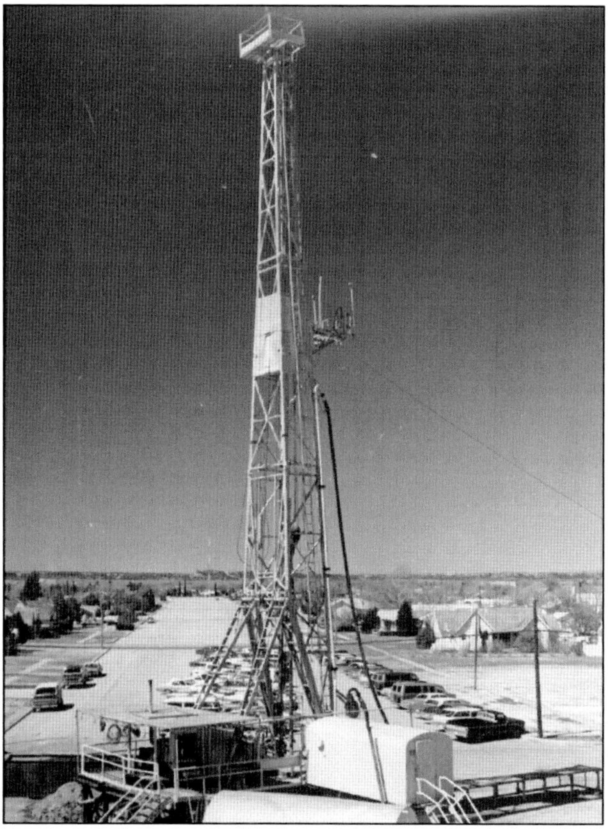

This 1979 photograph, taken by Ed Neff, shows the George R. Brown drilling rig on the west side of the courthouse. Oil is big business in Garza County. At the well site, a sign stood for many years identifying the well as "#B 38-CP–completed June 8, 1979, producing 43 barrels of oil per day from a depth of 3,100 feet." With an average annual production in excess of 7 million barrels from approximately 2,300 wells, the oil industry of Garza County generates an annual payroll in excess of $4 million and pays more than 70 percent of the taxes collected by the city, county, and school district. The photograph below shows the pump jack that replaced the rig and remained at the site for more than 20 years. (Both, courtesy Marie Neff.)

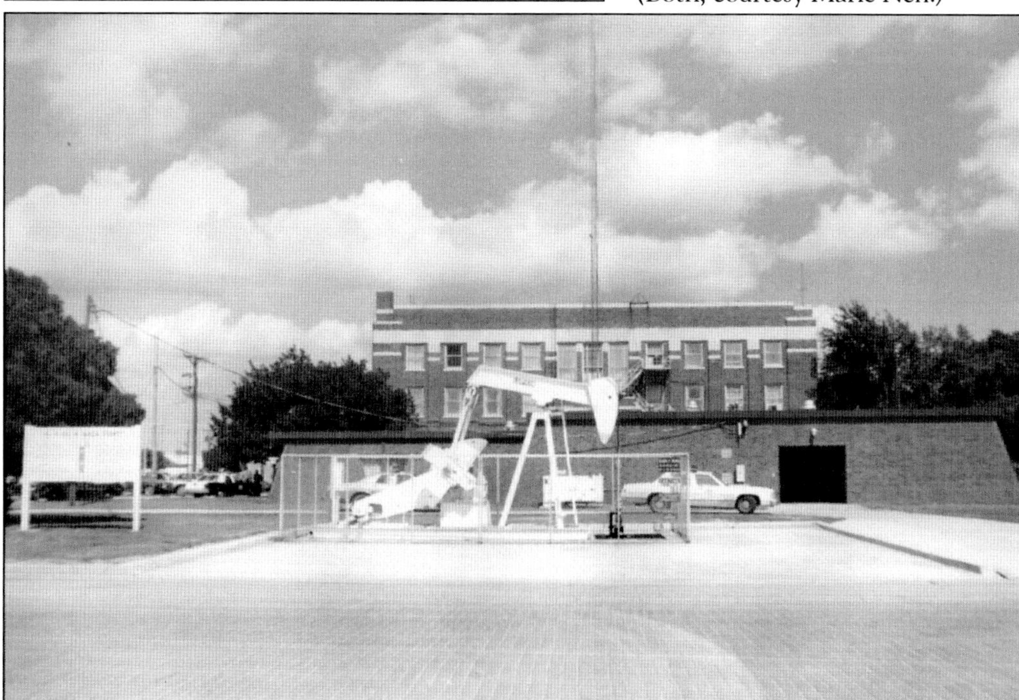

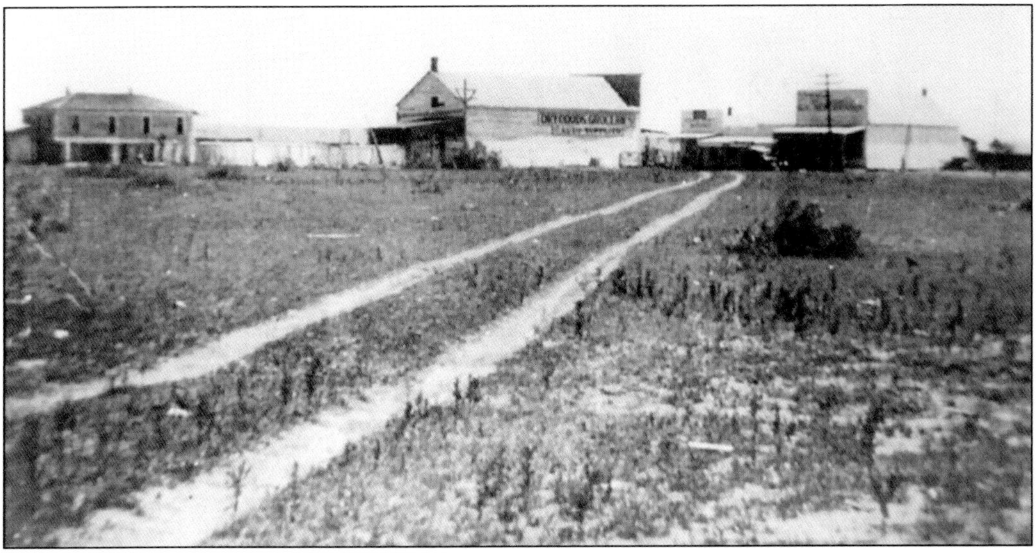

Justiceburg, formerly known as Leforest, is located 15 miles southeast of the town of Post. In 1910, Jefferson Davis Justice purchased the land and granted a right-of-way to the Atchison, Topeka, and Santa Fe Railroad. The railroad was completed in 1911, and the town was renamed Justiceburg. After the town site was platted in 1912, numerous businesses cropped up, complete with a train depot and school. Eventually the town failed, leaving only the school and post office, both of which eventually closed. The old town may have vanished, but the people remain.

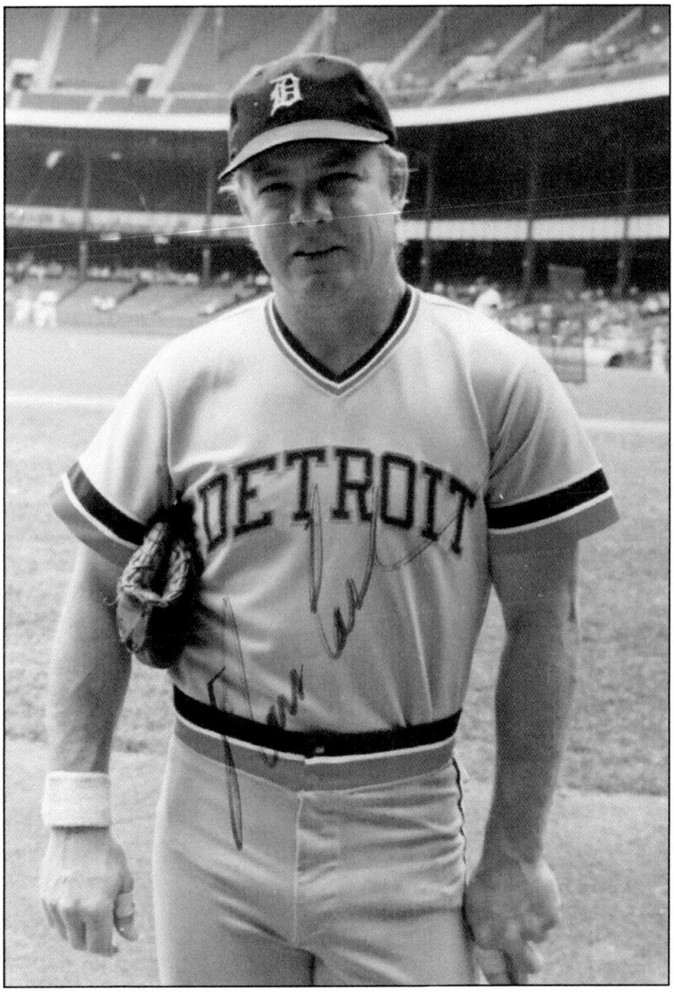

Norman "Stormin' Norman" Cash is a native son of Justiceburg and a graduate of Post High School. Norm played for the Detroit Tigers, winning the American League batting championship in 1961. Post honored his memory by renaming the Post Baseball Stadium as Norm Cash Field.

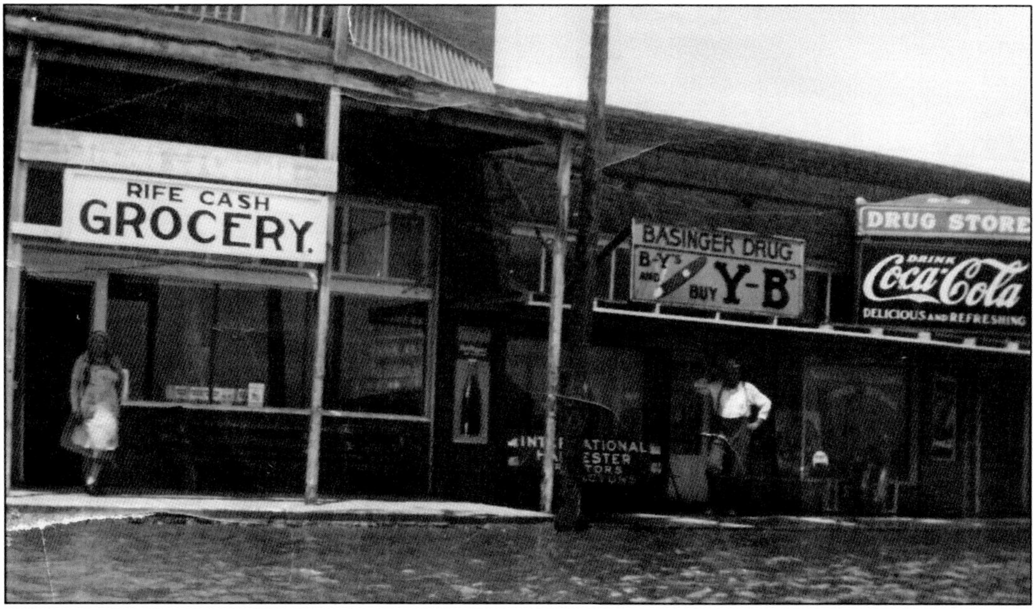

The 1941 flood at Southland made Main Street look like a river. In the image above, Dora Basinger is standing at the grocery store, and Elec Basinger is at the drugstore. The town of Southland got its name from its location in the southern portion of the V Ranch. When the railway was completed in 1910, the town began to prosper, boasting a dozen businesses, a bank, a newspaper, several churches, and a school. The Depression caused the bank to fail, and in time the other businesses began closing. The Southland Independent School District has remained strong, and the six-man Southland Eagles football team is the pride of the community. Below is a photograph of the Southland Hardware and Dry Goods Store, taken in 1932. Pictured below are, from left to right, George Basinger, Iva Basinger, unidentified, S. N. Hendrix, and unidentified.

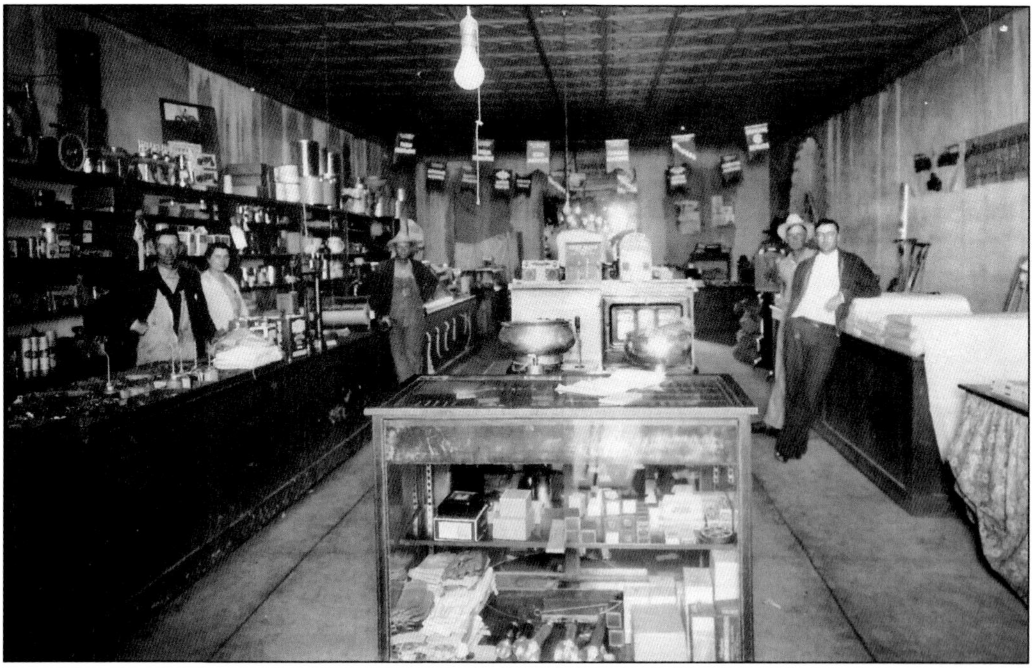

The first and only female sheriff of Garza County, Ruby Claborn was offered the job after her husband, L. A. "Fay" Claborn, died in office on February 10, 1970. He had served as sheriff for 10 years. Ruby Claborn vowed to keep the peace until a successor could be duly elected in November 1970.

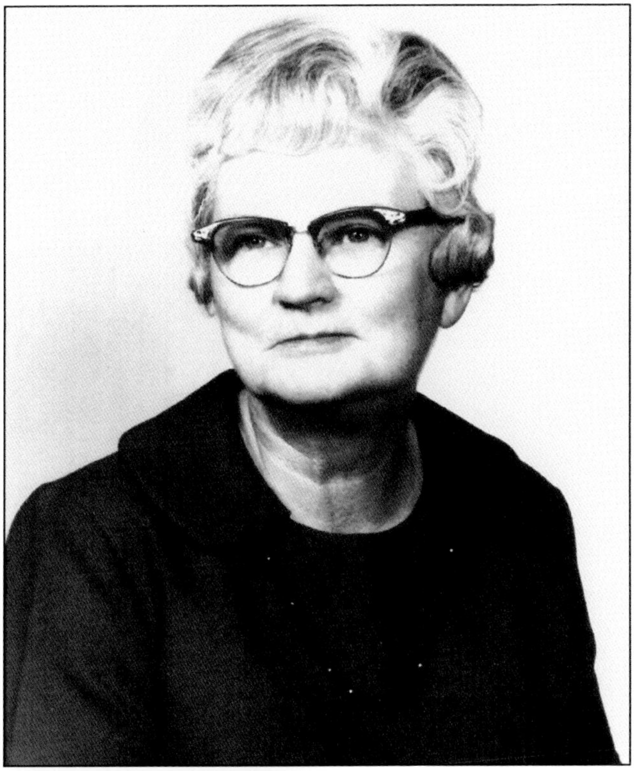

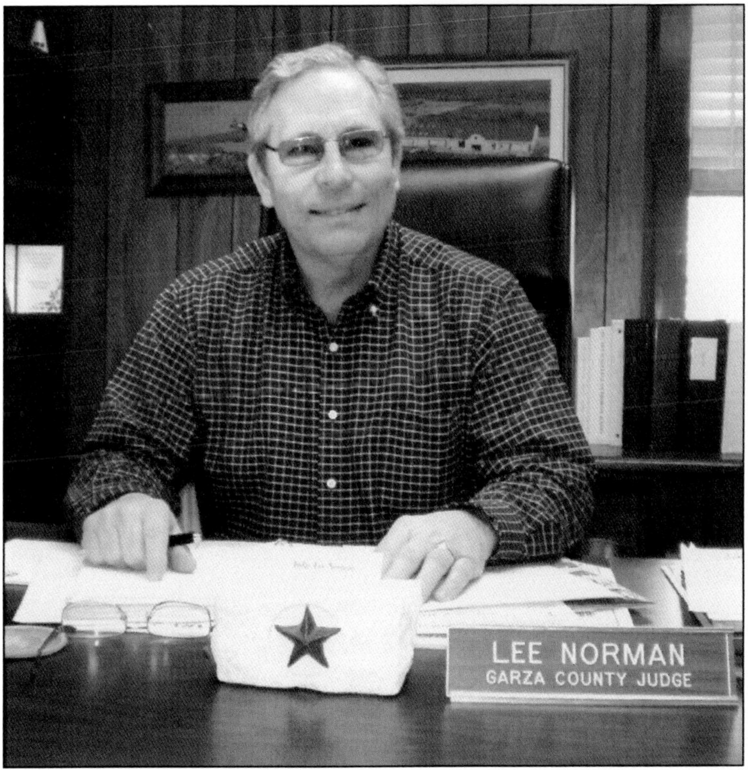

Garza County judge Lee Norman is a descendent of a pioneer family, and he keeps that heritage in mind. He actively participates in the improvement of Post and Garza County. He is a farmer, a former commissioner, and a county judge who juggles a schedule that only his wife, Marsha, can comprehend. Both are civic-minded, serving on boards of organizations or as volunteers.

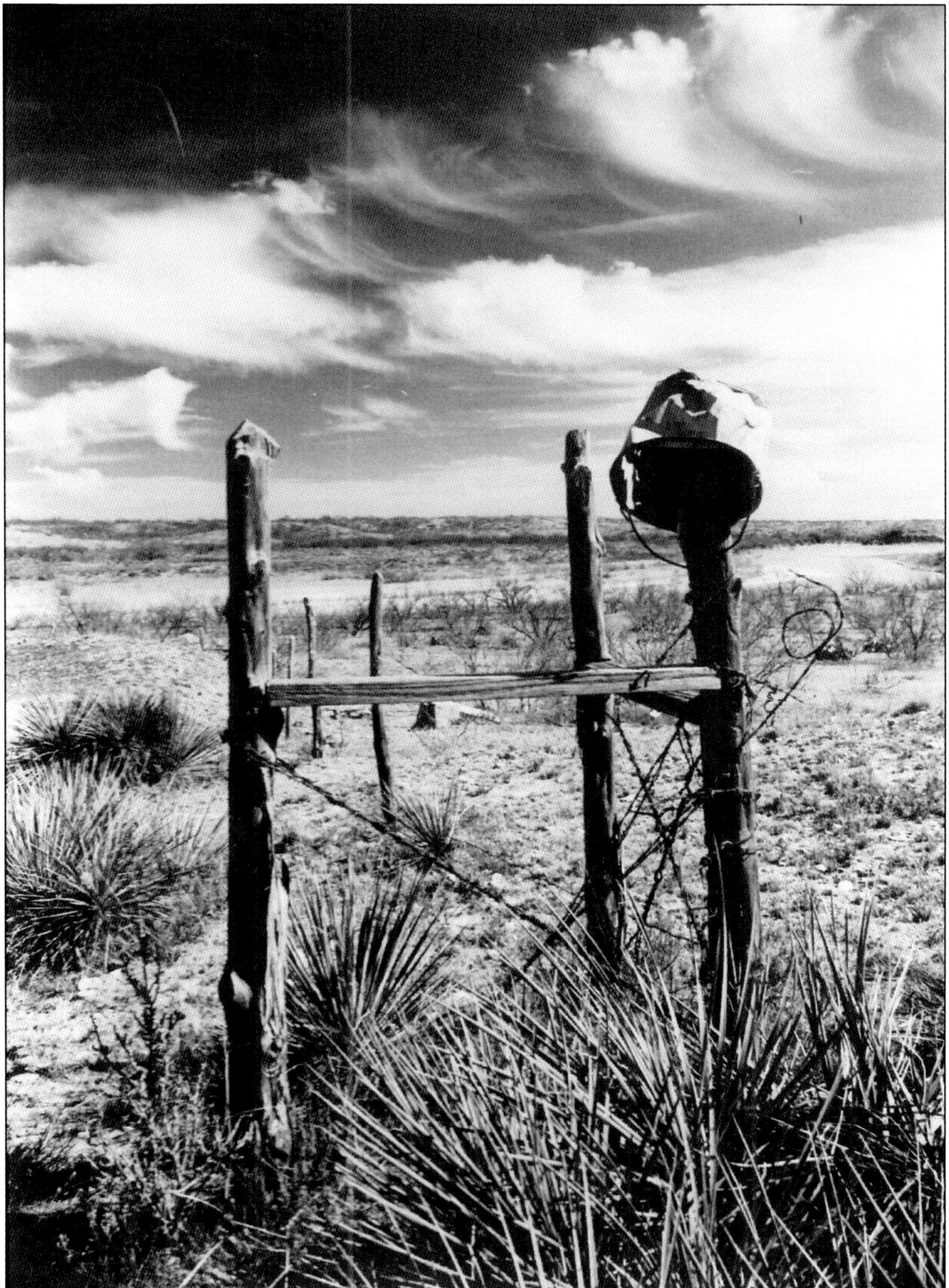

This beautiful landscape near the bank of the North Fork of the Double Mountain Fork of the Brazos River is a familiar rural scene in the county. A fence post is the final resting place of an old bucket that has seen better days, though it holds firm, even with the force of wind in the clouds. (Courtesy Marie Neff.)

Three

School Bells Toll

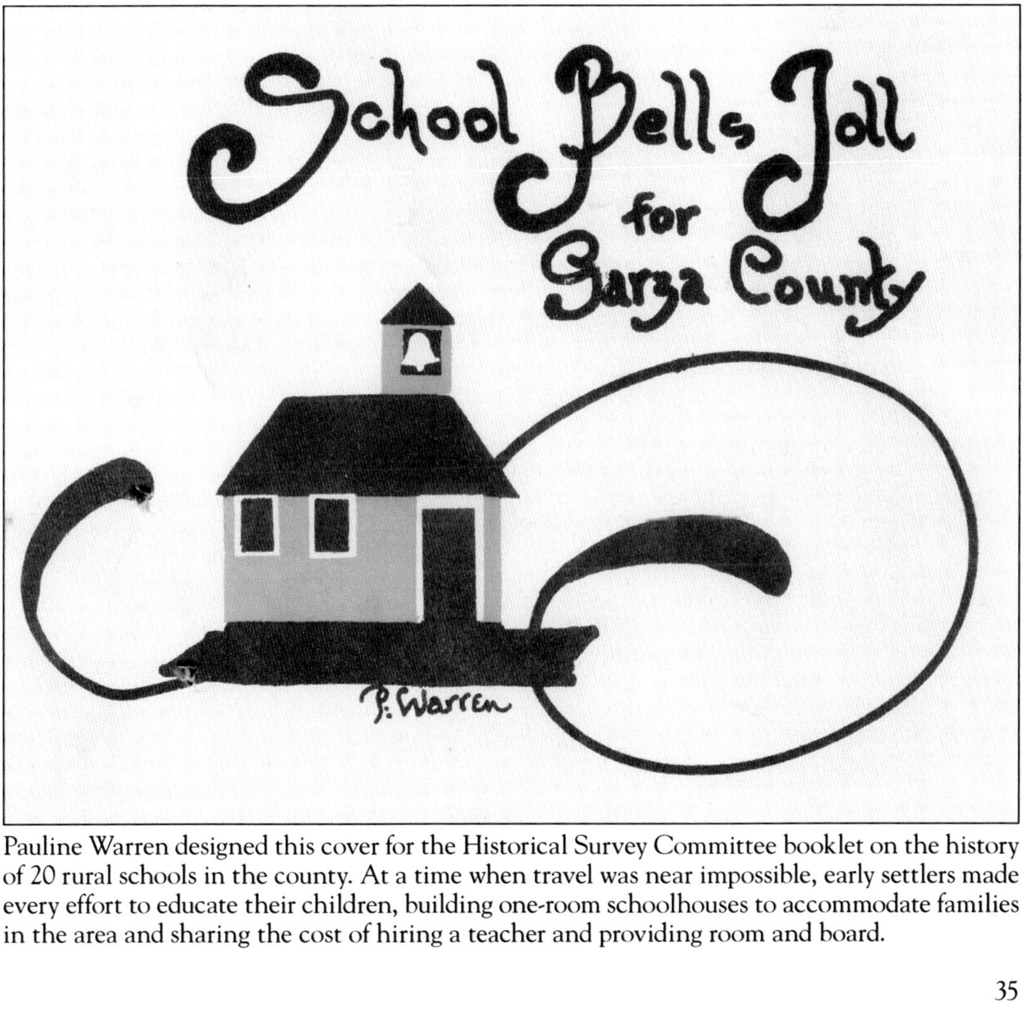

Pauline Warren designed this cover for the Historical Survey Committee booklet on the history of 20 rural schools in the county. At a time when travel was near impossible, early settlers made every effort to educate their children, building one-room schoolhouses to accommodate families in the area and sharing the cost of hiring a teacher and providing room and board.

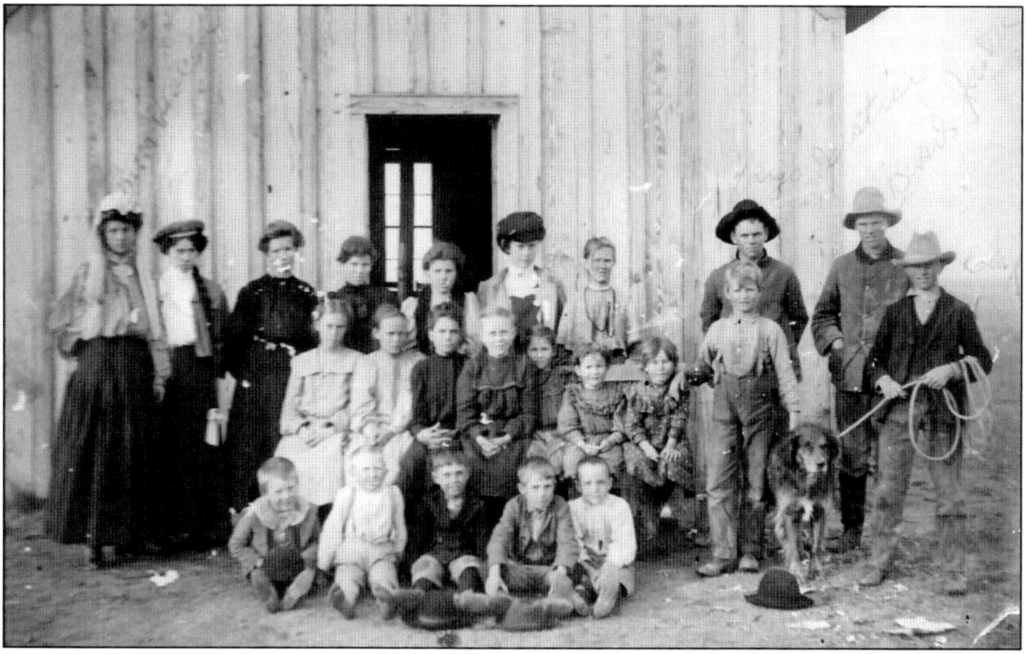

The above photograph shows the 1905–1906 class at the Graham School. The Joe McMahon family moved to the area in 1902. Only one house could be seen from the home site, a half-dugout later known as Graham Chapel. The community was also later called by this same name. Within a few months, the Wilbourn, Graham, Hughes, and Justice families, among others, moved to the area as well. The five families met to discuss the need for a school for their children. Money was raised, and lumber was hauled from Big Spring to build the school on land donated by McMahon. In 1904, the first teacher, Mabel Farmer, was hired for three months. The next year, Verna Elkins rode horseback every day from the Llano Ranch, where she lived, to teach at the school. She earned $60 per month by 1908. Expenditures for the 1908–1909 school term were only $390. The 1908 photograph below is of the Graham Singing School, taught by O. B. Crowley.

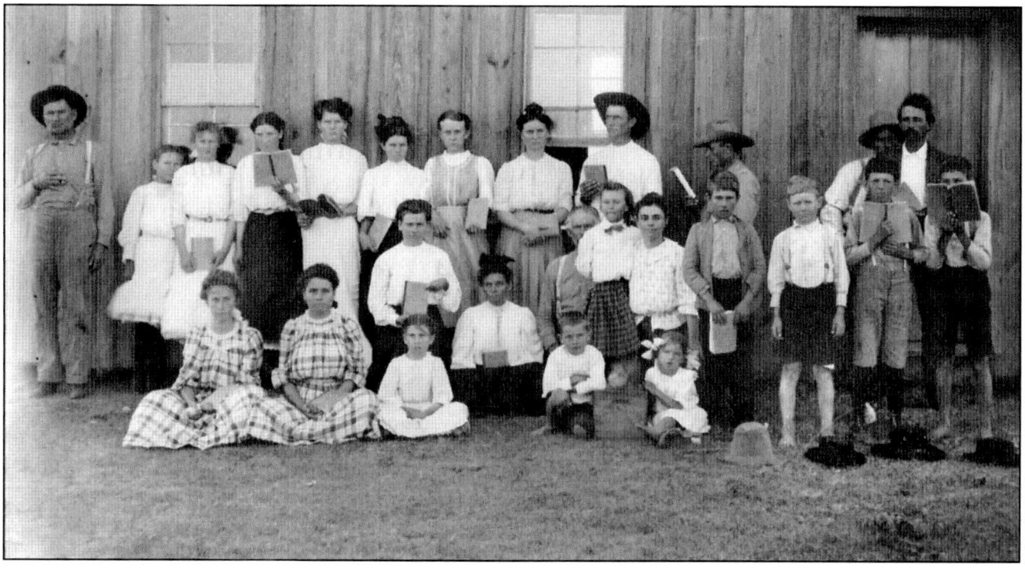

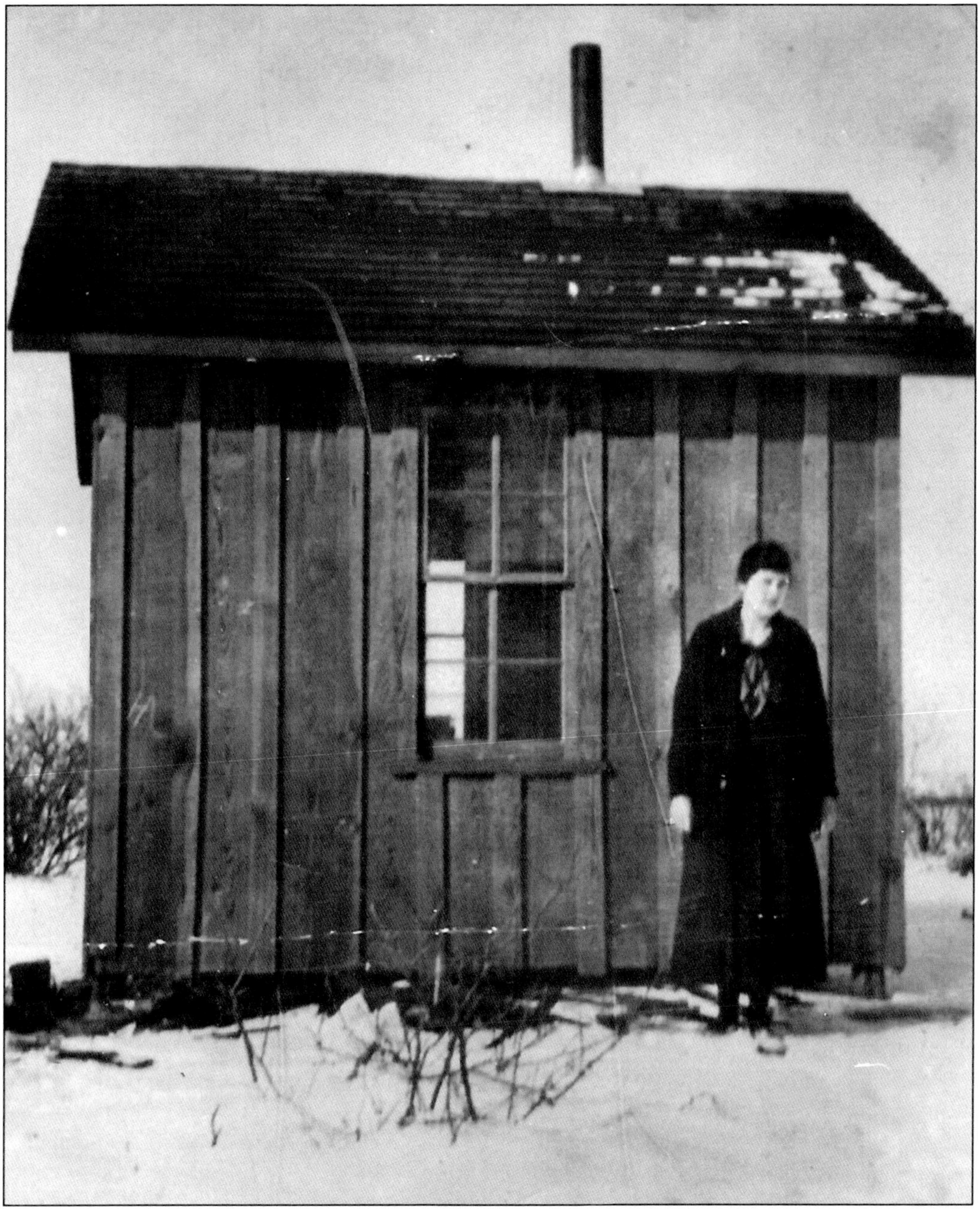

Lois Baird Williams stands by a one-room schoolhouse in 1917. Williams came to Post from California in 1916 to teach school, with plans to live with her uncle Dr. A. R. Ponton, chief surgeon at the Post Sanitarium. Her first teaching experience was at the Lindsey School, located 15 miles west of town. Ten pupils attended, including the two Lindsey boys, in grades first through ninth. She stayed in the country through the week and came to town on weekends. The next year (1917) Williams taught at the Leonard Barrow ranch, 25 miles northeast of town. Williams recalls the trip to town was no easy matter, with 14 gates to open and crossing (and stuck many times in) the Yellowhouse River. The trip took an entire day. After World War I she married Dr. D. C. Williams.

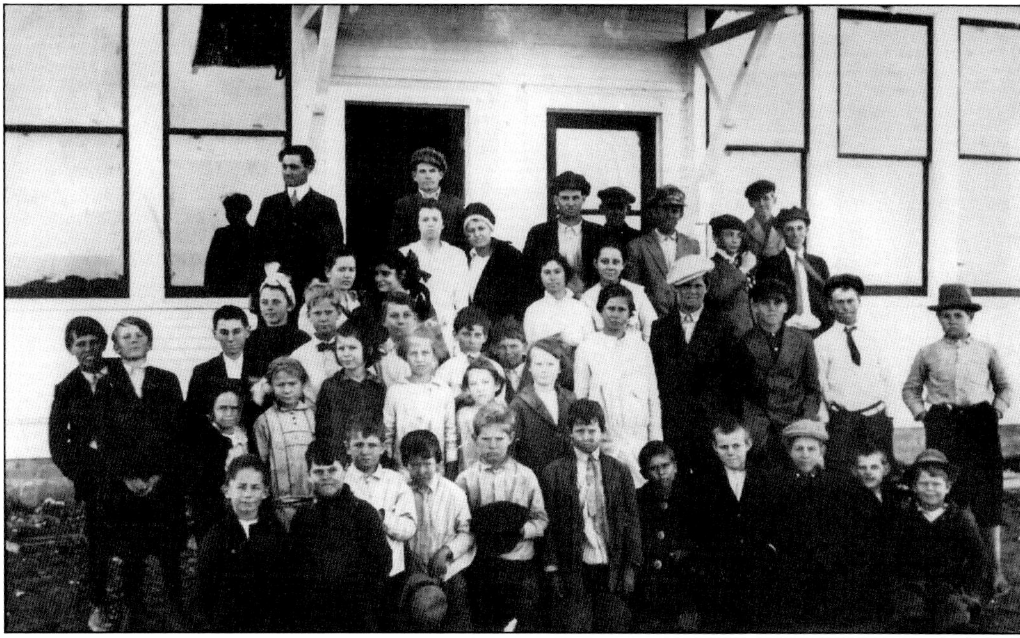

The 1915 photograph of the Pleasant Valley School features teacher Sam Carter and children from the following families: Durham, Franklin, Robinson, Williams, Spence, Smith, Pierce and Redman.

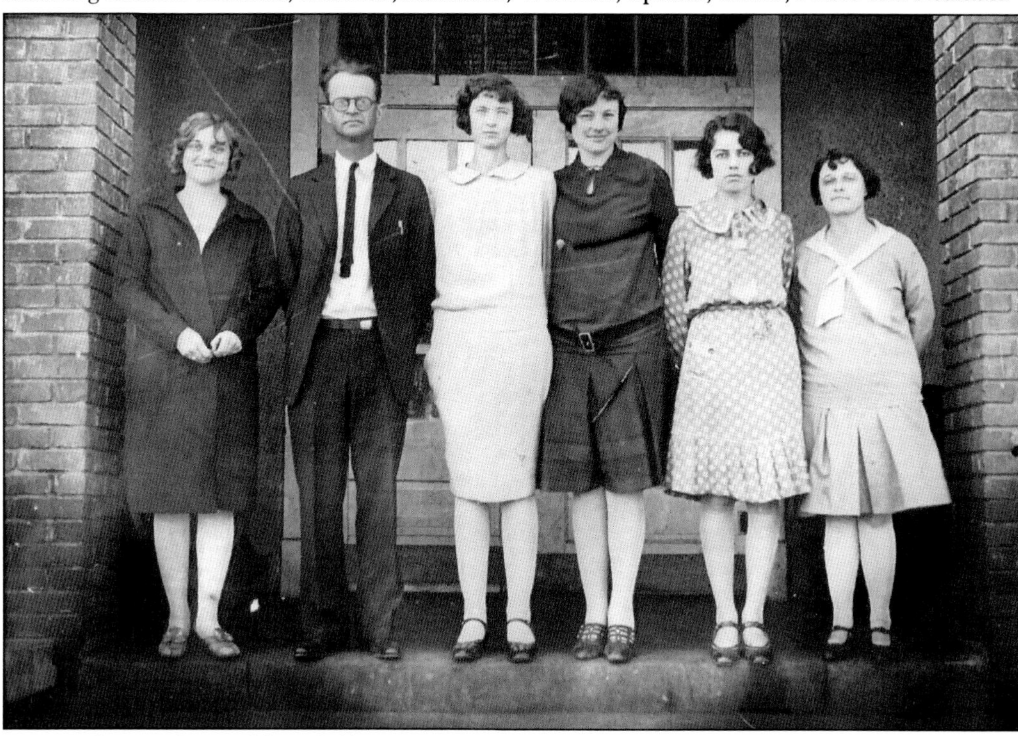

Dean Robinson (second from left) came to Garza County in 1926 and served as superintendent of the Close City Independent School District until 1934. That same year he ran for and was elected county superintendent. Robinson was reelected for eight consecutive four-year terms without ever having an opponent. Pearl Story is standing third from left.

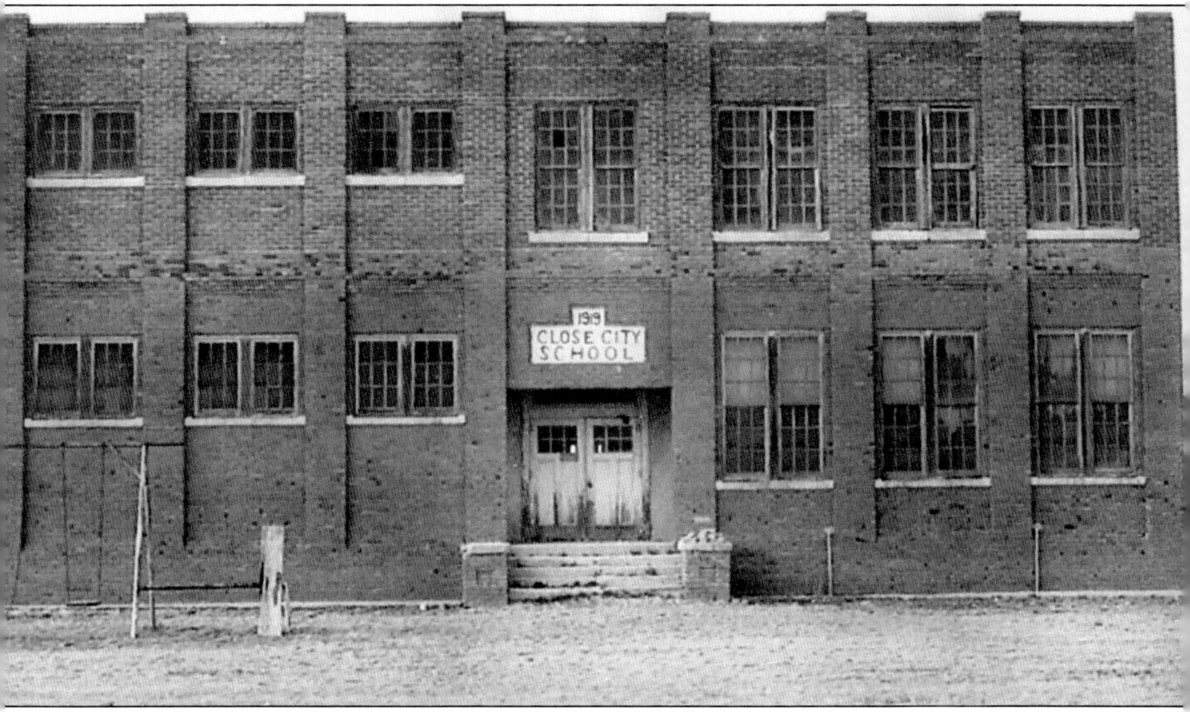

In 1909, Close City students attended school in the one-room wooden commissary building, from the original town site of Post City before the relocation below the Caprock. The first teacher was Mrs. J. E. Crowder, who received $50 per month. Before long, a second teacher was needed, and another room was added. Mrs. Paul Duren recalls the great times they had at the little school and how they had box suppers to raise money for the purchase of basketball suits and baseball uniforms; how there was no parking lot full of colorful cars, but saddle horses or horse and buggies that brought the kids to school. In 1919, George Samson and Jimmie Napier built a new brick schoolhouse, which served the community well until 1965, when Close City School was consolidated with Post.

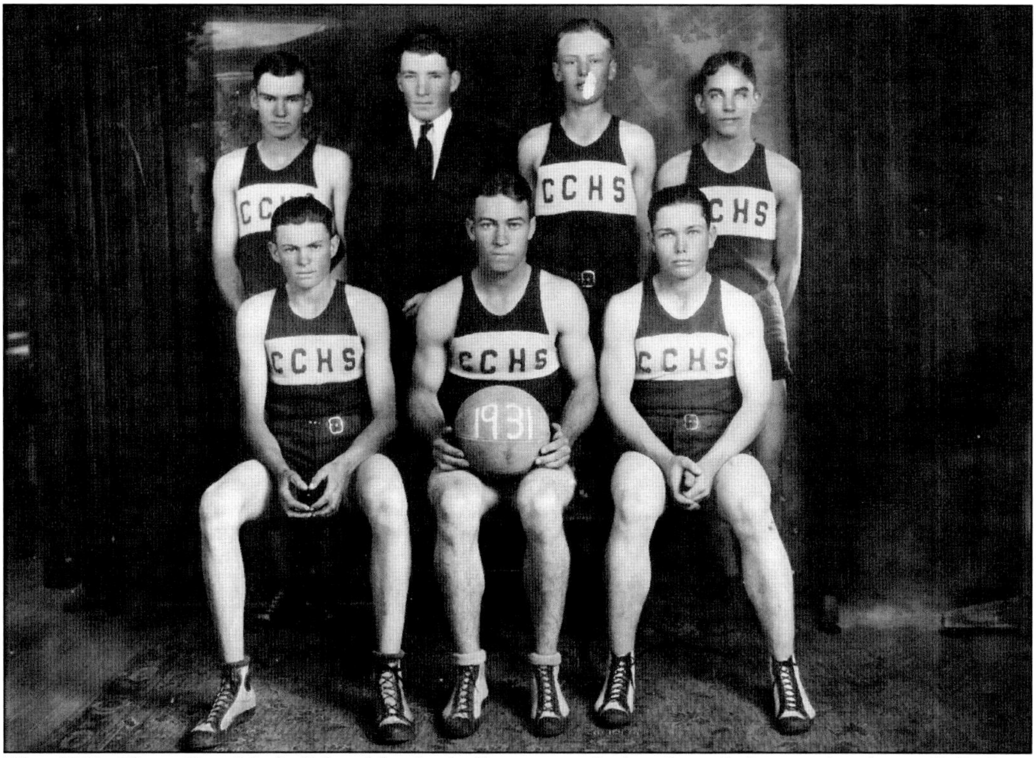

The 1931 Close City High School basketball team includes, from left to right, (seated) Robert Louis Mason, Travis Lloyd, and W. C. Bush; (standing) Conner Howell, coach Davis Pound, Loyd Roberts, and Gomer Custer.

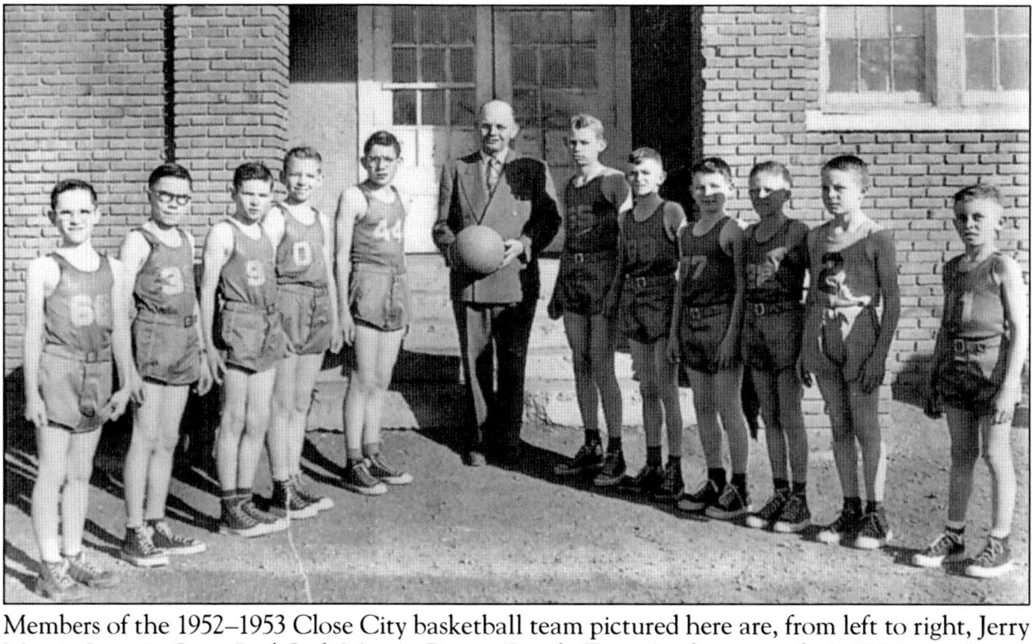

Members of the 1952–1953 Close City basketball team pictured here are, from left to right, Jerry Morris, Lonnie Gene Peel, Jack Morris, Bunny Smith, Ernie Popham, coach A. T. Nixon, Harry Smith, John Shultz, Jimmie Redman, Ronnie Morris, Robert Lewis, and Tommy Young.

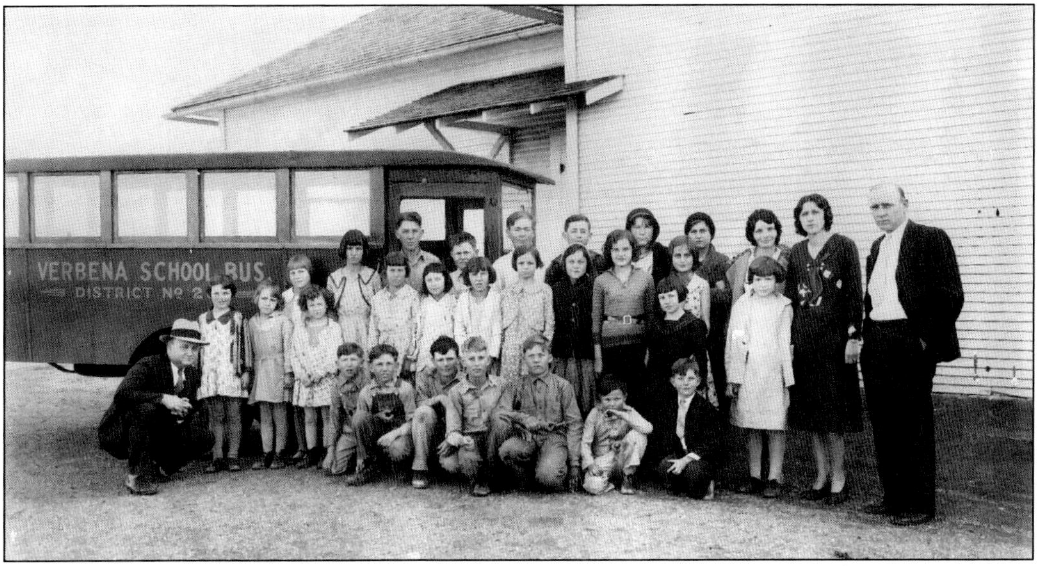

In the 1911–1912 school year, the Verbena School employed J. M. Mayfield at $60 per month for seven months, for a total of $420 for the year. Later two teachers were hired, and a large room was added, along with a house for the teachers and bus driver. A teacher's husband usually drove the bus. Most children were always happy when school was out but were eager to start again in the fall.

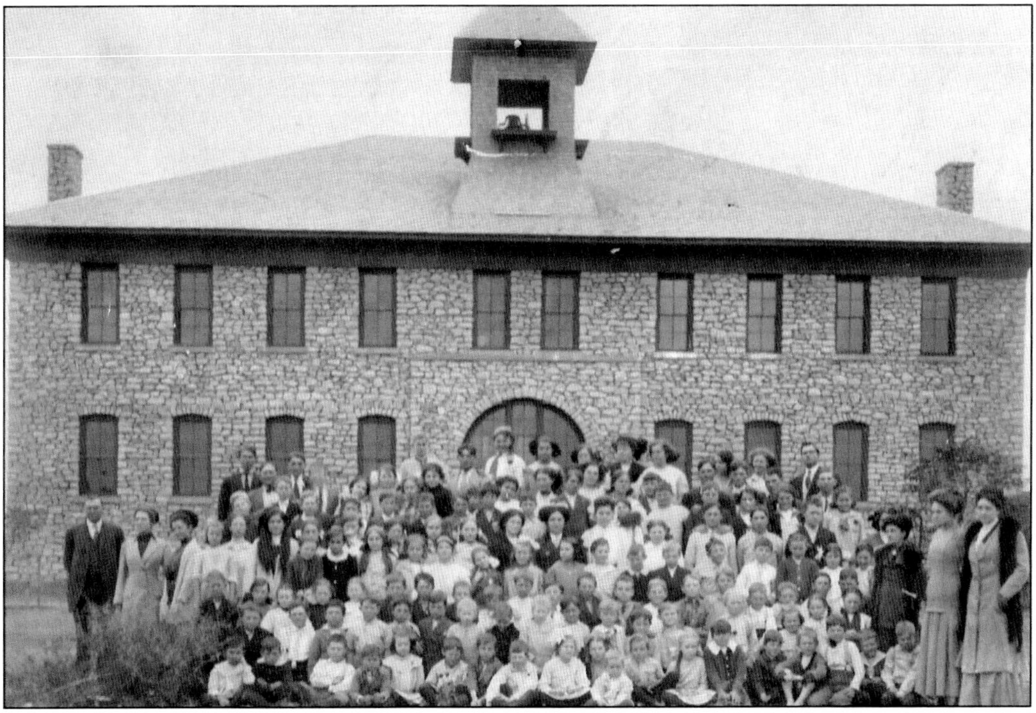

The 1911–1912 student body poses in front of Post City Rock School. The first Post City teacher was J. E. Crowder, who received a salary of $100 per month for seven months. Other disbursements totaled $277.86. This included the purchase of 25 desks at $4.85 each. Before long, the Post school employed six teachers and H. C. Zorns as principal.

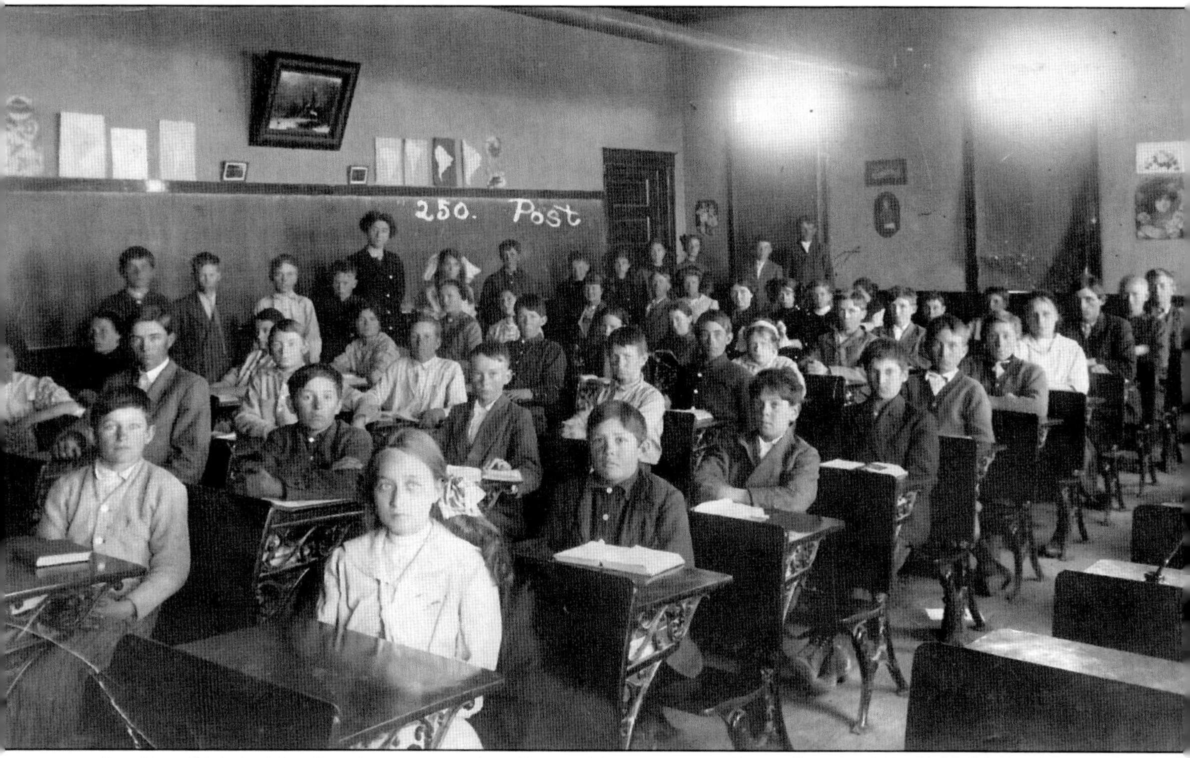

In the 1911–1912 school year, teacher Pannel Brown stands in front of the blackboard next to her class. Students are, from left to right, (first row) Madge Godfrey, Harry Askins, unidentified, Eudy ?, Roy King, Possum Reed, unidentified, ? Kuykendoll, Harry Lindsey and two unidentified; (second row) David Hume, Dexter Woods, Fletcher Thomas, Oscar Graham, unidentified, Mae Weakley, Wilford Stovall, Claude Stovall, and two unidentified; (third row) Paul Duren, Oscar McGinty, and eight unidentified; (fourth row) Eldridge White, Celia Mae Mason, unidentified, Hazel Murray, Gladys Everett, Susie Graham, Zelma White, and two unidentified; (standing) three unidentified, Walter Boren, teacher Pannel Brown, Lura Morrow, and seven unidentified.

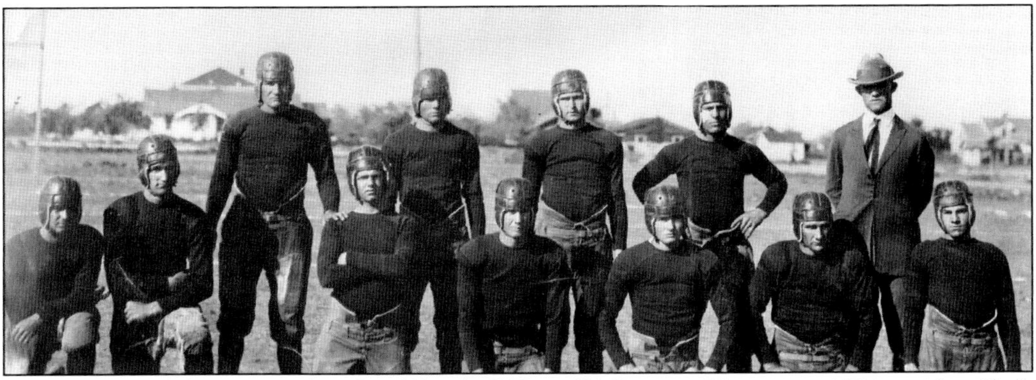

No members of the Post High School Football Team B1 District Champs in 1924 are identified. Of the 20 boys in the football program, 11 were seniors. Claude Brannon, from Denton, coached the team.

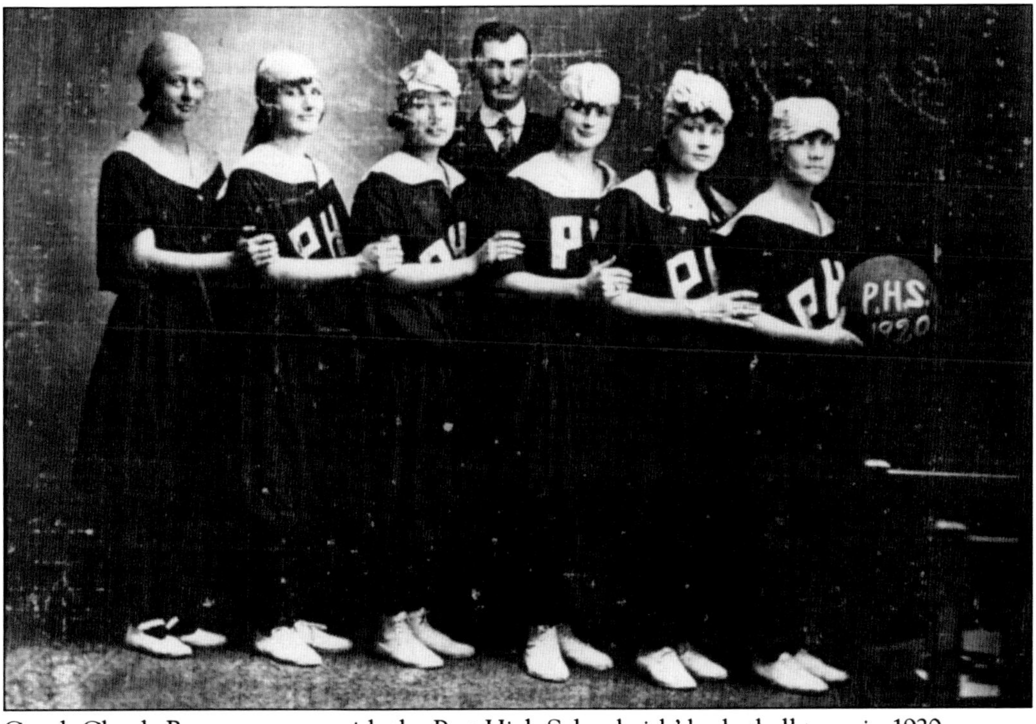

Coach Claude Brannon poses with the Post High School girls' basketball team in 1920.

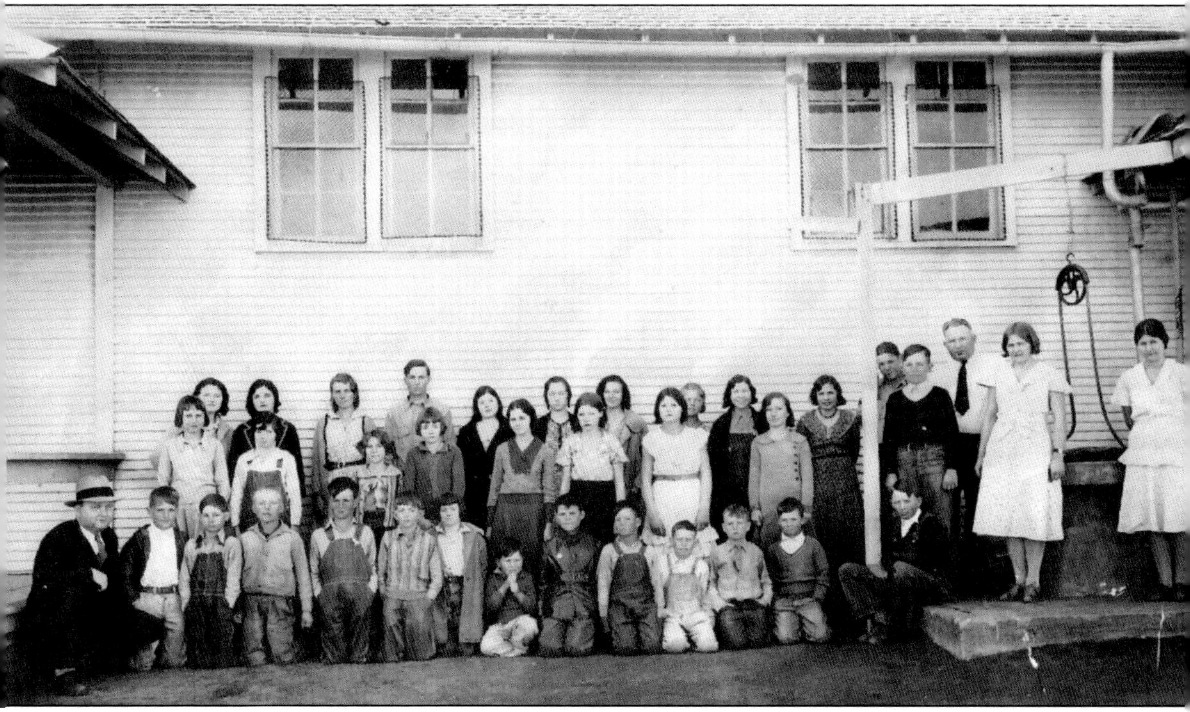

This c. 1940 photograph was taken at the Grassburr School. Gracie Houston, a teacher at Grassburr in 1935, described the school as having a cistern, a four-room house for the teachers, grass burrs, rattlesnakes, and a tennis court. Many folks in the area have fond memories of the school and community. Tommy Puckett confessed to smoking in the toilet, catching it on fire. Billy Jean Cross recalled how volunteers purchased lunchroom groceries and supplies, and how rattlesnakes limited outdoor activities, especially from May through October. Jet Puckett drove the school bus until around 1963. Only a few students are identified in the photograph. They are (first row) Orville Sewert (third from left), Tommy Puckett (eighth from left), Jimmy Puckett (ninth from left), and Russell Wilks Jr. (fourteenth from left); (second row) Clara Sewert (fourth from left) and Evelyn Barrow (fifth from left); (third row) Rosa Lee Cross (second from left), Lucille Wilks (sixth from left), and Willie Lou Barrow (ninth from left).

Jack Kirkpatrick was a graduate of Post High School and Texas Tech University. Kirkpatrick played quarterback for Texas Tech from 1952 to 1955. His honors include most valuable player of 1953, all-conference in 1953, and playing on the 1953 Gator Bowl winning team. Kirkpatrick was inducted into the Hall of Honor in 1971.

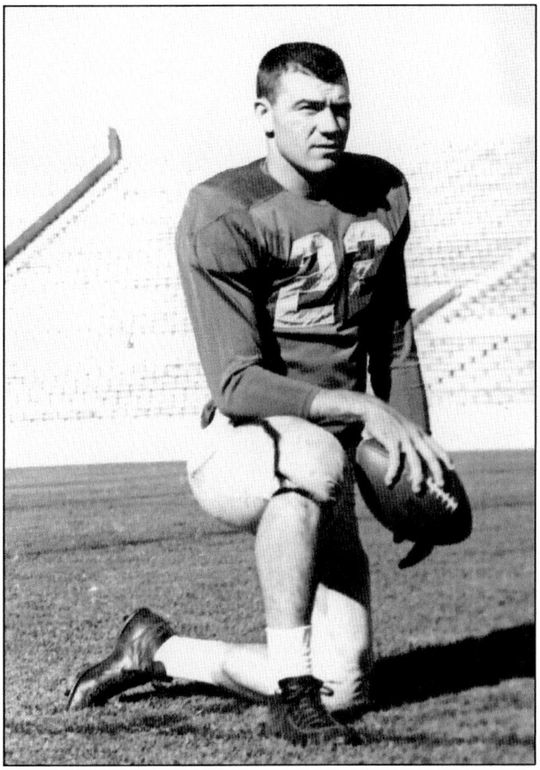

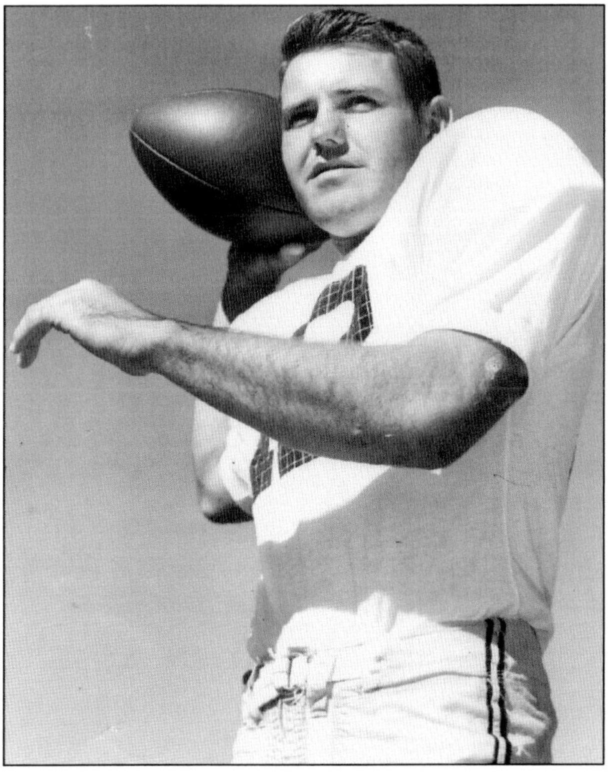

James A. Williams graduated from Post High School in the class of 1957. He was placed on the All-American football squad of the National Junior College Athletic Association, inducted into the Top of Texas Football Hall of Fame in 1983, and honored by the Amarillo Referees Association with the Coach of the Year Award in 1988.

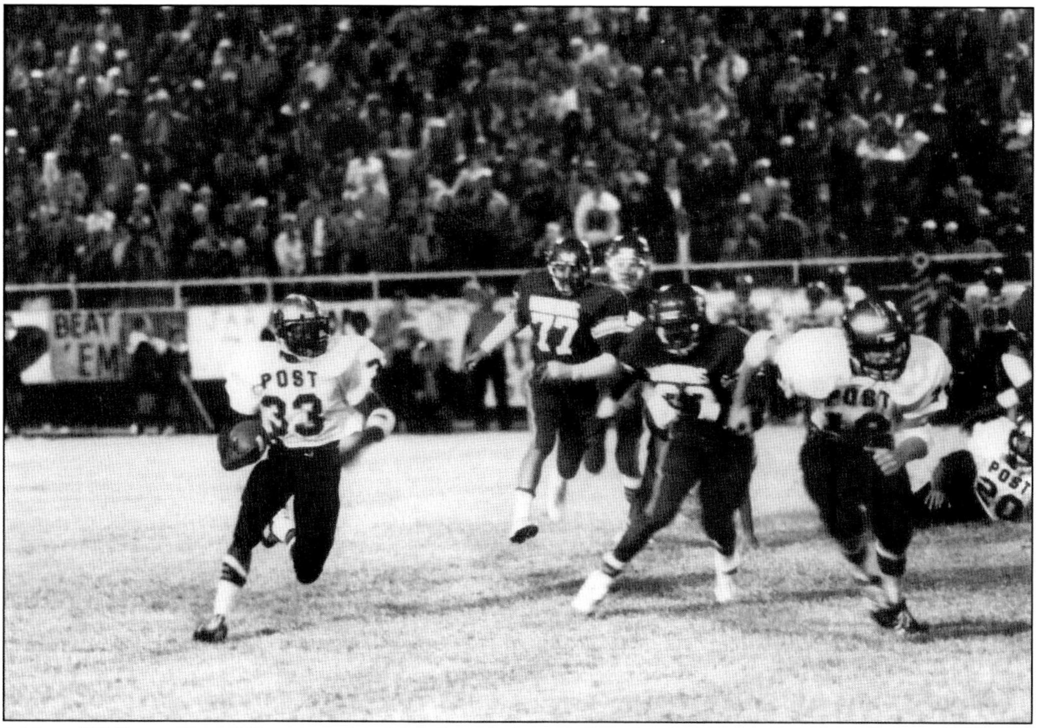

Milton Williams (no. 33), quarterback Joel Kirkpatrick (no. 10), and Michael Olison (no. 20), keep the fans on their feet during the 1983 season. All the players were real sports hero to the fans in Post. Williams received All-District First Team offense, All–South Plains defense, and player of the year honors. Olison and Kirkpatrick won All-District honorable mentions.

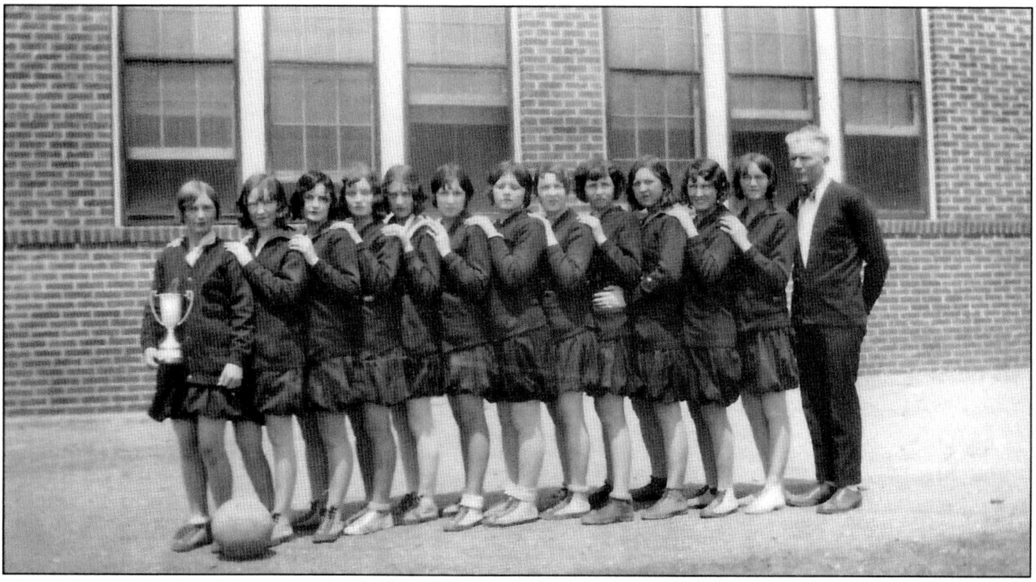

The 1930 Southland girls' basketball team won the championship, known as state champions today. A Mr. Smith was the coach and superintendent. Among those pictured are Ruby Basinger, Opal Basinger, and Ailene Gray.

Four

An American Icon

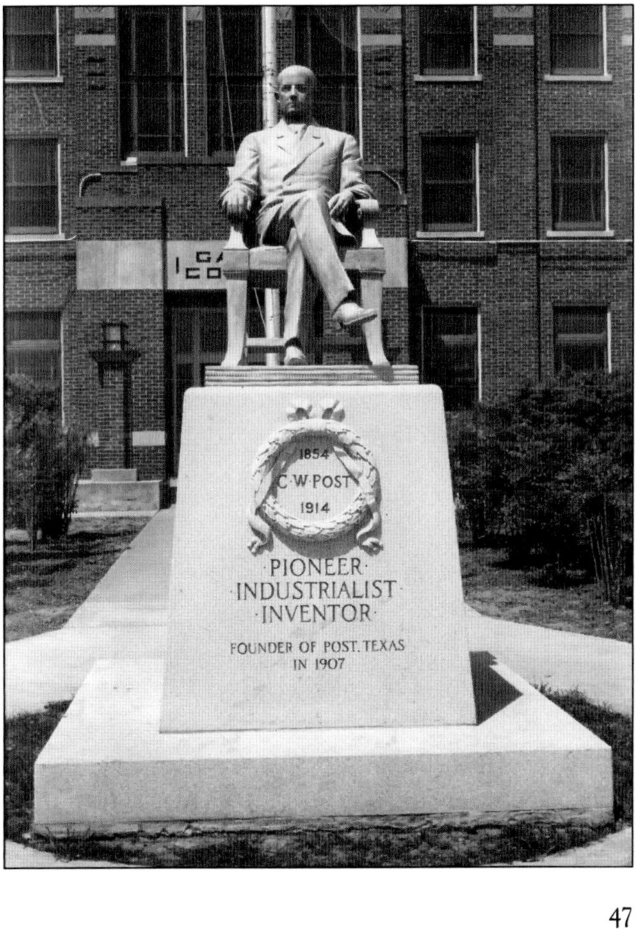

The statue of C. W. Post sits on the courthouse square, facing the main street of the city he founded, Post City, Texas. Marjorie Merriweather Post had the statue made in honor of her father. The text reads, "C. W. Post 1854–1914, Pioneer, Industrialist, Inventor, Founder of Post Texas in 1907." Those few words make a powerful, condensed statement that accurately describes the life of this great man.

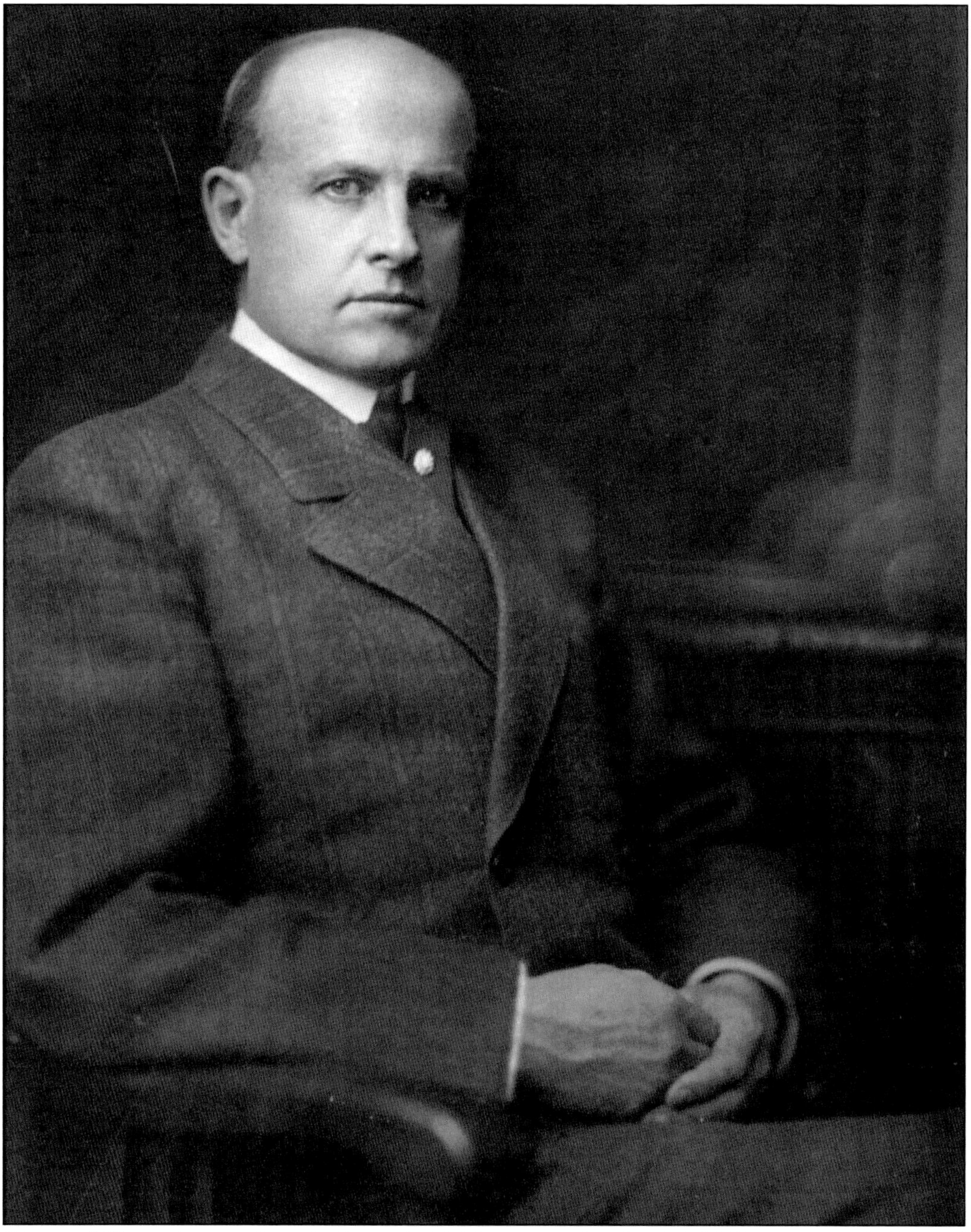

Charles William Post was born in Springfield, Illinois, on October 26, 1854, to parents Rollin and Caroline Post. His father, a forty-niner, was reared in an agricultural background, and his mother was a published poet. C. W., known as Charlie to his family, grew up in Springfield just a few blocks from a man who would become America's 16th president, Abraham Lincoln. Ironically, both young men from the neighborhood would be destined to achieve great fame. It would take a complete book to tell C. W. Post's story. In 1874, he married Ella Letitia Merriweather, his childhood sweetheart, when he was just 20 years old. They had one daughter, Marjorie, born on March 15, 1887.

Pictured around 1920, Marjorie Merriweather Post was C. W. Post's beloved daughter. She accompanied him everywhere, whether to a factory or to the board room of his company. He groomed his only child from an early age, preparing her for the future when she would become the sole heir to his cereal empire. She was destined to achieve greatness, being called "the Heiress" and "An American Empress."

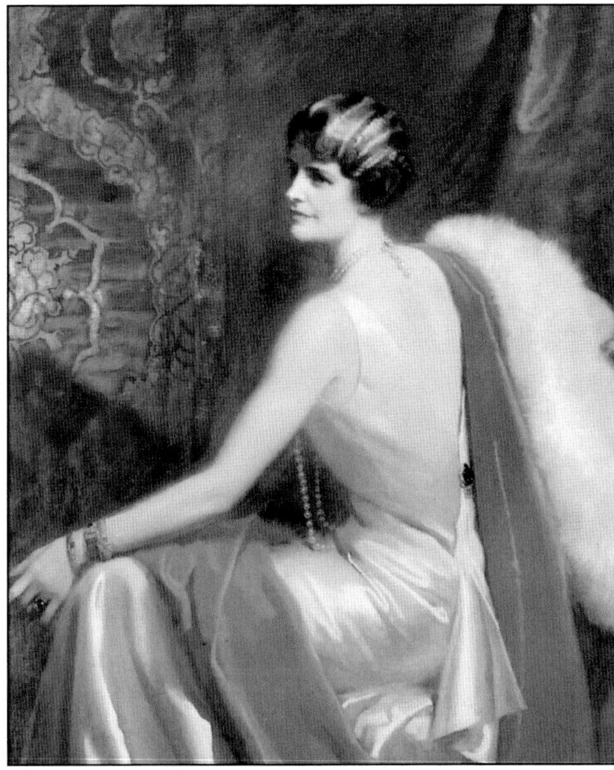

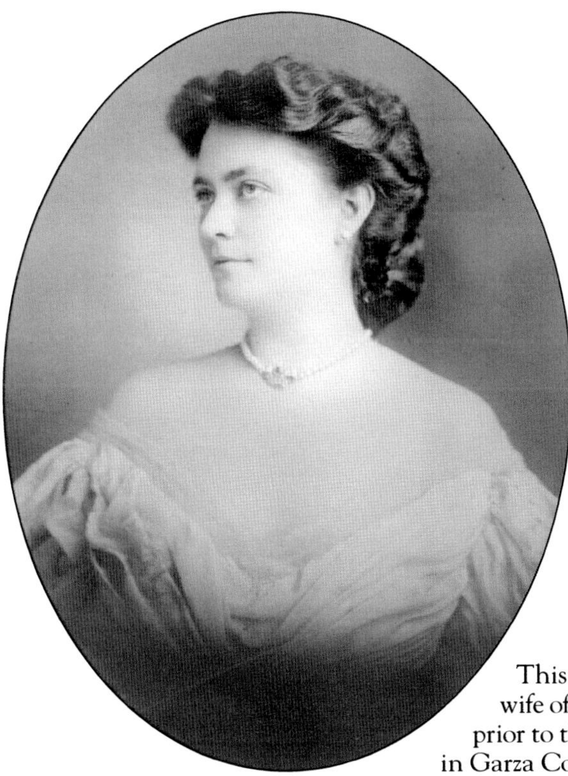

This lovely lady is Leila Young Post, the second wife of C. W. Post. The couple married in 1904, just prior to the time when Post began searching for land in Garza County. Leila had been a secretary for Post.

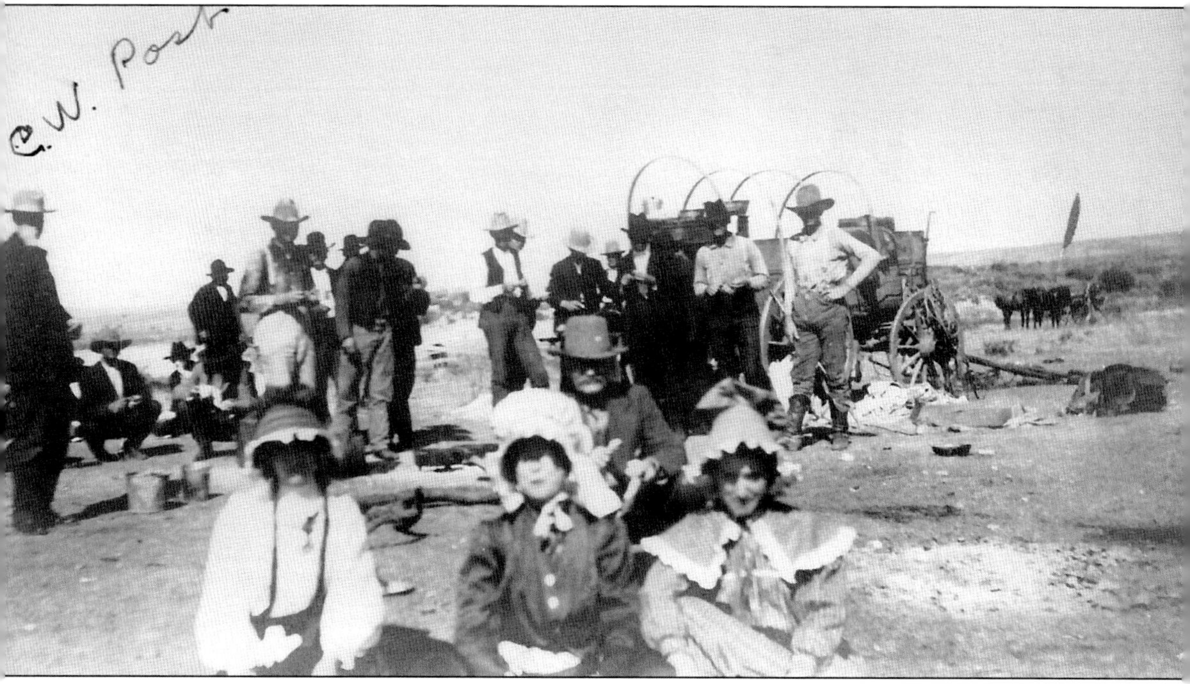

This 1907 photograph shows C. W. Post and his associates somewhere on the plains. From left to right, Dorothy Howe, Leila Post, and Lucile Stevens are seated in front. After numerous trips during 1905 and 1906, C. W. Post had purchased about 333 square miles of land, much of which was located on the plains and below the Caprock, called the breaks. By 1907, Post was ready to begin his colonizing efforts to create a town for the people, surrounded by farms. After the 1880s, the country had begun to recognize the merit of agriculture and what part it played in the economy. Post had great plans of making that a reality in West Texas and hired a manager to oversee his company, chartered by the State of Texas as the Double U Company.

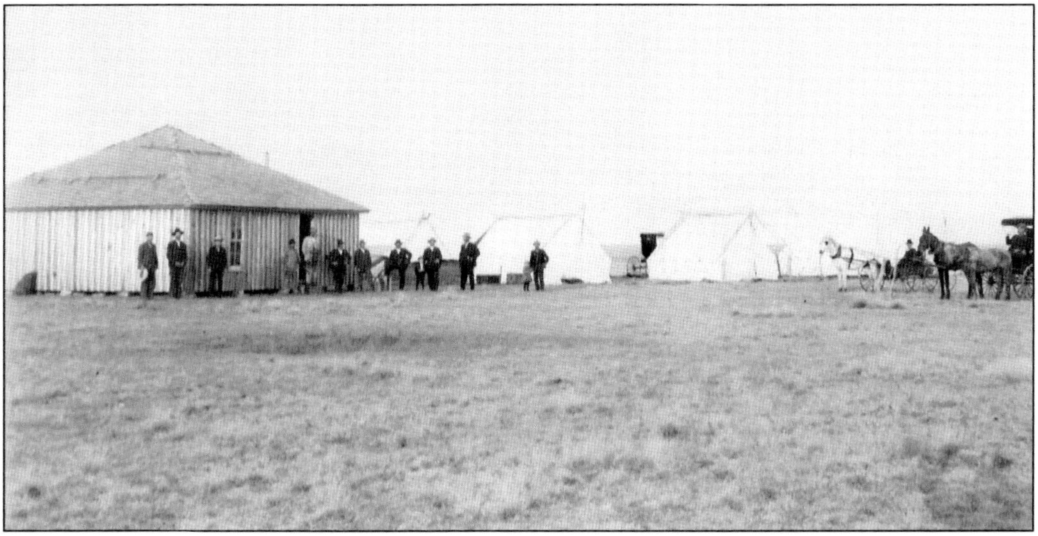

This 1907 photograph is of the first town site. Tents sit in the background. The first months proved to be a false start, as surveyors discovered the site chosen by Post for the town was not located in the center of the county, as required by Texas law. Post ordered all construction halted, and a new site was staked below the Caprock.

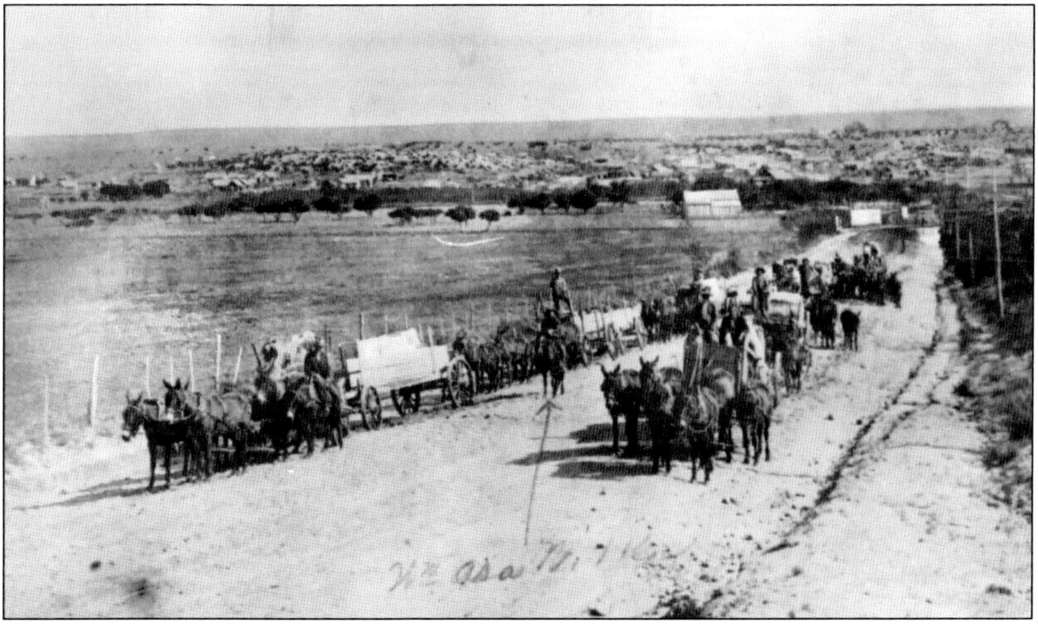

The Double U wagons shown here are leaving Big Spring. In February 1907, the Double U Company mule train, consisting of 24 new wagons loaded with supplies, pulled by 72 of Missouri's finest mules, took off from Big Spring, the closest rail head. A 70-mile trip lay ahead to reach the new town site of Post City. Wagons and stock probably arrived on the train.

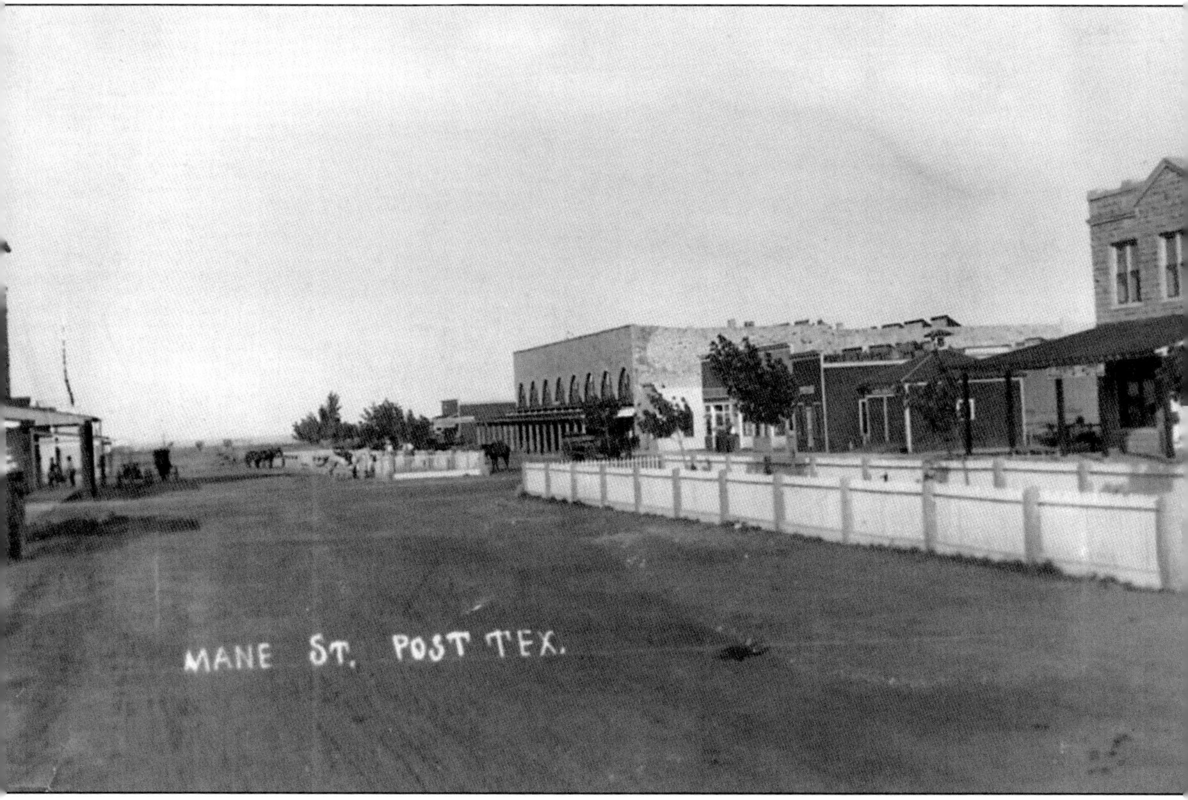

This photograph of Main Street in Post City reveals the new town that has begun taking shape. The arched buildings are the Double U Company stores. On the far right is the new Algerita Hotel, named from the Algerita bush, a beautiful shrub with little red berries and prickly leaves. By 1911, Post City began to prosper. C. W. Post ordered the town's rapid expansion to slow up to allow the economy to adjust itself and to quit relying on the Double U Company. The transition was a little painful for a while, but by the end of the year, the population had increased to 1,500, almost double the previous year. While blasting a road coming off the cap, a limestone deposit was discovered, which would prove to be a great source for building materials for homes and businesses.

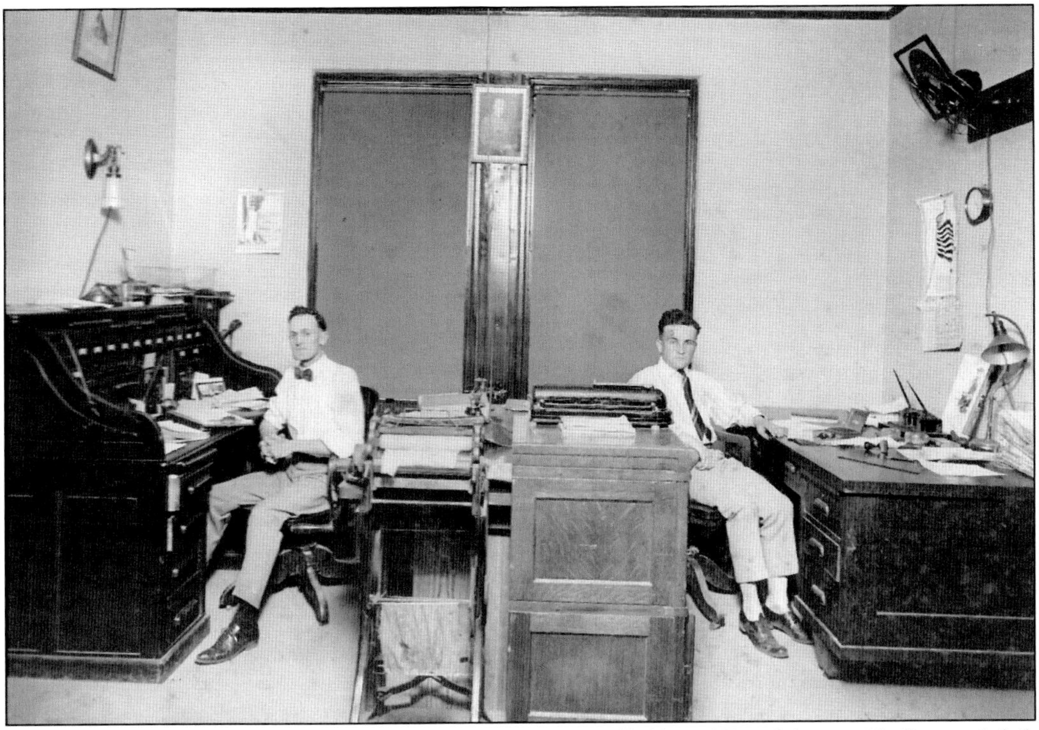

The Double U Company bookkeepers are James Durrett (left) and Don Murray. To Durrett's left is an early version of a copy machine, now in the collection of the museum. A portrait of C. W. Post is hanging at the top of the window.

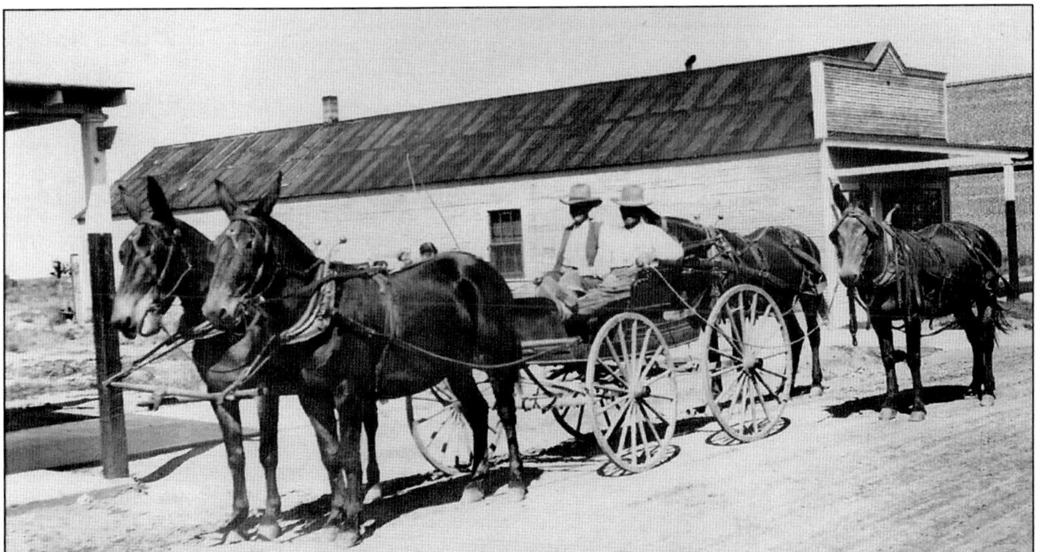

This is an early photograph of C. W. Post's prize mules, probably taken around 1908. Seated in the buggy are Uncle Tom Stevens (left) and Post. The building in the background was the newspaper office. Stevens was a Fort Worth banker who scouted the area for available lands for Post to buy.

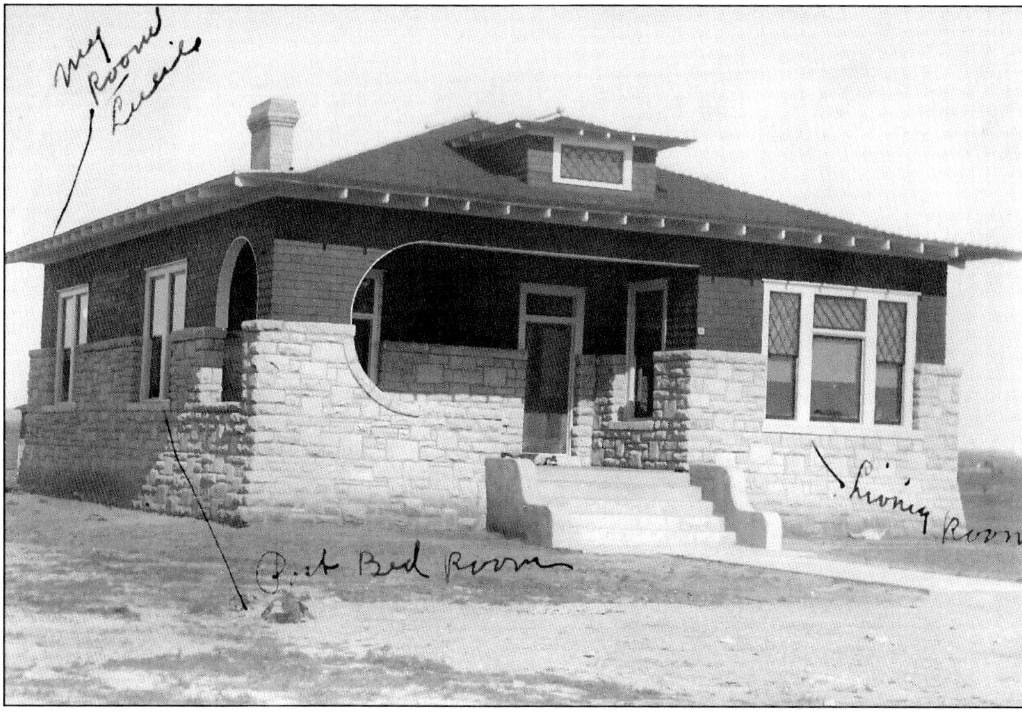

The first house (pictured above), built in 1907, was this little cottage constructed of native stone as a residence for C. W. Post and his family. Those on the front porch of the Post cottage (shown below) are, from left to right, Lucile Stevens, Dorothy Howe, C. W. Post, Leila Post, Uncle Tom Stevens, and Mrs. T. P. Stevens. Apparently this was young Lucile's first visit (of many to come) as guest of the Posts. This delightful lady never married and lived to be 101 years old. She was clipping grass near her driveway when her neighbor accidently hit her with her car, ending Lucile's long, full life. Many of the earliest photographs were taken by her and were later donated to the museum. She also wrote on every picture.

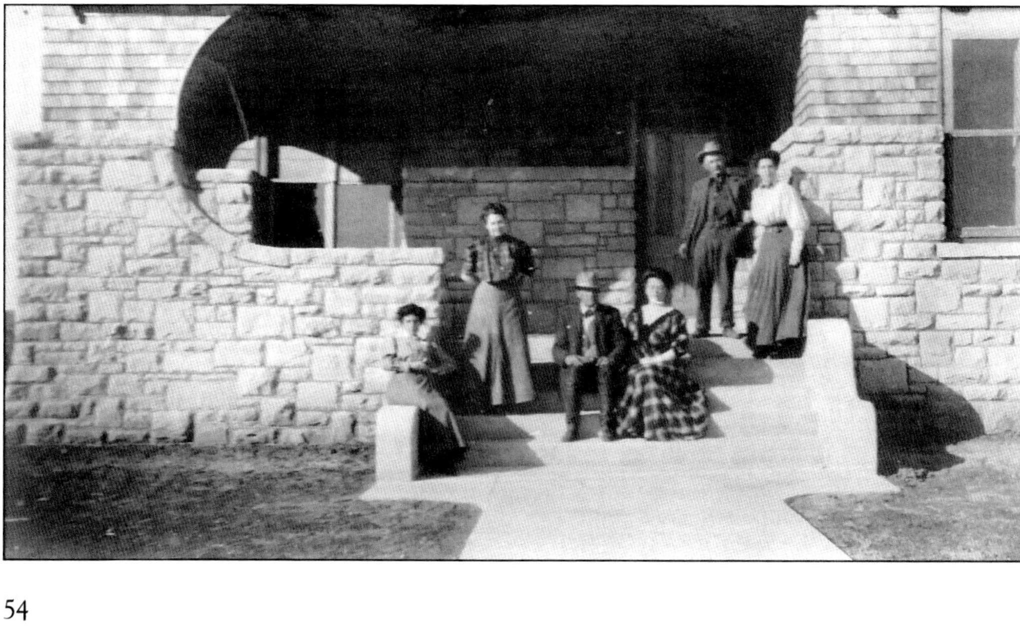

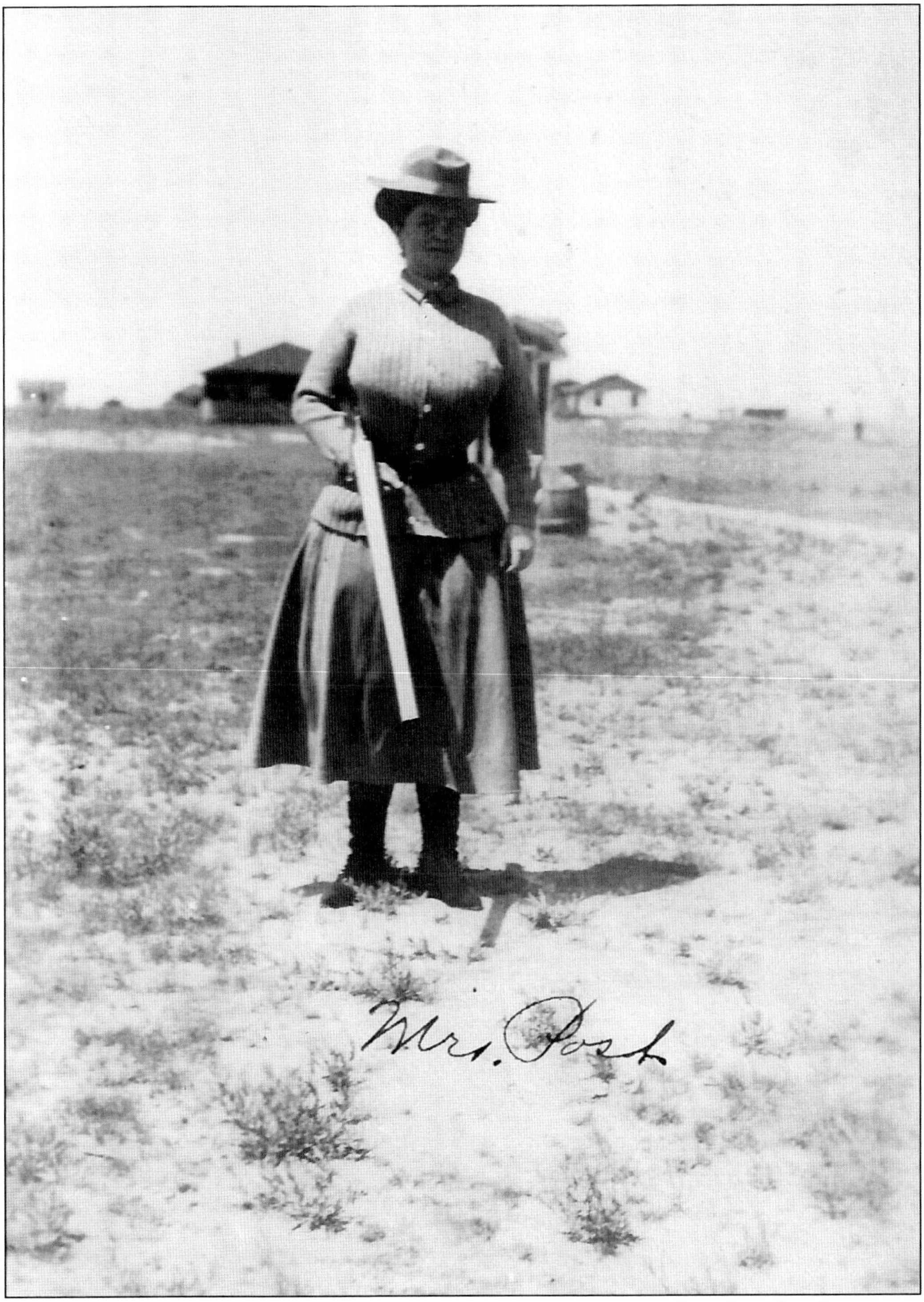

This 1908 photograph shows Leila Post. She seems to have adjusted to the role of a pioneer woman, at least in training, carrying the large gun with ease. C. W. Post was an avid hunter and gun collector, providing Leila with her own personal firearms instructor.

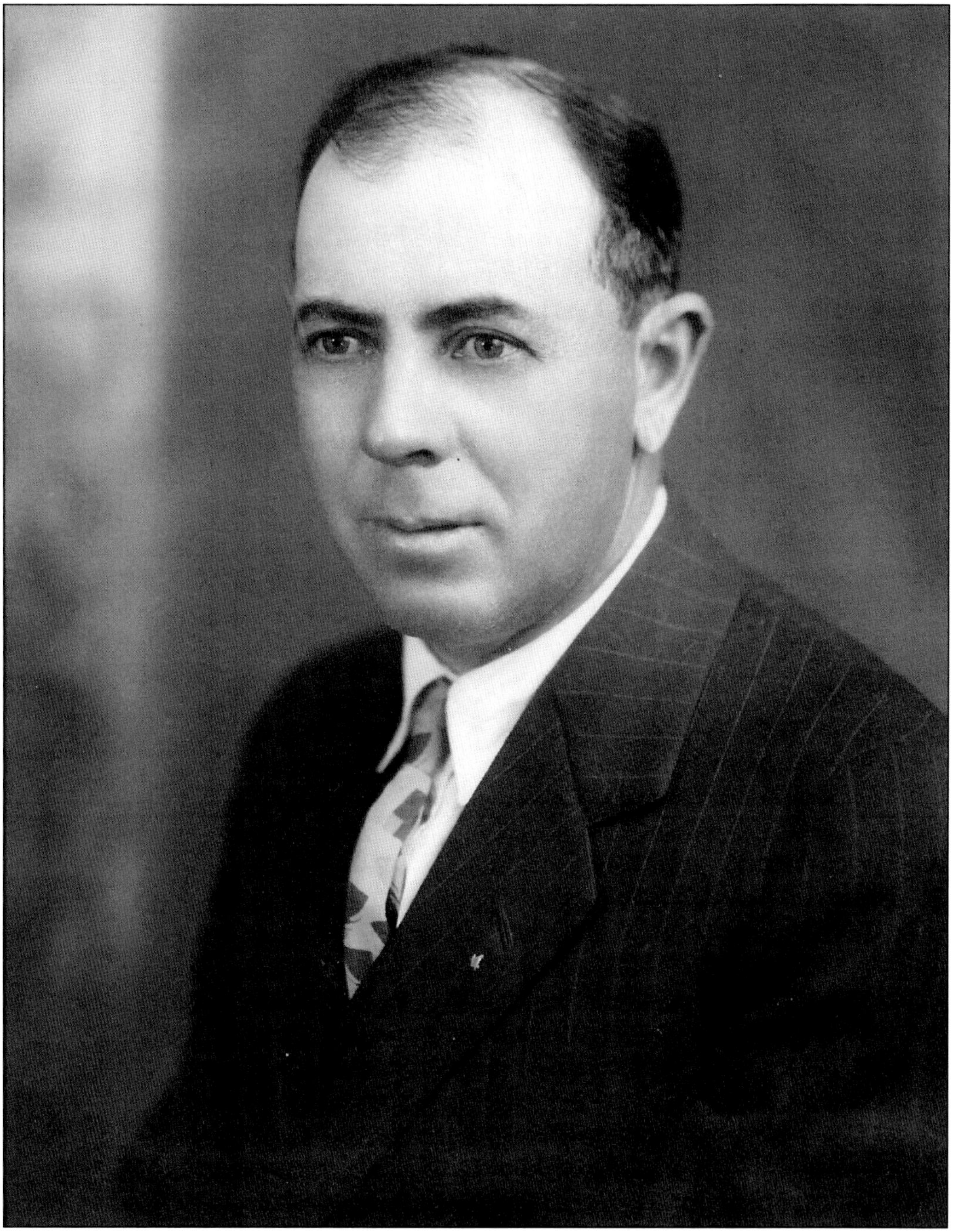

George "Scotty" Samson, a stonemason from Scotland, came to Post in 1907. Samson and fellow stonemason Jimmie Napier were working in Georgetown when they heard about a fellow named C. W. Post building a town in West Texas. Their job was about to end, so they decided to send a telegram of inquiry, which read, "C. W. Post-What about a job for two stonemasons?-signed George Samson and Jimmie Napier." In about two weeks an answer arrived, "Come at once, plenty of work-signed C. W. Post." Jimmie volunteered to go check it out. Two weeks later, George joined him. Post soon made him foreman over stonework.

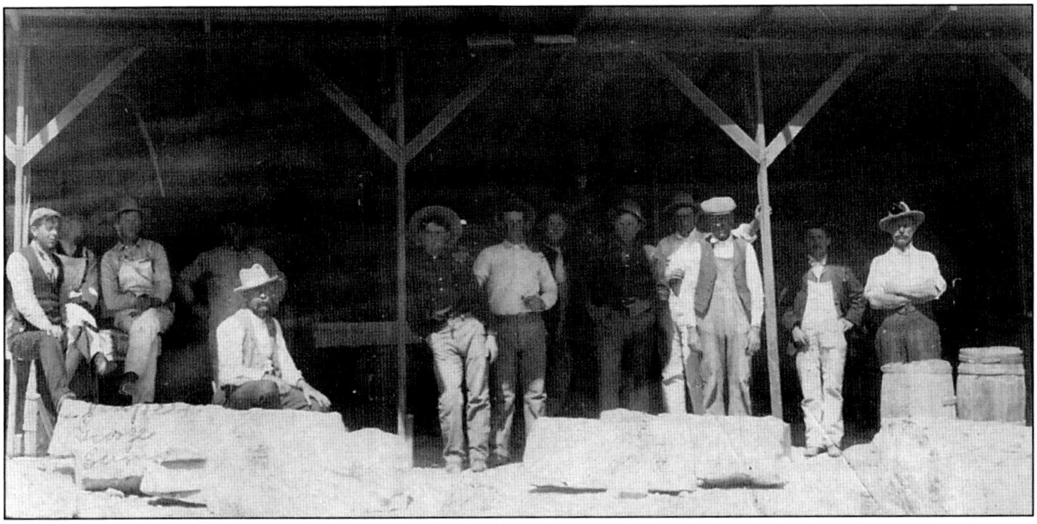

Stonecutters George "Scotty" Samson (far left) and Jimmie Napier (sitting on large stone) pose with coworkers at the stonecutters shed in 1907. Finding these two young stonemasons to make use of the limestone quarry was a real windfall for C. W. Post and for the town.

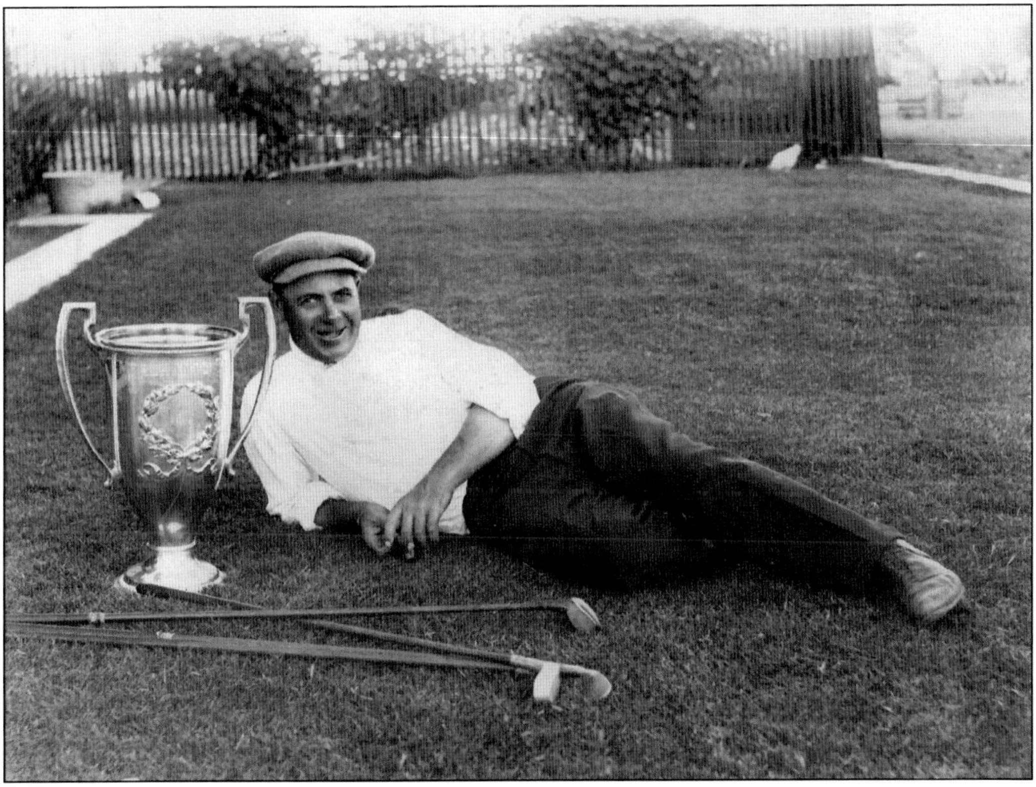

Golfer George "Scotty" Samson poses with the winning cup. In 1912, many changes were happening in Post, one being the laying out of a golf course. Golf was appropriately called cow pasture pool at that time, and the course wrested from the cows at Post City was hailed as the first golf course west of Mineral Wells. C. W. Post provided a cup for the annual competition and played when in town. Scotty seems to be the winner this year.

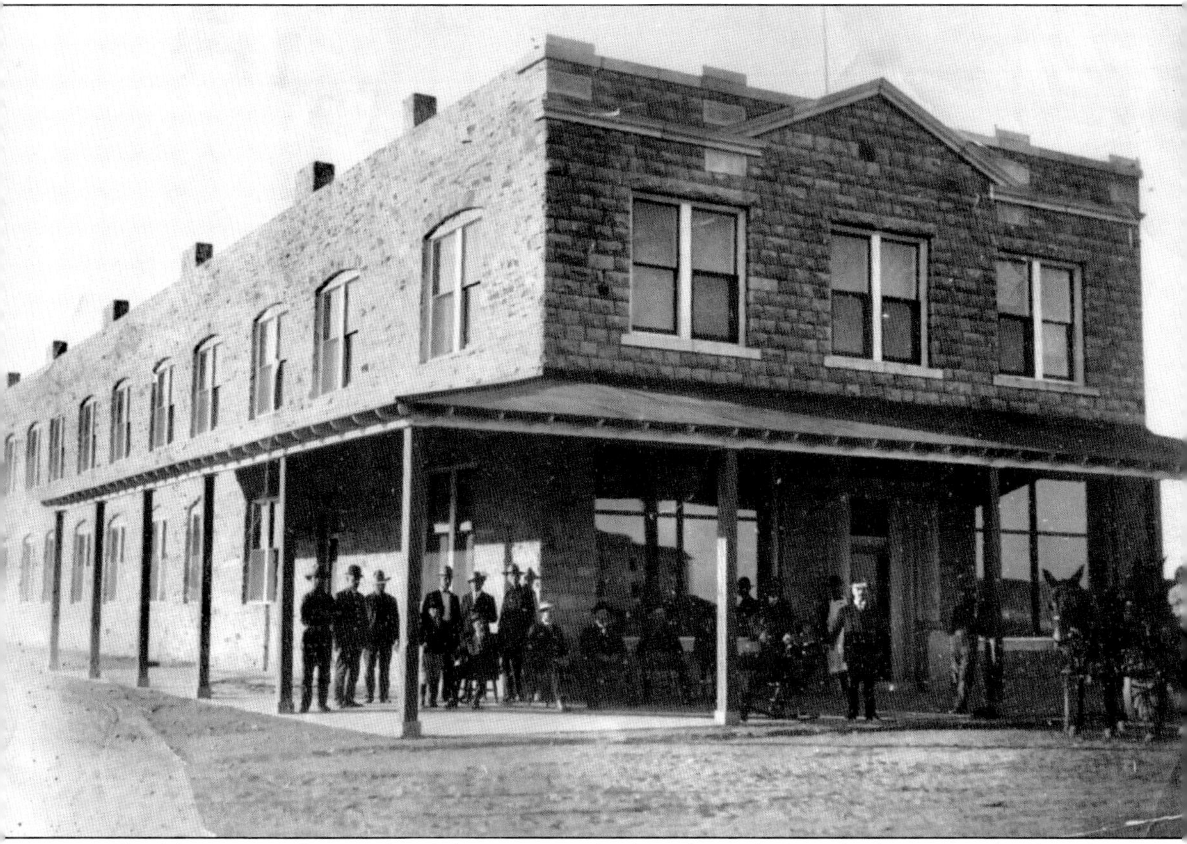

The Algerita Hotel opened on July 17, 1908. It had 30 elegantly furnished rooms with all modern improvements, including bathrooms, flushing water closets, and a fine barbershop. The rate per day for workmen was $1, and $2 for the best in the house. The hotel became a favorite spot for parties. Christmas 1908 was one such gathering; every room was taken, with two or three people in each bed. The occasion was the Grand Cowboy Ball, held the night after Christmas, which was attended by 150 people dancing until dawn. In 1909, C. W. Post came to town and stayed at the Algerita. The next day he claimed the mattress was so hard he could not sleep, so he ordered new ones to be put on top of the old ones in each room, along with larger sheets and more blankets.

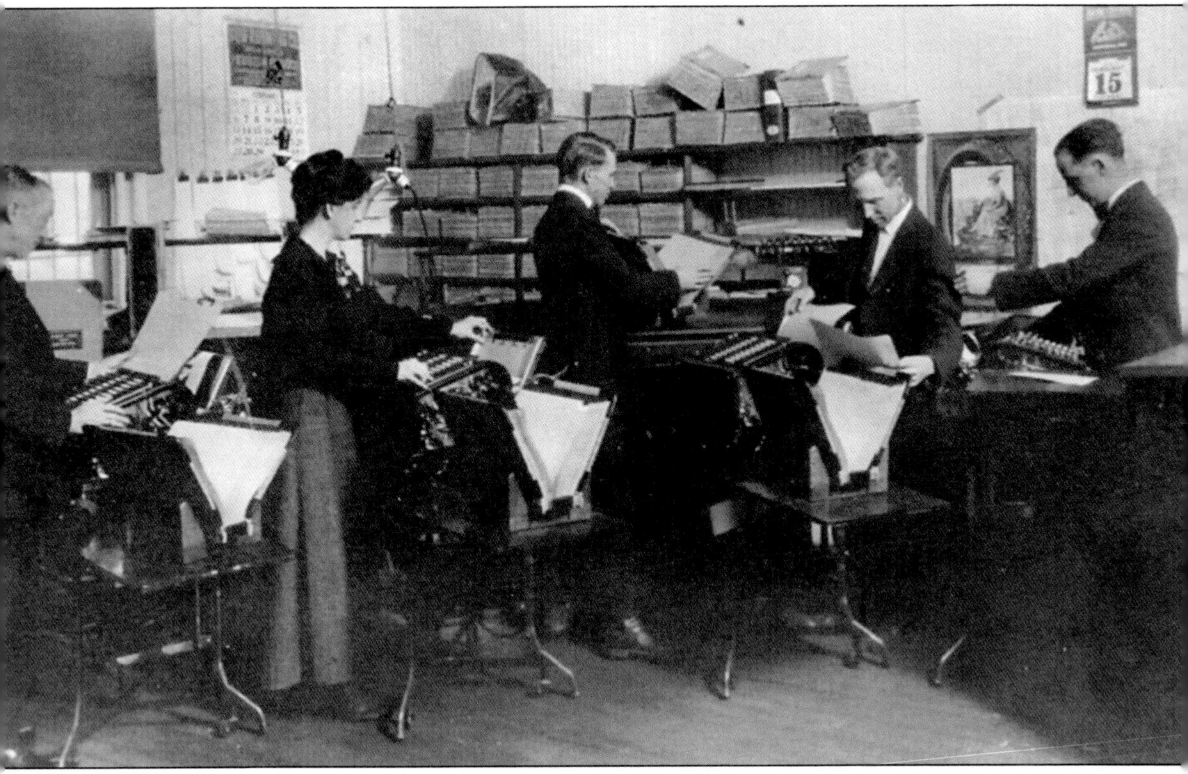

The First National Bank of Post opened for business on July 31, 1909. The five individuals in the photograph are not identified, but they seem to be efficiently taking care of business. The bank opened with a capital stock of $50,000, with C. W. Post holding the controlling interest of $26,000. The first location of the bank was in one of the Double U Company store buildings. Opening day netted a total of $16,109.50 in deposits. A new bank building was constructed in 1916. One of Post's recommendations to the bank was that it should provide itself with a .44 Colt, double action, with either a 6- or 8-inch barrel. Post was said to be an expert on firearms, but the purchase was never confirmed. At any rate, the bank was never robbed.

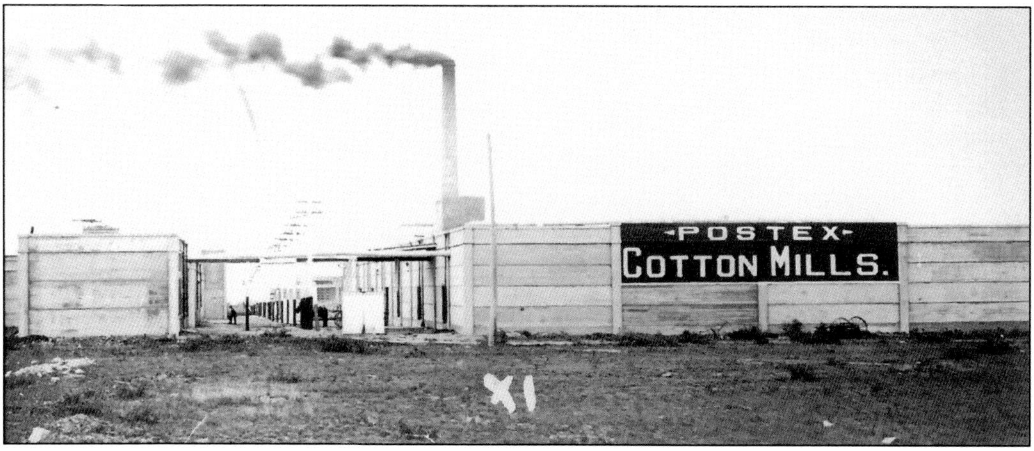

C. W. Post began planning the Postex Cotton Mill (pictured above in 1913) in 1911, and it was in full production by May 1913. His goal was to bring locally grown cotton from the field to the cotton mill, which would manufacture sheets and pillowcases under the trade name of Garza and Postex. The plant was said to be the first of its kind in the nation and possibly in the world. The cost of building Postex was $650,000. Post not only created jobs for the people, but an economic base that would sustain the area for the next 70 years. After Post died, the Post family continued management of the mill through its New York offices until the plant was sold in 1945. In 1955, Burlington Industries, the world's largest textile manufacturer, purchased Postex and operated the plant until 1983. The 1913 photograph below shows the heavy machinery operating in the mill.

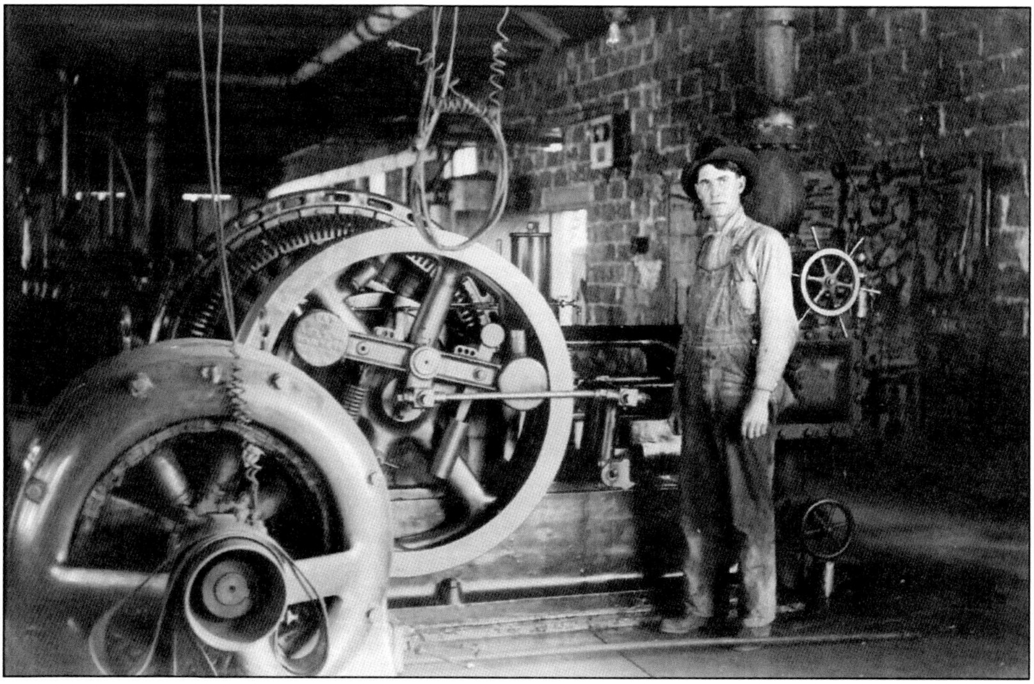

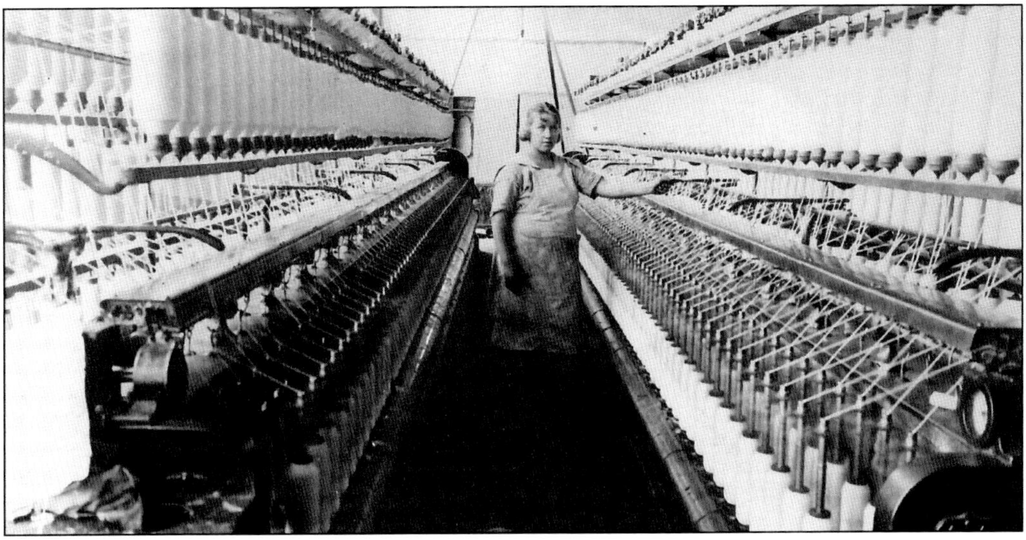

The 1913 photograph above was taken in the spinning room of Postex. In 1905, C. W. Post said, "A large industry reminds me of a big clock. The face is like the factory grounds, the workmen move about like the hands, and are seen most, the foreman, bookkeepers, cashier, timekeeper, superintendent and heads of departments are the wheels, and away back there somewhere is the boss, the mainspring that must be strong and kept wound up to keep the hands and wheels going; but every piece is important, and each must do its part, and do it faithfully." The 1913 Postex Mill photograph below was taken in the bleach room, where J. C. Coal (above), Jim Hare (left), and Leslie Cartright (right) are running cloth.

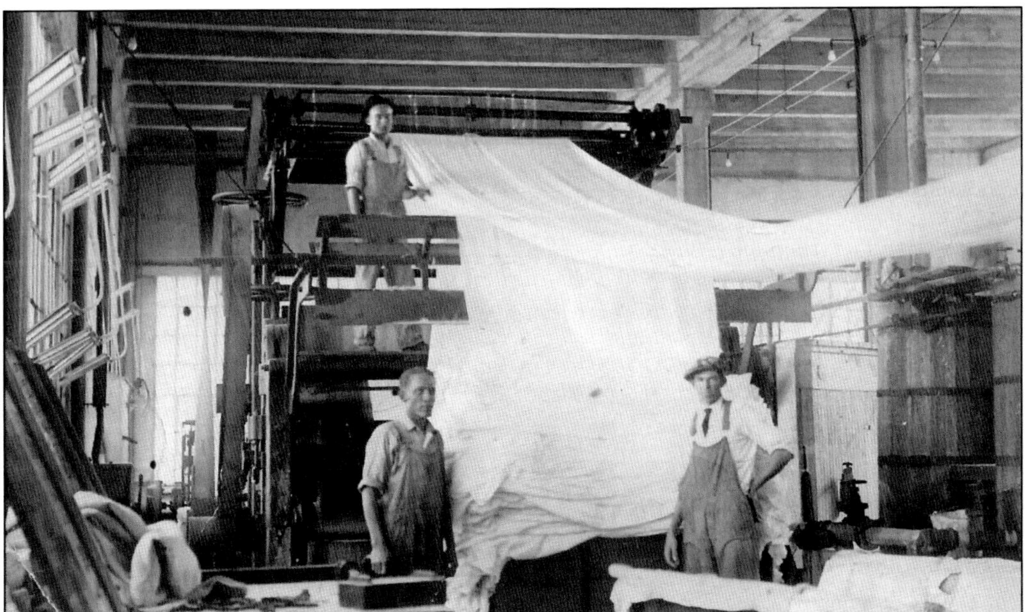

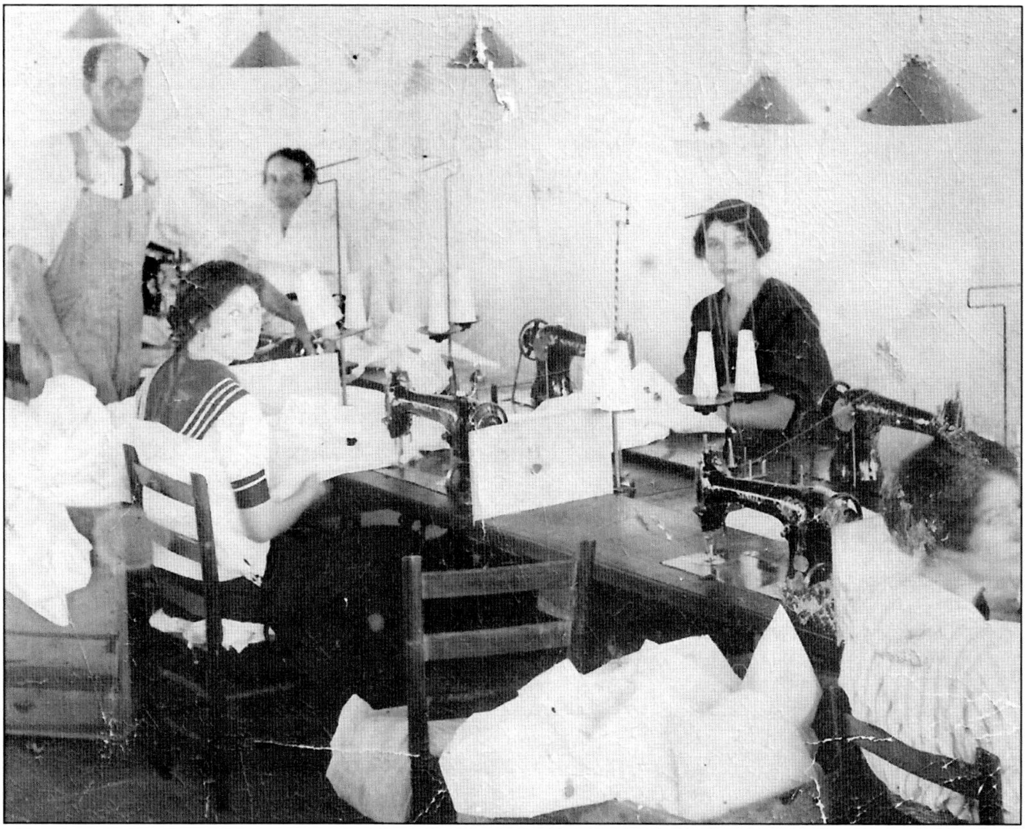

This 1913 photograph (above) shows workers in the sewing room of the Postex Cotton Mill. The 1957 aerial view below shows the vastness of the plant itself. The homes are mill houses available for the employees. The old smokestack still stands as a landmark that can be seen from miles away. Locals still miss the whistle that signaled shift changes and even the traffic jams on Main Street.

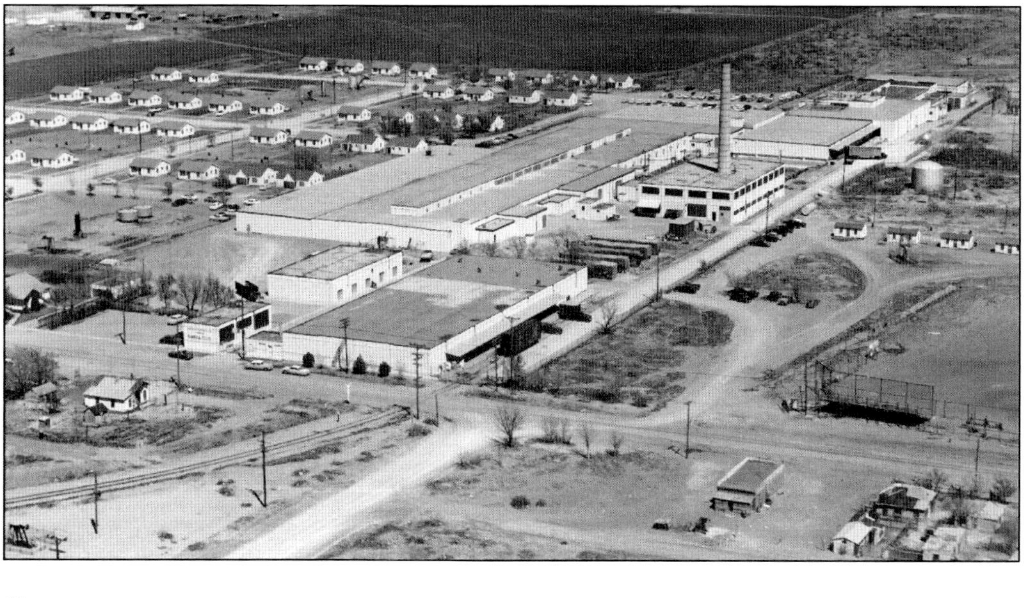

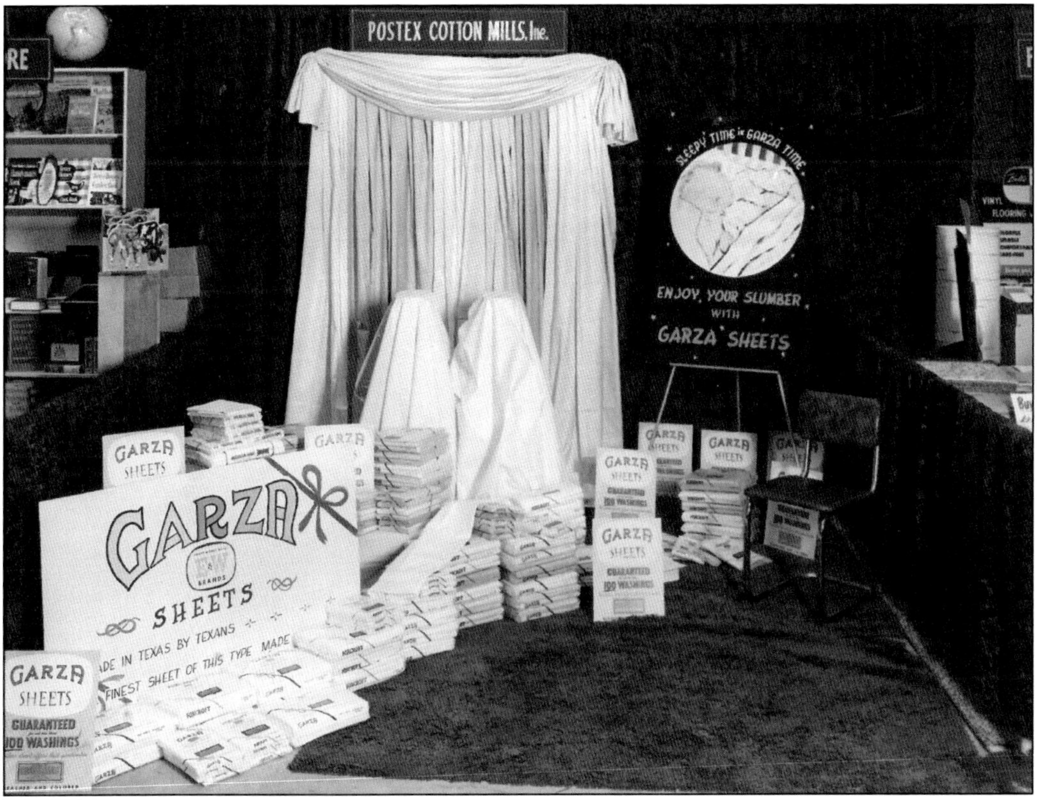

The Postex Cotton Mill Exhibit at the Lubbock Fair in 1955 (pictured above) featured "Garza sheets and pillowcases, made in Texas by Texans, guaranteed for 100 washings." The image below shows one of the Post farmhouses, built by the Double U Company. When prospective colonists came into town to see the farms, the first thing they saw was a 32-by-8-foot sign that read, "C. W. Post Home Farms. Tracts of 160 to 320 acres improved and ready to farm. Houses designed by good architect. Farms complete with all necessary buildings, silos, fences, wells, tanks, etc. Terms: Cash two dollars per acre and one dollar seventy-five per acre each year until purchase price is paid with interest at four percent." By July 1915, three hundred farms had been sold. By January 1, 1916, that number increased to more than 400 farms and ranches sold.

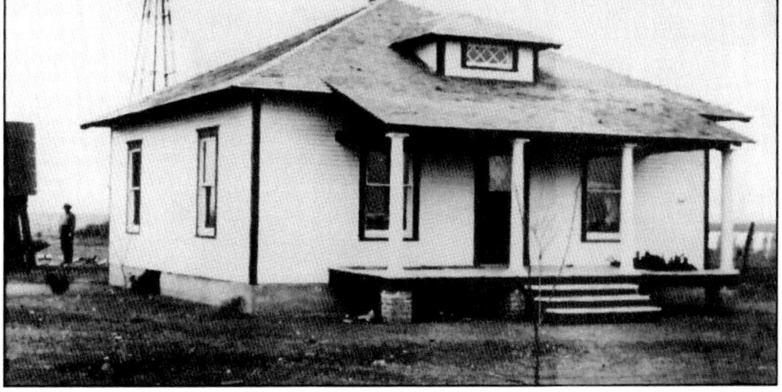

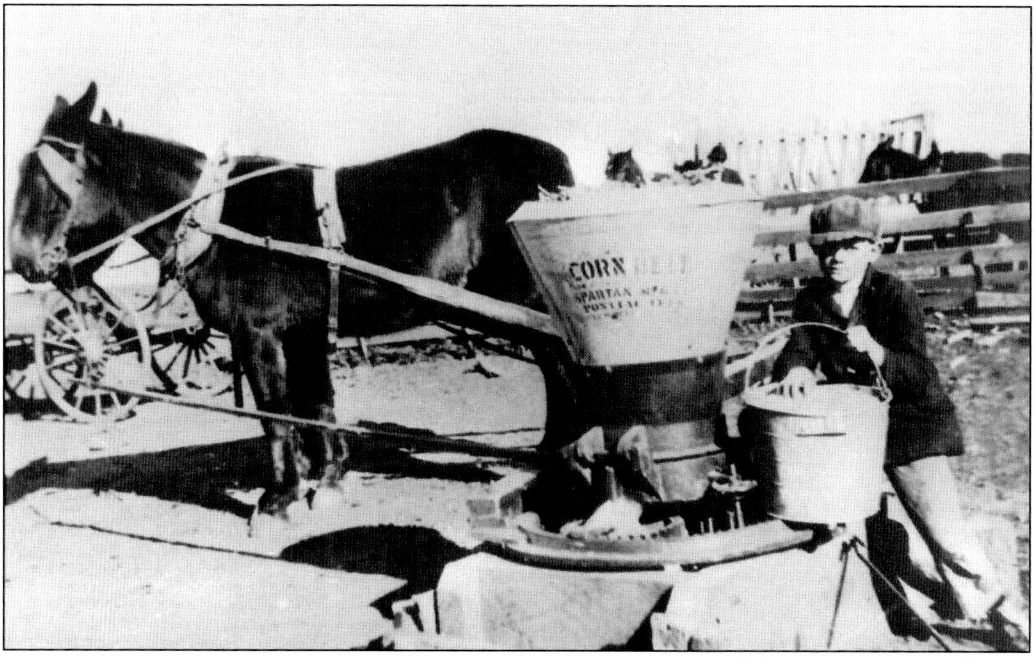

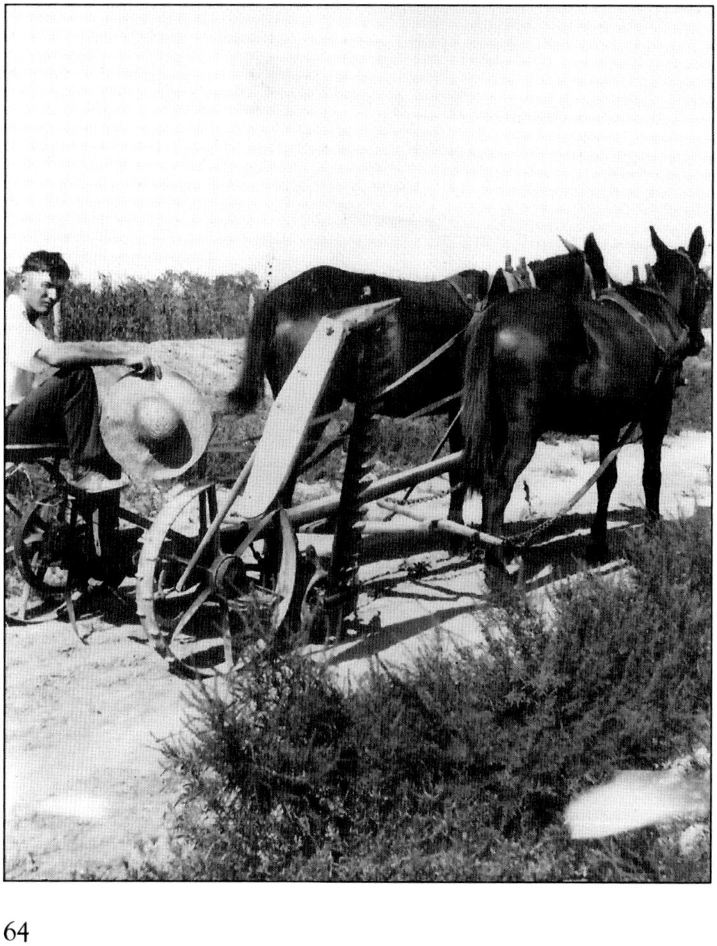

The young man in the above image is operating a mule-drawn feed grinder in 1920. C. W. Post's experimental farming project started with 320 acres of land on the plains and another 320 acres in the breaks below the Caprock Escarpment. These projects were a process of elimination for what would or would not grow in the area. Post was keen on planting fruit trees, and each farm of 80 and 160 acres was provided a 3-acre orchard. The 1923 photograph at left shows Oscar Sinclair on a mule-drawn hay mower.

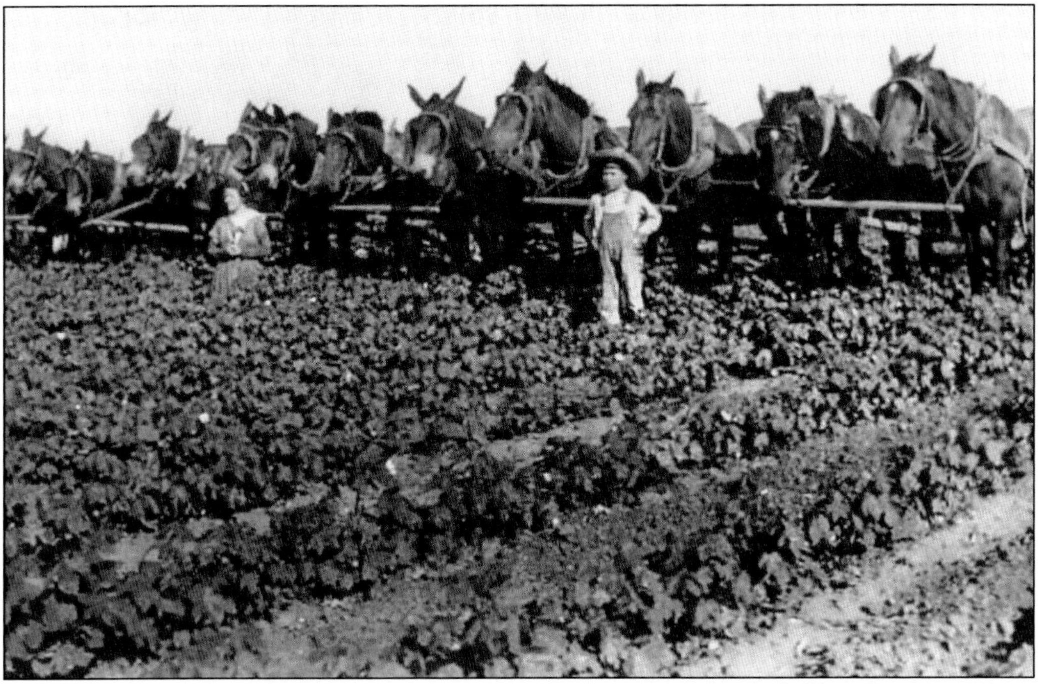

This early photograph, taken at the Thuett farm, shows Myrtle Thuett (left) and son L. G. Jr. in the cotton field. L. G. Sr. and hired hands are likely behind the line of mules and horses. It would be interesting to know how many plows they were pulling. In 1918, Lawrence Gregory Thuett Sr. went to investigate farming opportunities in West Texas, purchased 160 acres from the C. W. Post Estate, and in time he acquired more land for his farming operation. The property was passed on to his son, L. G. Jr. The land remained in the family and is now farmed by grandsons Ronald Thuett and Jerry Thuett. The tractors shown below were massive machines for the time and even had canopies to give a little shade. (Both, courtesy Ron and Nancy Thuett.)

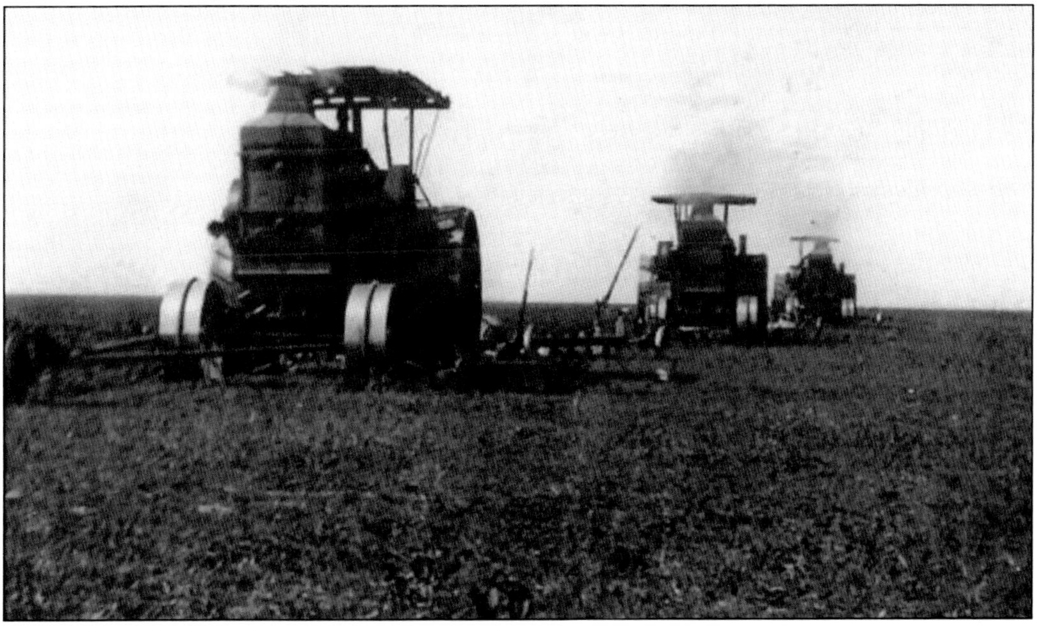

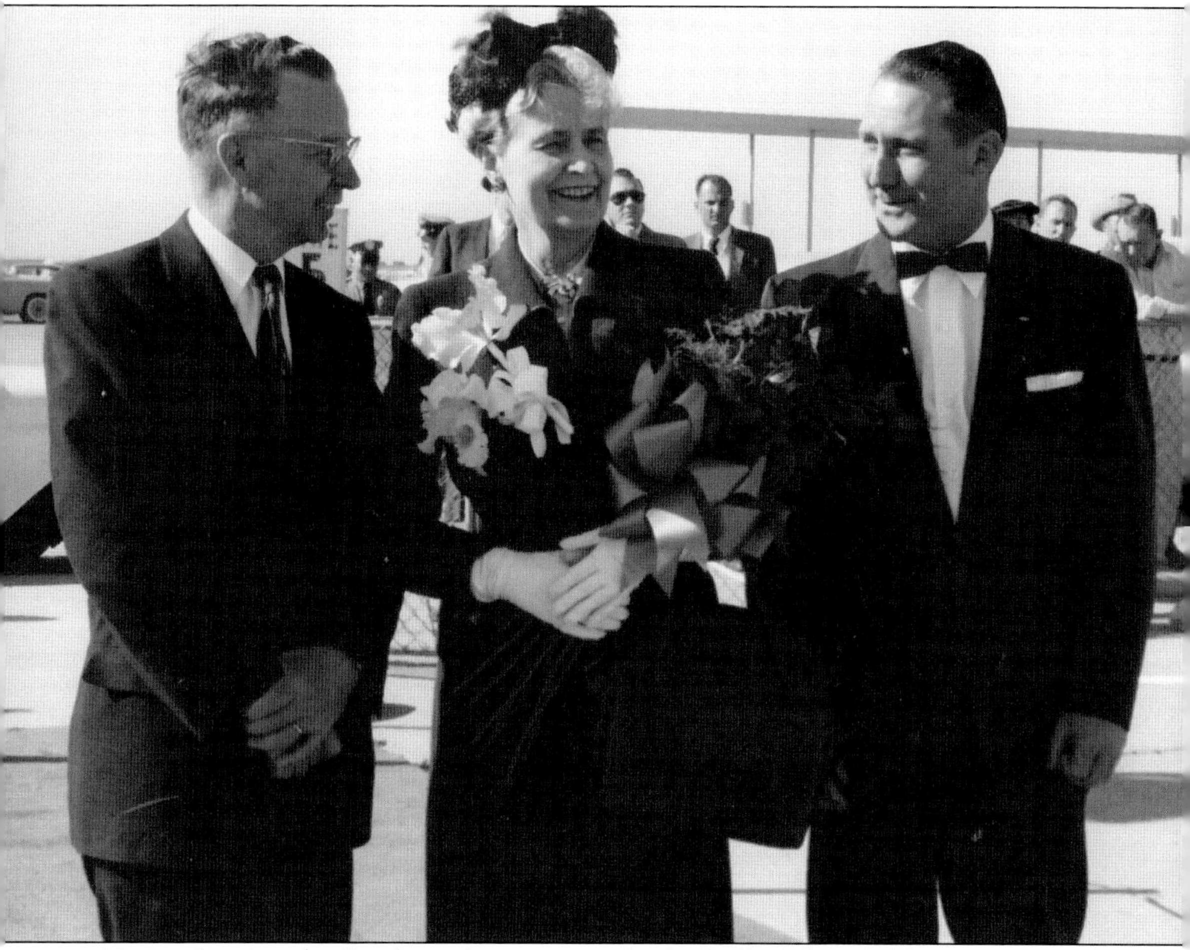

Marjorie Merriweather Post (center) came to town for the Golden Jubilee Celebration in September 1957. On her right is Russell Worgess, mayor of Battle Creek, Michigan, and the gentleman on her left is Post's mayor, James Minor. Post wears a beautiful orchid corsage. She raised orchids in the hothouse at Hillwood, her home in Washington, D.C. That tradition continues at the Hillwood Museum.

Five

Gateway to Post City

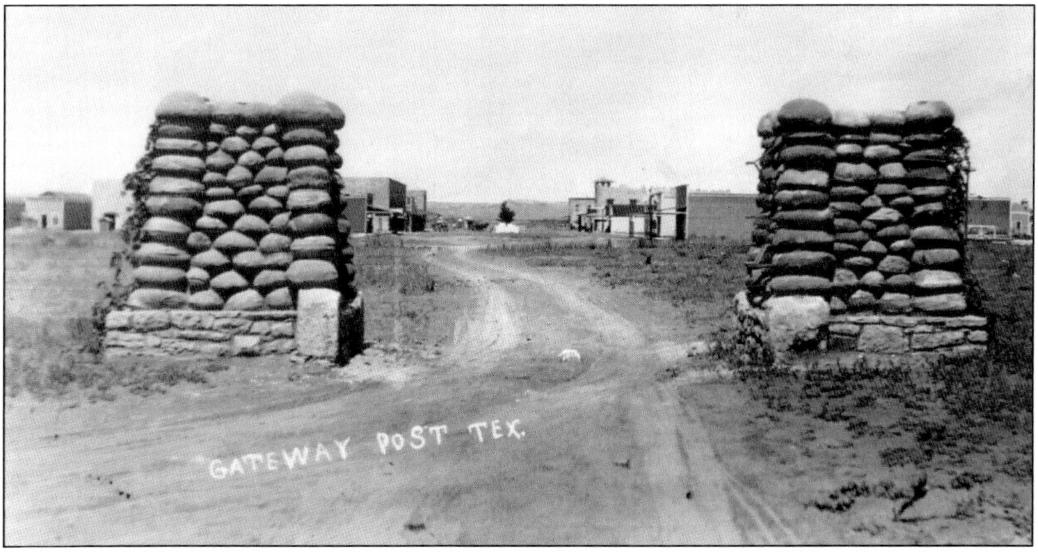

C. W. Post was intrigued by the shape and color of the unusual round rocks found in the county. He ordered the rocks harvested after big rains and stored them for future use. Stonemason Scotty Samson used the stones to build the gate shown in this 1907 image at the east end of town, but a runaway team demolished it, and the stones were again placed in storage.

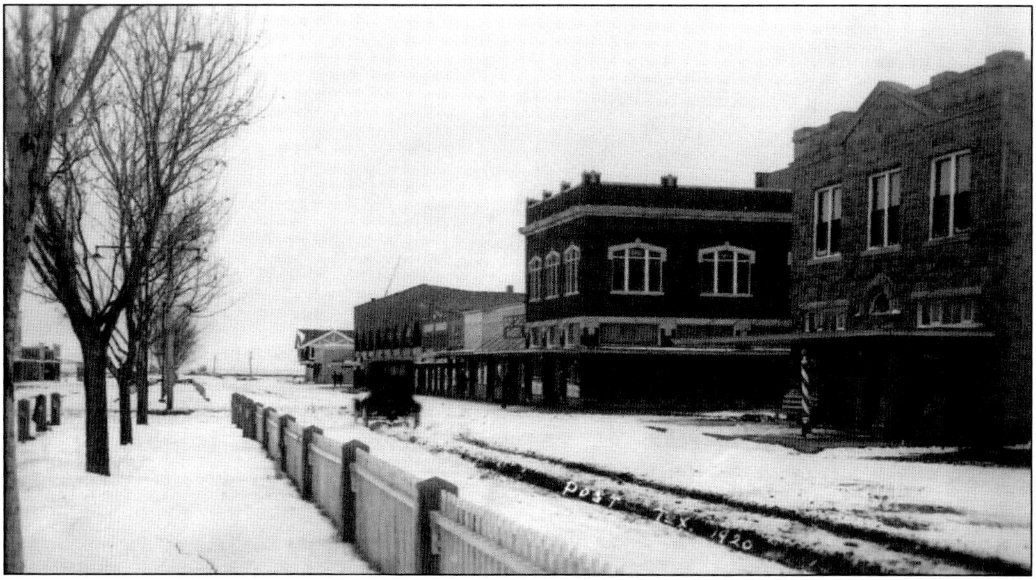

This 1920 scene of a snow-covered Main Street shows the progress made during a 13-year period. What was once a prairie now sported two-story buildings, grocers, drugstores, hardware stores, a bank, a 30-room hotel, and more. The building on the right front is the first hotel, the Algerita, built in 1908 and later called the Rogers Hotel. The next building to the left housed C. W. Post's offices.

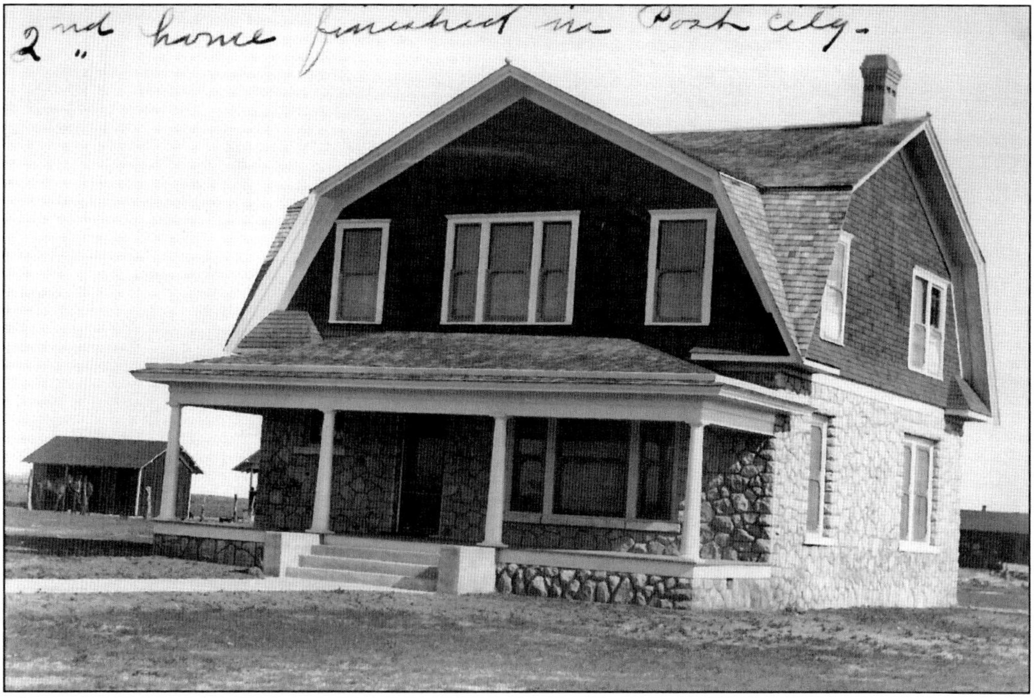

This 1907 image shows the W. O. Stevens residence, the second home built in Post. Stevens, formerly of Bridgeport, came highly recommended for an opening for a cashier at the new bank. He was hired and at the same time was made a Double U Company manager by C. W. Post. Stevens was the half-brother of Uncle Tom Stevens, a trusted friend and associate of Post.

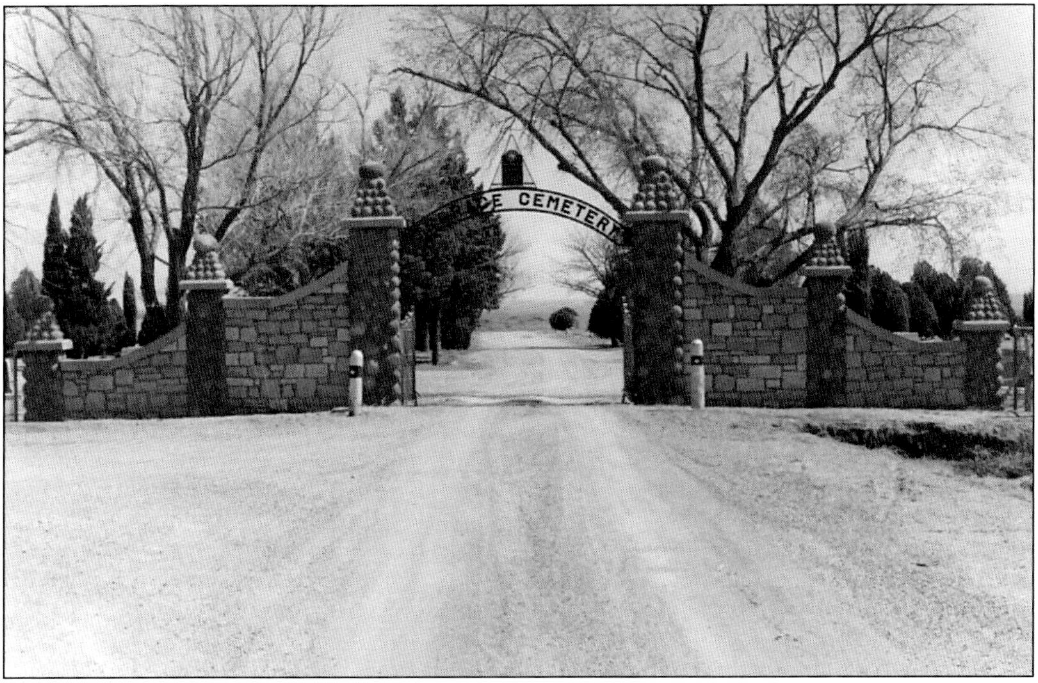

Scotty Samson used saved stones to create an entrance gate to the Terrace Cemetery (pictured above), designed after a similar gate near his home in Scotland. After the second death in Post in 1908, it became apparent that the town needed a cemetery. A request was made to C. W. Post. He replied that he personally wished that there were no need of any such spot, but that affairs must be conducted in accordance with the dictation of a power much superior to human intelligence. He gave his approval and provided the board with a complete plan for driveways, plots, and fencing. The date of the Terrace Cemetery photograph (below) is probably 1909. It would appear that the Woodsman gravestones were being placed.

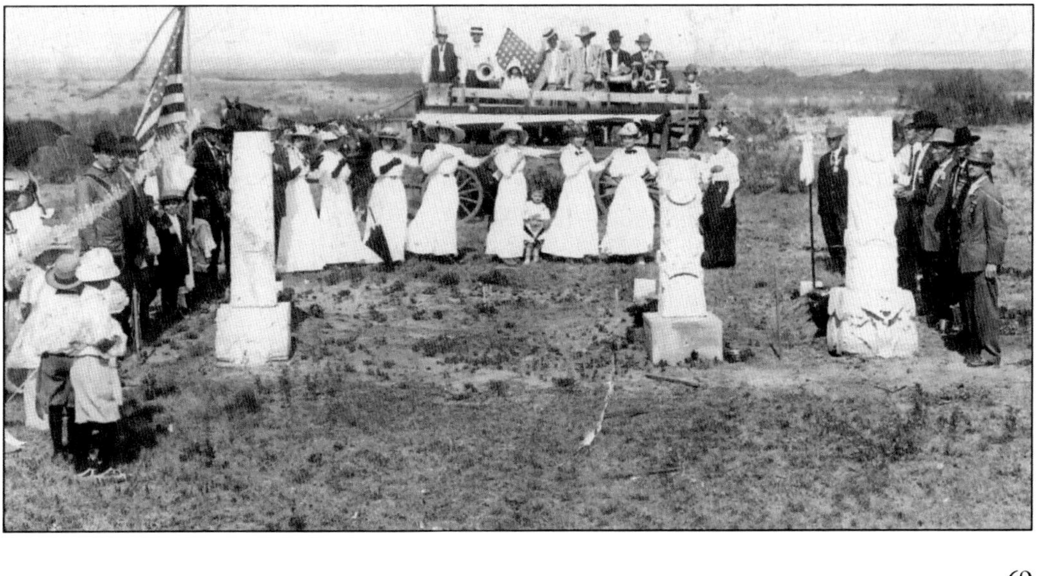

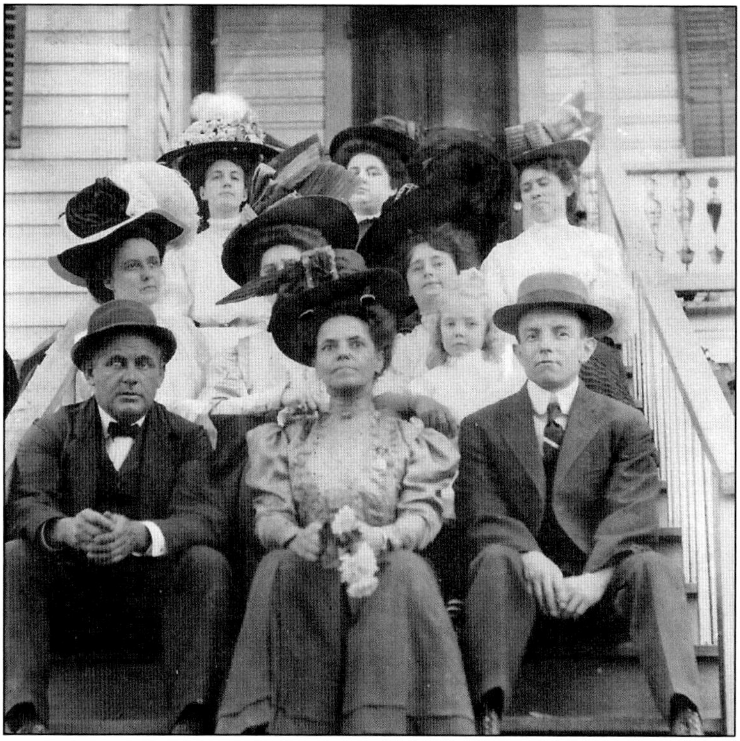

E. A. and Eva Warren (seated, front left) are the only people identified in this photograph. Everyone is decked out in his or her finest; ladies with beautiful hats and dresses, making a true fashion statement in the rural West Texas town of Post City. The striking group reflects that early residents exuberated great pride. Mrs. Warren wears a split skirt.

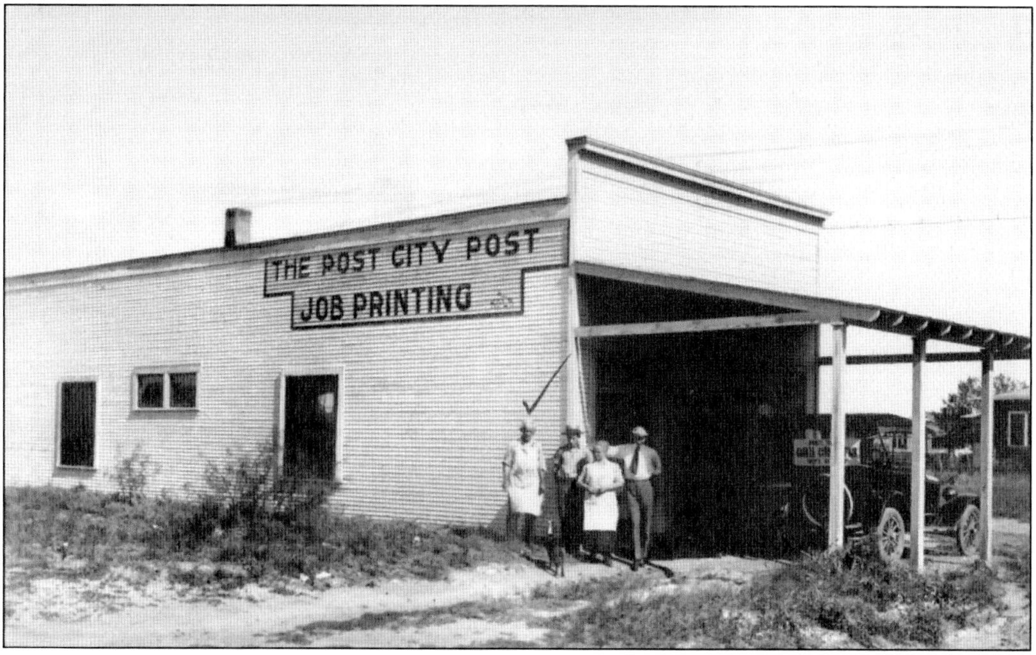

At the time of this photograph, E. A. Warren Sr., editor and publisher, owned the *Post City Post*. Its first owner was Hal Murray. Later the business name was changed to the *Post Dispatch* by E. A. Warren Jr. In this image are, from left to right, E. A. Warren Sr., Eddie Warren, Pauline Warren, and Emile Gandin A banner on the automobile advertises the Garza County Fair in September. A porch post obscures the year.

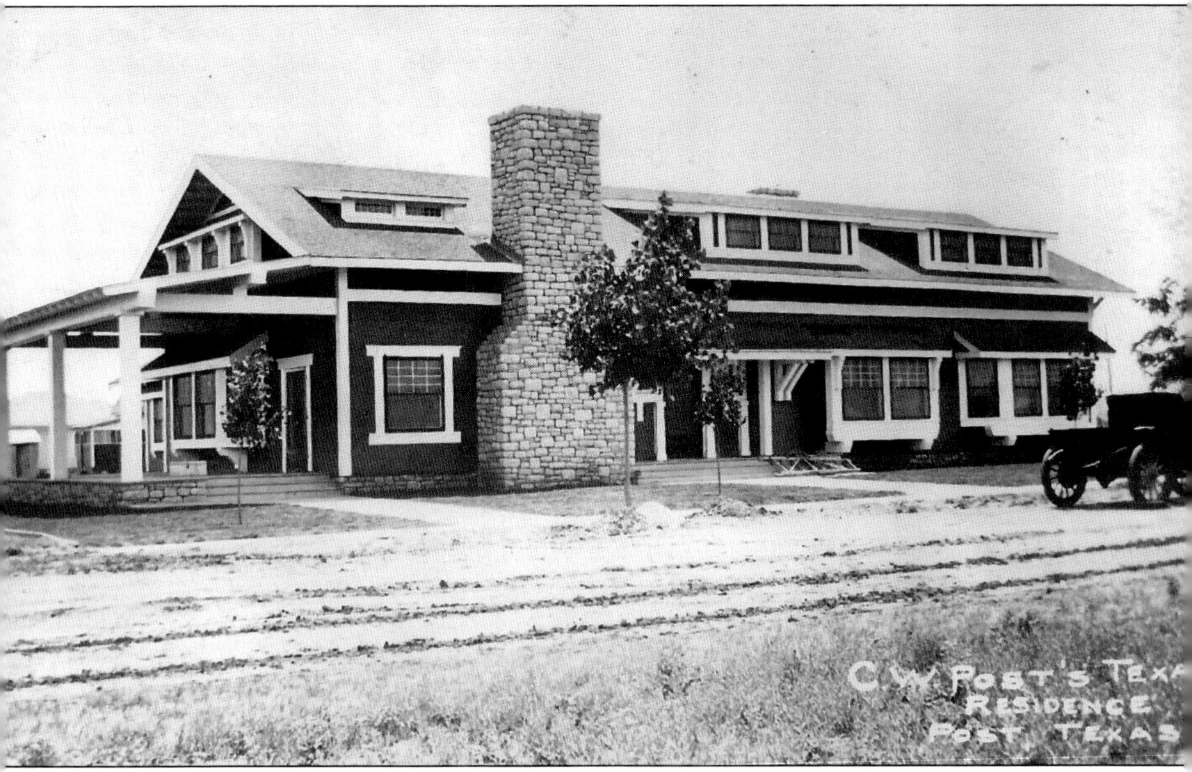

C. W. Post decided to build a home in Post City. He took great care in the planning and building of the house, which featured six bedrooms and six bathrooms, selecting furnishings that included hand-painted leather wallpaper. A Persian rug completely covered the floor, and chairs were stamped leather. The huge living room has a massive fireplace. The house was finished by September 1913, but due to pressing business that delayed his planned trip to Post City and then his illness, Post was never able to enjoy the comforts of his new home. He passed away on May 9, 1914, at age 59.

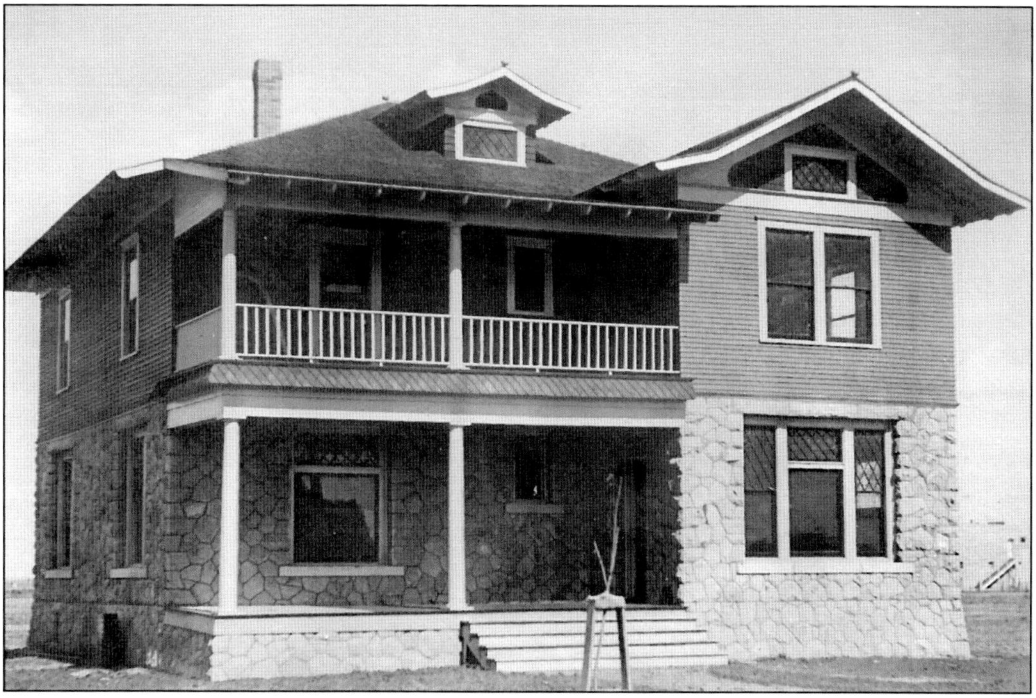

Built by a Mr. Fairbanks, the first superintendent of the Postex Mill, this was later home to the Guy Speck family. Early houses in Post were of many different styles, with some constructed of native stone and others of wood or combinations of the two. In 1908, C. W. Post set the price on town lots at $90 to $500, depending on location. He also fixed prices for houses from $800 to $5,000, depending on the number of rooms.

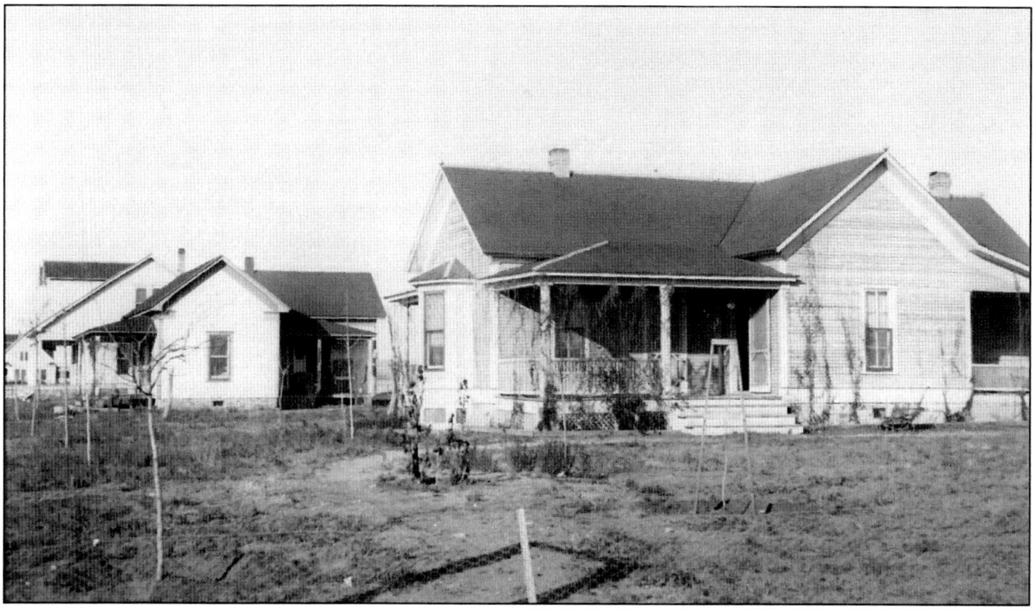

The house at far left is the home of H. B. Murray, the first county-district clerk, who was elected in 1907. The middle dwelling belongs to the Elkins family, and the home on the right belonged to the first sheriff, O. B. Kelley.

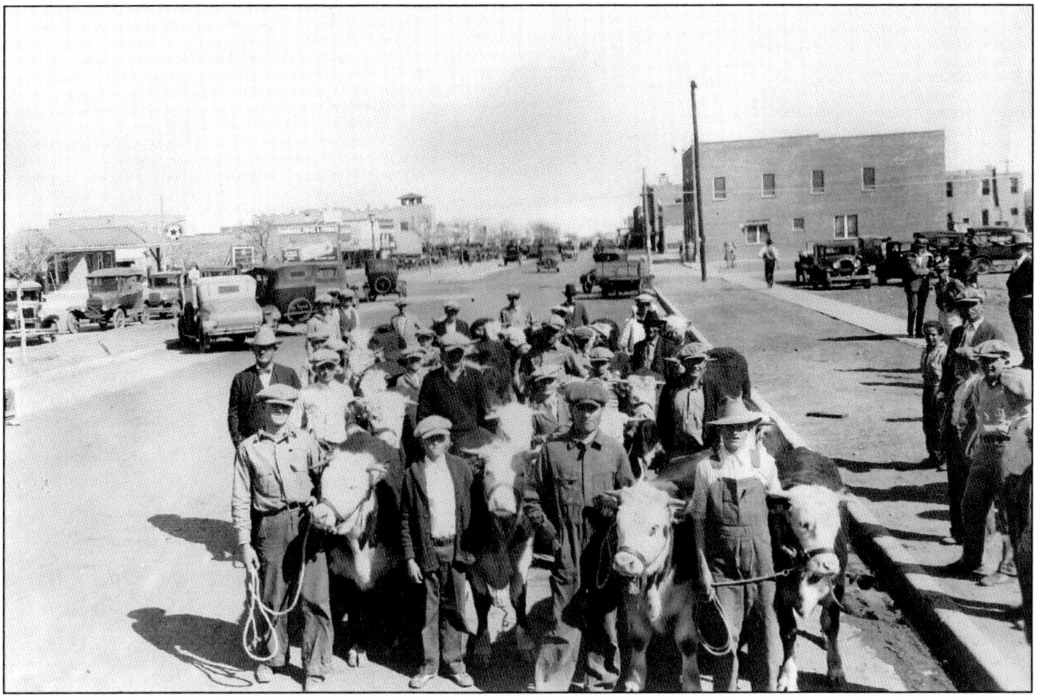

This 1928 photograph shows a large group of 4-H boys with their stock show animals, cattle from the OS Ranch. Giles Connell is the gentleman in the dark suit. The winners of that event pose in the image below.

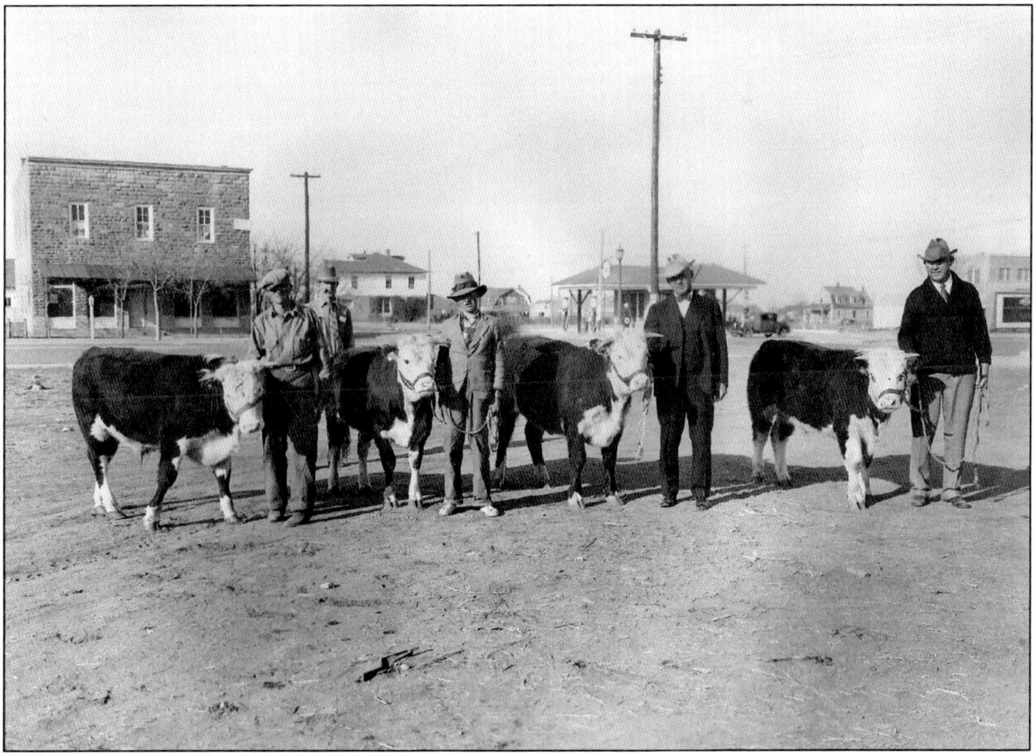

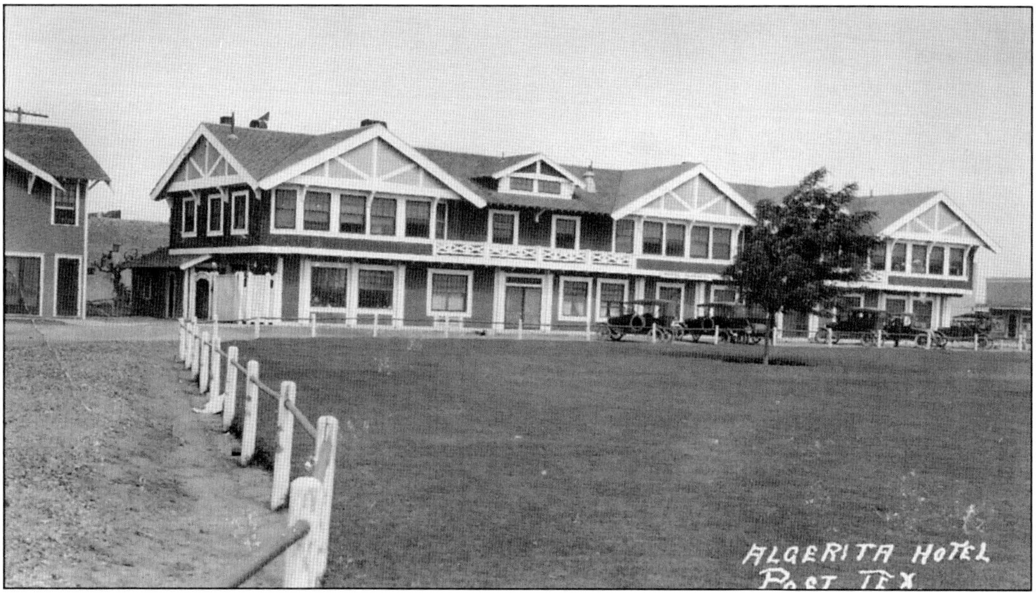

The second Algerita Hotel (pictured above) was built near the Santa Fe Depot to be more convenient for travelers arriving by train. The building was said to be a real showplace and was the site of many social gatherings. Sadly, it suffered a devastating fire and was completely destroyed. The photograph below features Charlie and Nancy Jackson, grandparents of Marie Neff and owners of the Railroad Hotel. This hotel was located near the tracks and provided easy access for men working on the railroad. The building is now the site of Calvary Baptist Church. (Both, courtesy Marie Neff.)

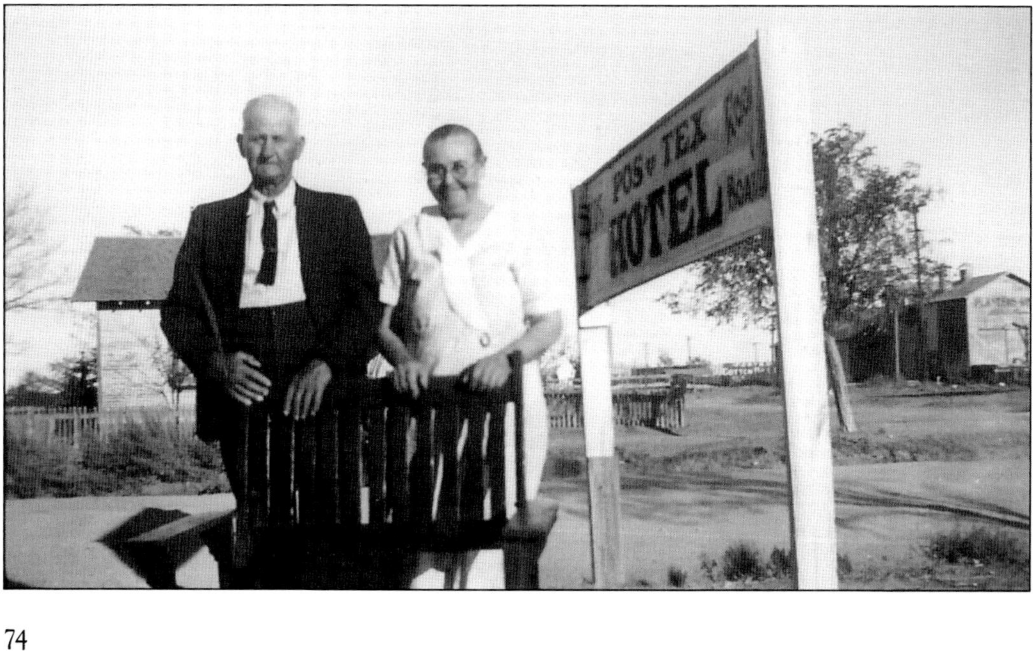

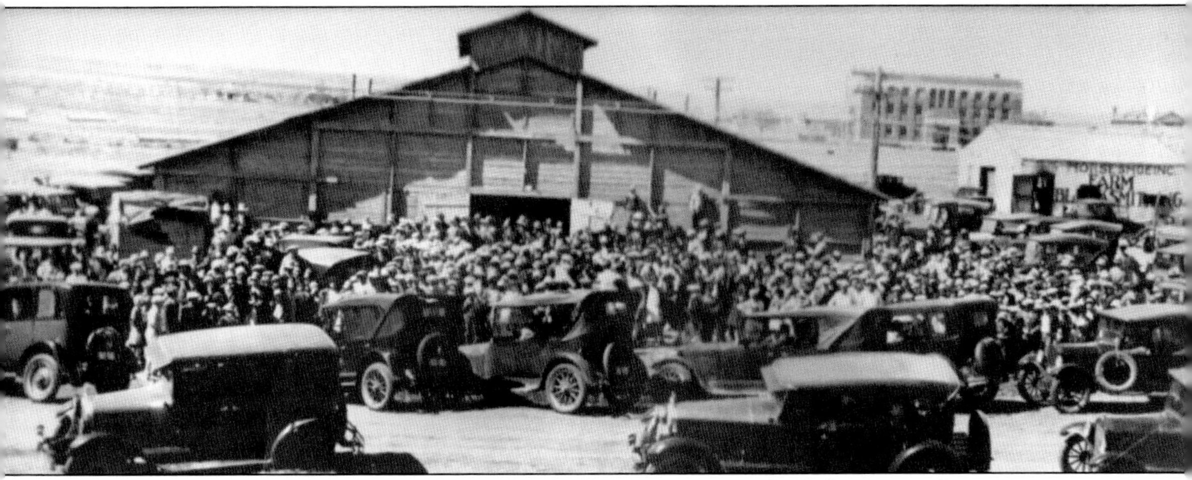

A county fair crowd gathers at the Mule Barn, built in 1922. The following information was attached to this donated photograph. "In 1922 when Rev. Finney, a well known evangelist, was coming to Post to hold a series of meetings, all the local churches pooled their resources and built this large building to accommodate the crowds. It was later called the Mule Barn and served many community needs. County Fairs, basketball games, school parties, Halloween parties, church meetings and numerous other community affairs were held here until it was demolished in 1936. One historic use was when it housed the Farm Exhibit created by Scotty Samson, which won first place in the State Fair in Dallas in 1926. The Garza County Courthouse can be seen in the background."

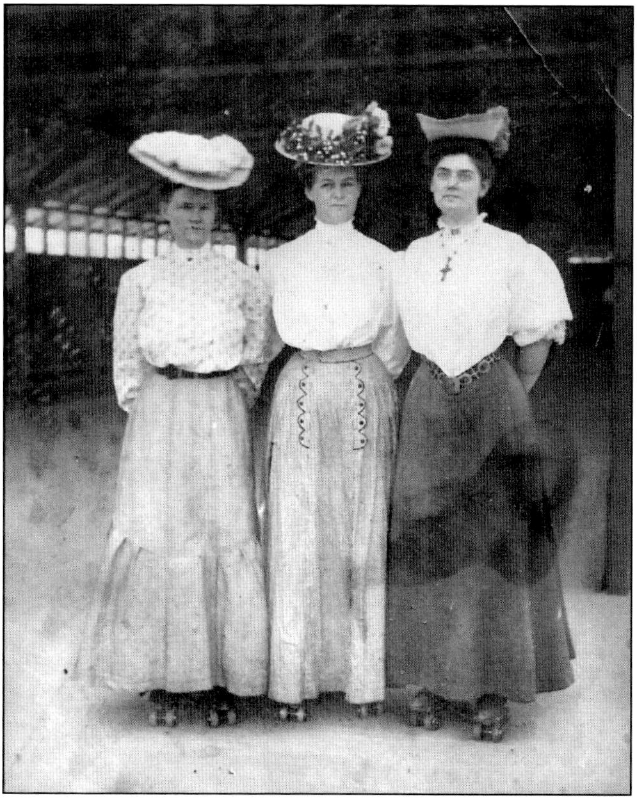

This c. 1915 photograph shows three unidentified young ladies. On roller skates, they are dressed in the latest fashion of the day, wearing beautiful hats.

This Post City baseball team photograph was taken in 1911 or 1912. Team members are, from left to right, (first row) Claud Hicks, Lois Stevens, and C. J. Dickinson; (second row) Floyd Tomes, John Herd, Nick Carter, Glen Brown, coach Ben Williams, Ray Spence, Lawrence Williams, Bob Bullock, and Ralph Hicks.

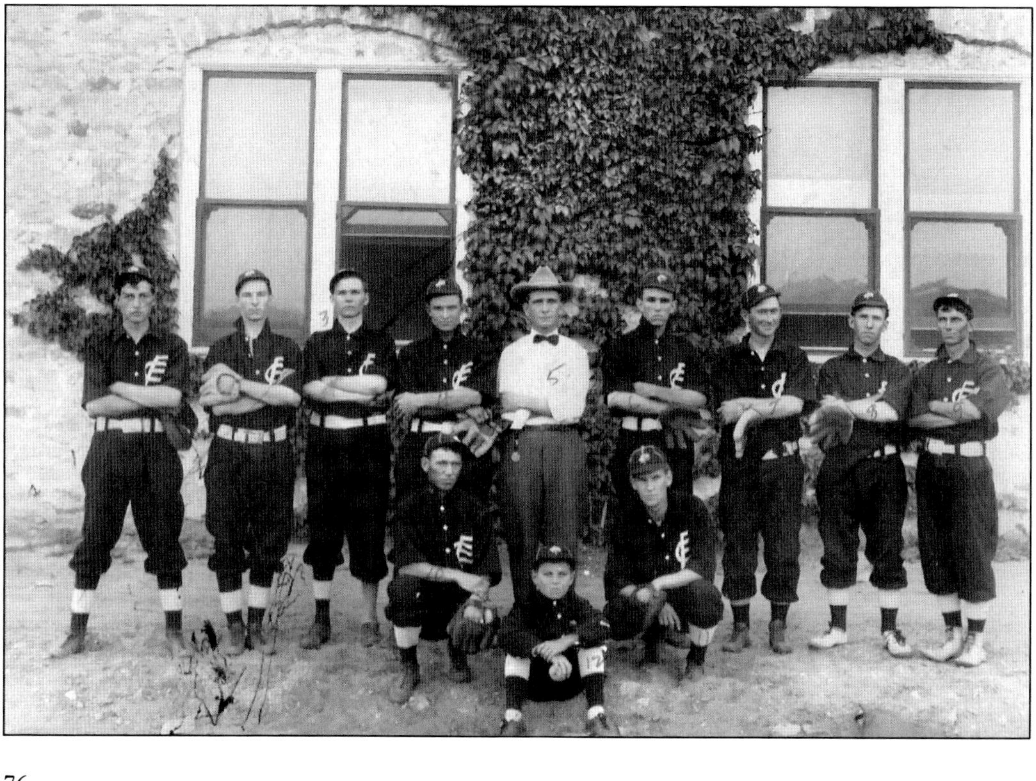

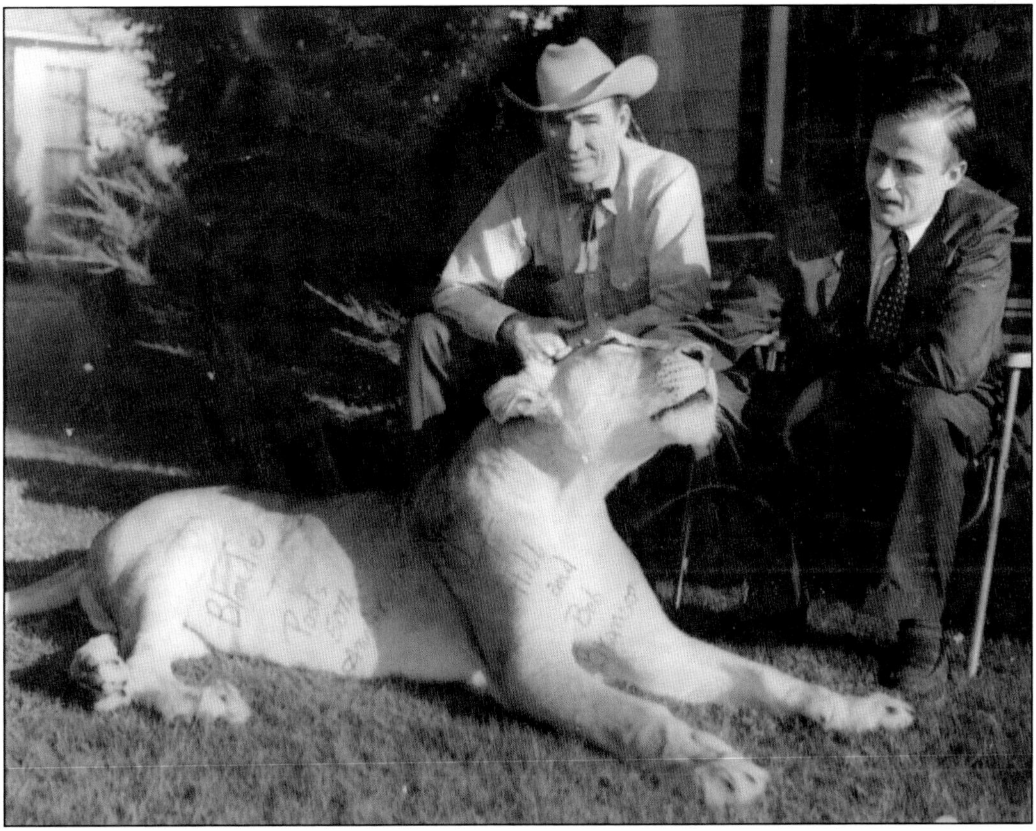

Charlie Hipp (left) and his pet lion, Blondie, were one of the attractions for C. W. Post's 50th anniversary celebration in 1957. In the photograph on the right is a Washington, D.C.–Battle Creek, Michigan, reporter, Bob Branson, who covered the event. Hipp was the uncle of C. R. Wilson, of Post.

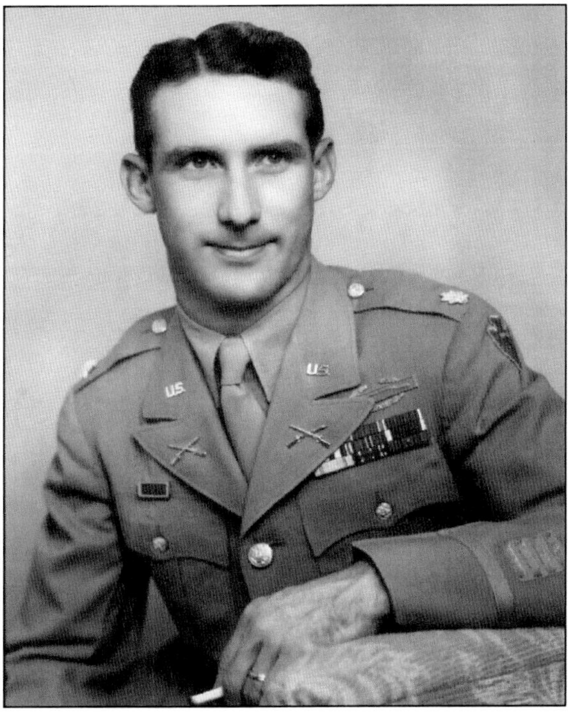

James Leroy Minor was inducted into the Texas Hall of State in 1952 for his outstanding military record. At age 25, Minor was the youngest lieutenant colonel in the armed forces, commanding an infantry battalion in combat. His battalion received the Presidential Unit Citation for its action in Selestat, France, in December 1944. Minor was wounded three times and was awarded numerous decorations and citations.

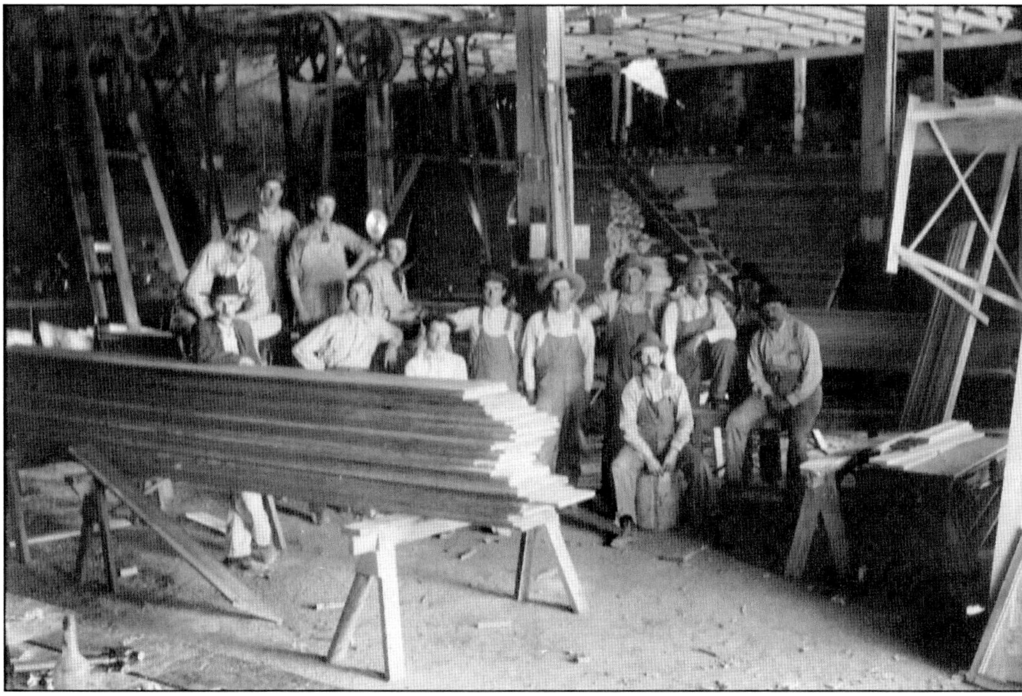

This Post Planing Mill photograph (above) was taken in 1917. The men are all carpenters except the farmer, standing by the lumber, who came to purchase some doors and windows. The only men identified are the three on the far right: a Mr. Larson (sitting on the keg), Jim Parker, and a Mr. Corley. The mill was created in 1907 by the Double U Company to process the lumber hauled in from the railhead as the town was being built. Powell and Williams later became owners of the planning mill. The photograph below was taken in 1920 at the Garza County Fair Celebration–Parade. The planing mill float is parked at the second Algerita Hotel, near the depot.

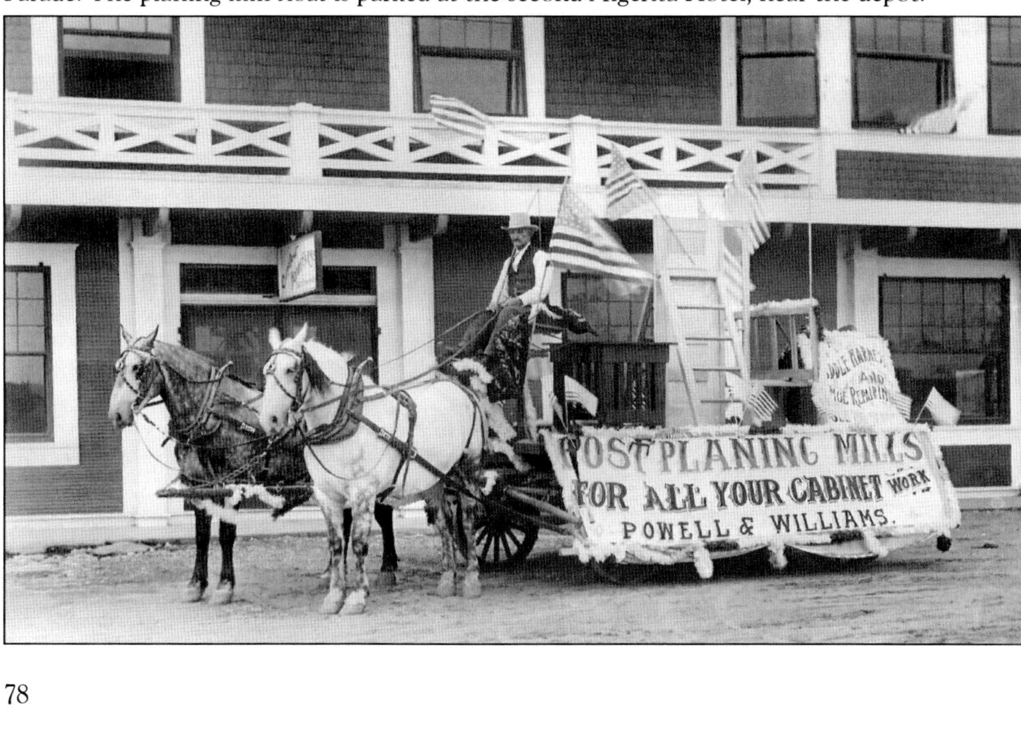

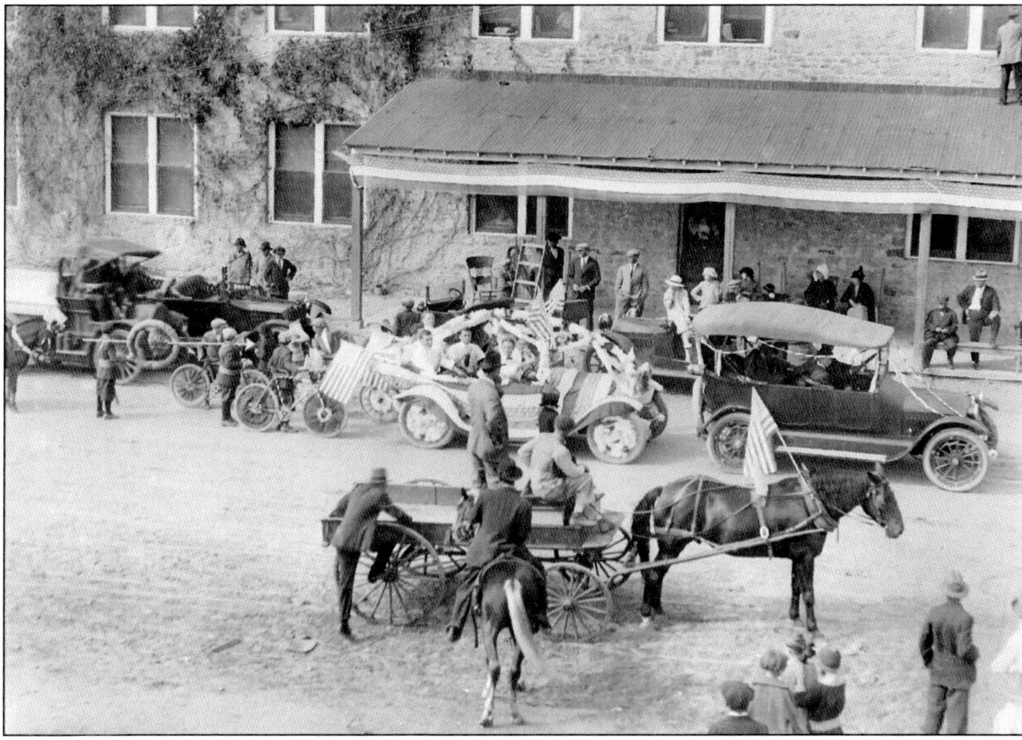

Floats are assembling at the old Algerita Hotel building, then known as the Rogers Hotel, on Main Street in 1920 for the Garza County Fair parade. Garza County folks love a parade, and every year has at least two, the annual rodeo parade and the lighted Christmas parade.

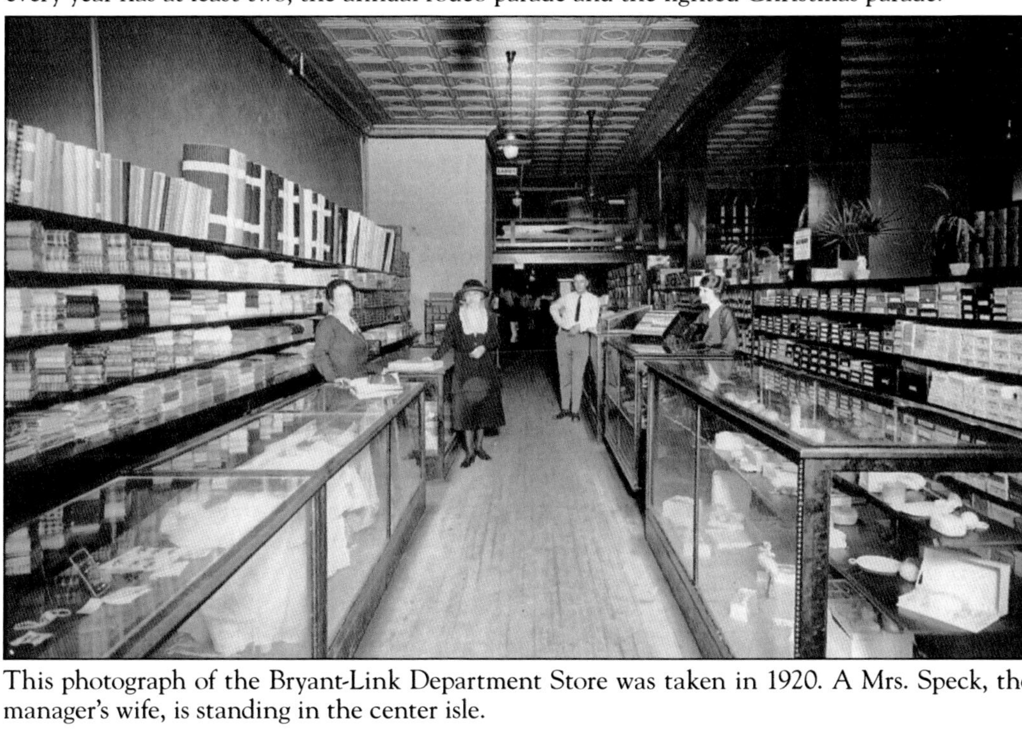

This photograph of the Bryant-Link Department Store was taken in 1920. A Mrs. Speck, the manager's wife, is standing in the center isle.

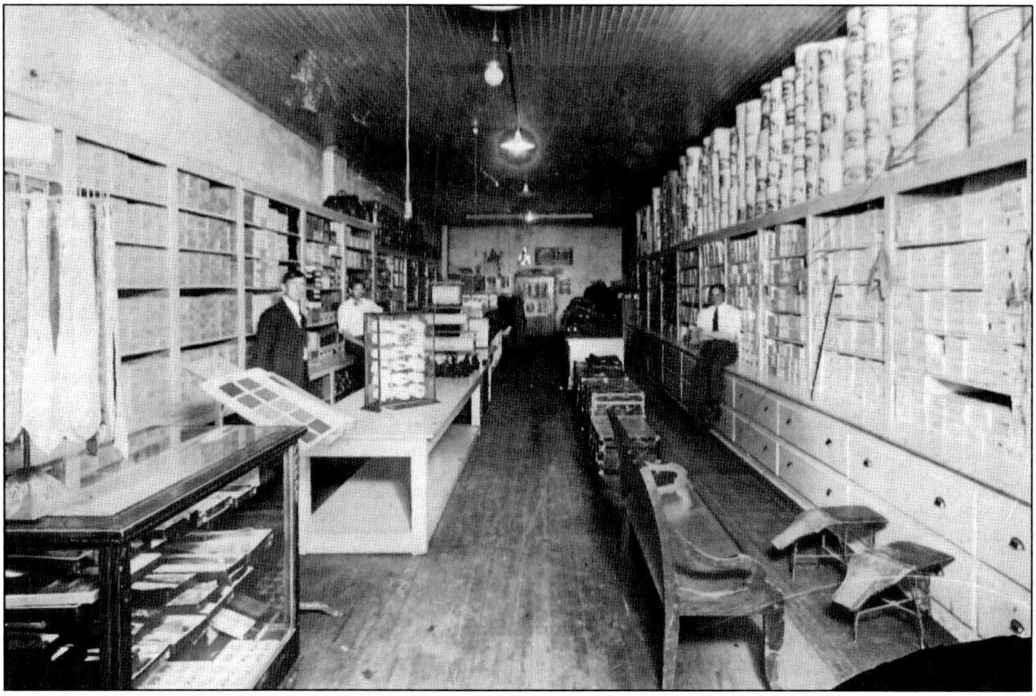

In this image from the early 1900s, Donald Alan Murray (right) sits in the men's clothing store he owns in Post. Judging from the large inventory of hatboxes, business was very good.

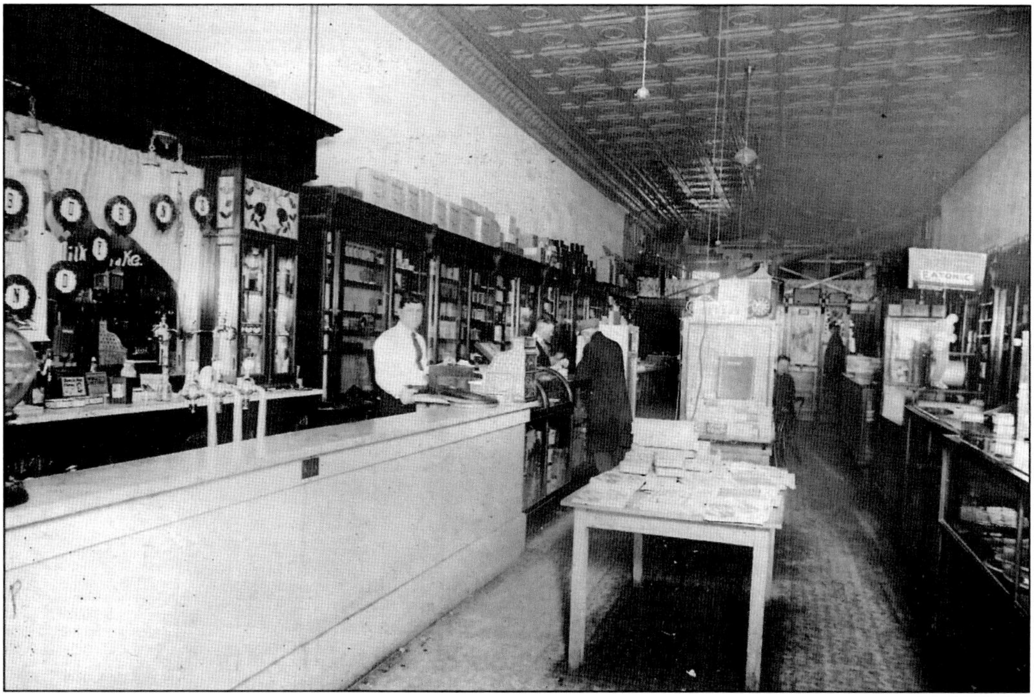

Behind the counter at the Warren drugstore are Bob Warren and a Mr. McAdoo. The soda fountain brings back great memories of a time gone by. There are no stools, but standing to wait for a delicious sundae, soda, or milk shake would likely have not been a problem.

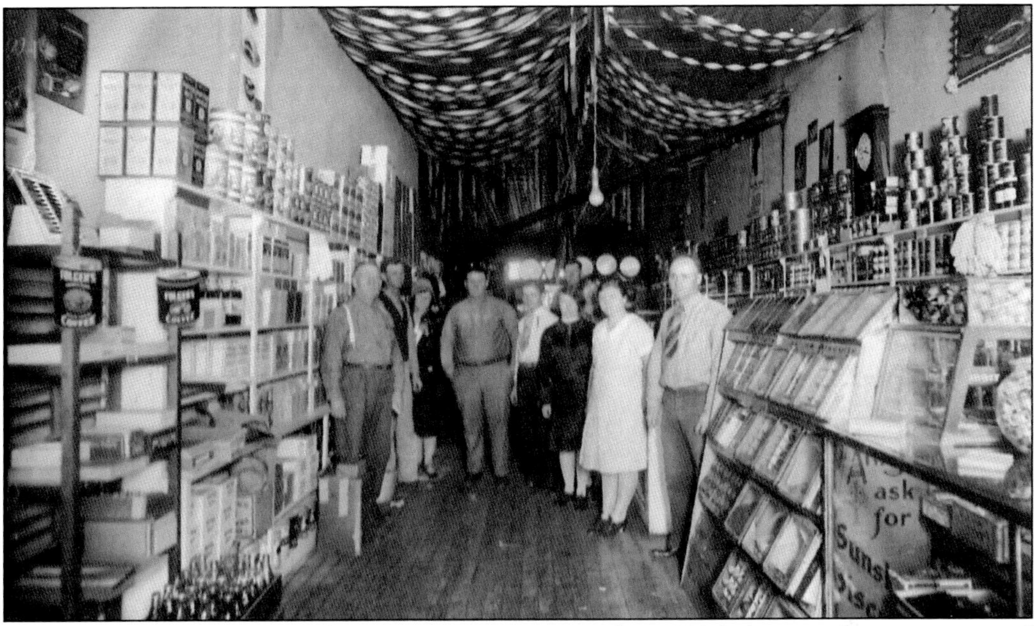

This photograph of the Gollehon grocery store was made in 1926. Apparently it was a special occasion, perhaps the grand opening. Identified in this image are owner-manager Lee Gollehon (far left), his son Robert (center), his wife, Lena Mae (Maxey), and son Elmer (far right). Following the passing of their father in 1929, Elmer started his own store in Hereford, and Robert continued the store in Post.

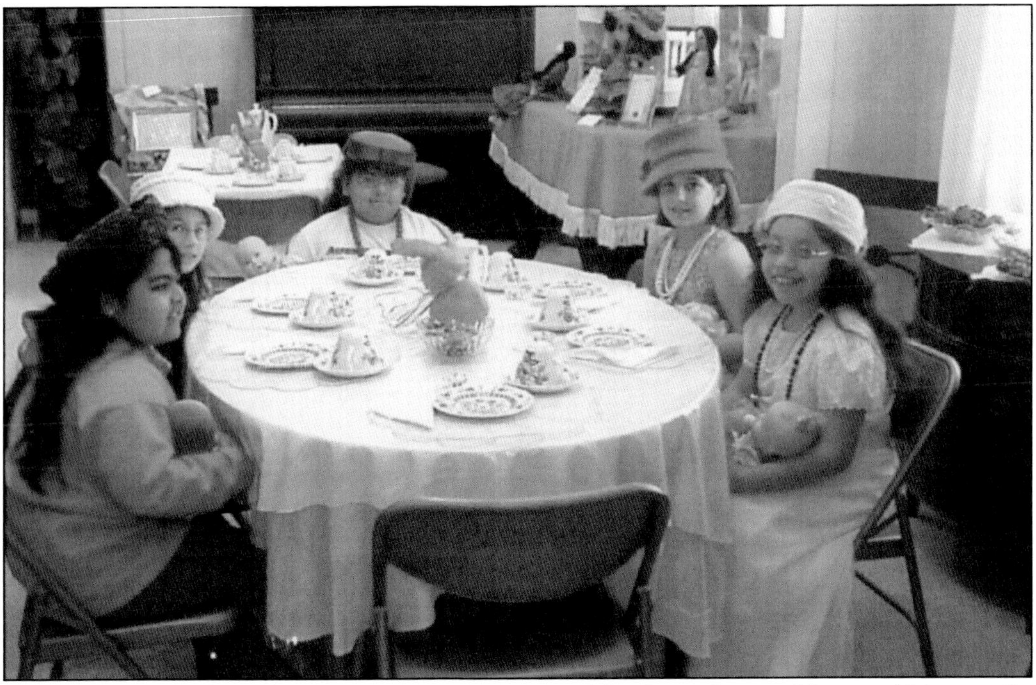

These students in the Kids N Art program are guests of the Garza County Historical Museum for a tea party during the doll show. Since this was their first tea party, they decided to dress up in vintage hats. All, even the art teachers, Linda Puckett and Jean Davenport, had a great time.

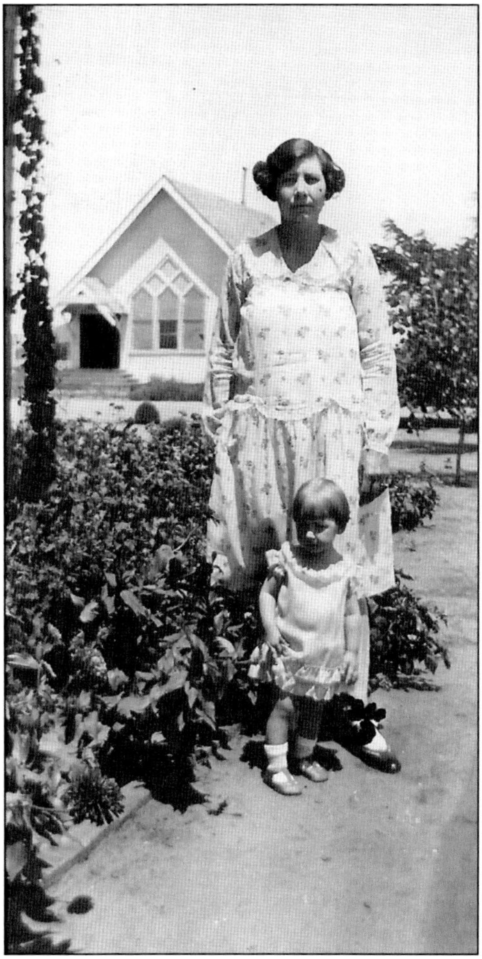

This 1920s photograph features Pearl Taylor and daughter Marie at their home on Avenue M in Post. Marie grew up to be an accomplished artist and director of the OS Ranch Art Museum in Post. The Church of Christ building sits in the background. (Courtesy Marie Neff.)

These young ladies are all dressed up and look as though they are enjoying having a day off. Big Marie is third from the left. (Courtesy Marie Neff.)

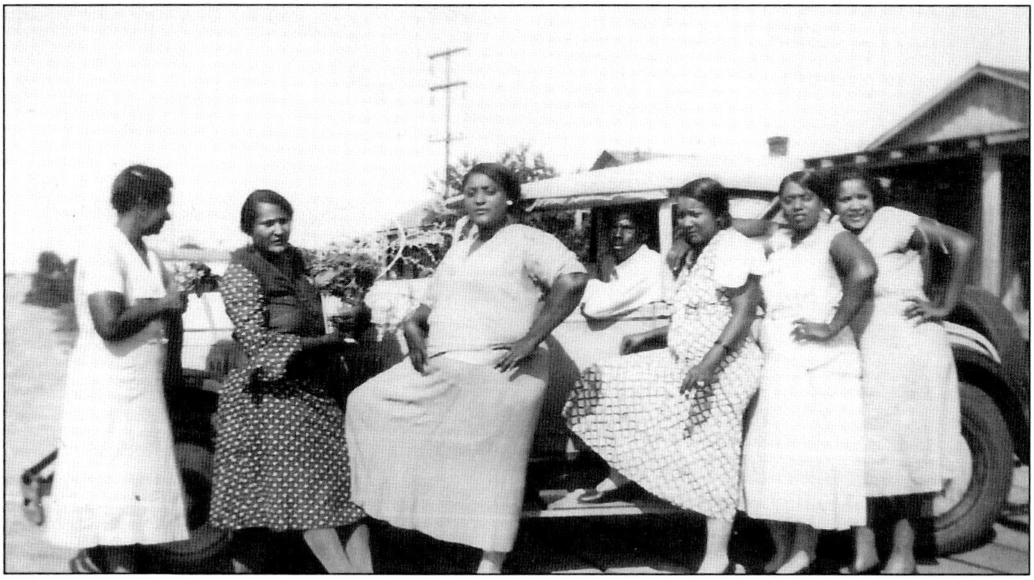

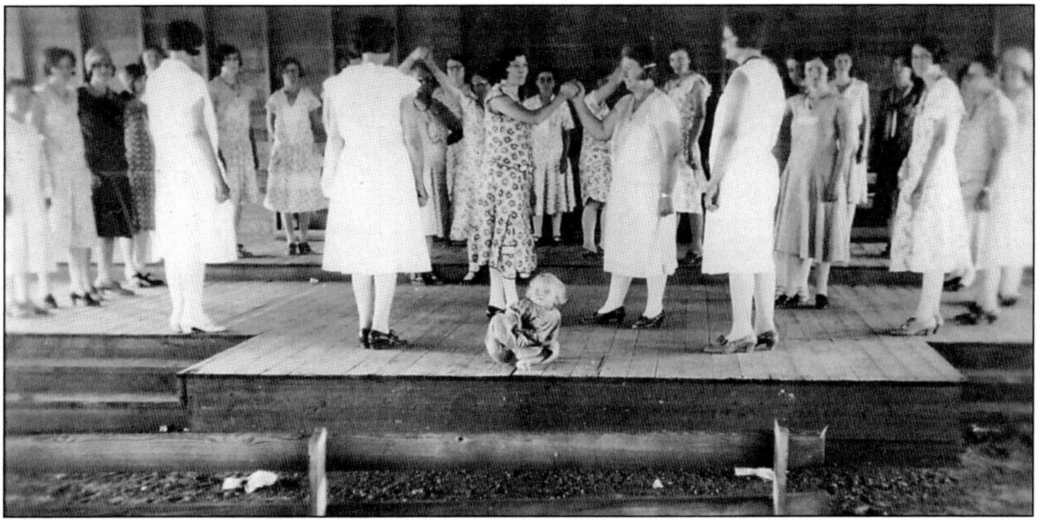

This group of ladies dances at Two-Draw Lake, probably in the 1940s. The child in front has tired of dancing and is giving himself a foot massage while he rests. Two-Draw Lake was a popular gathering spot for socials, boating, and fishing.

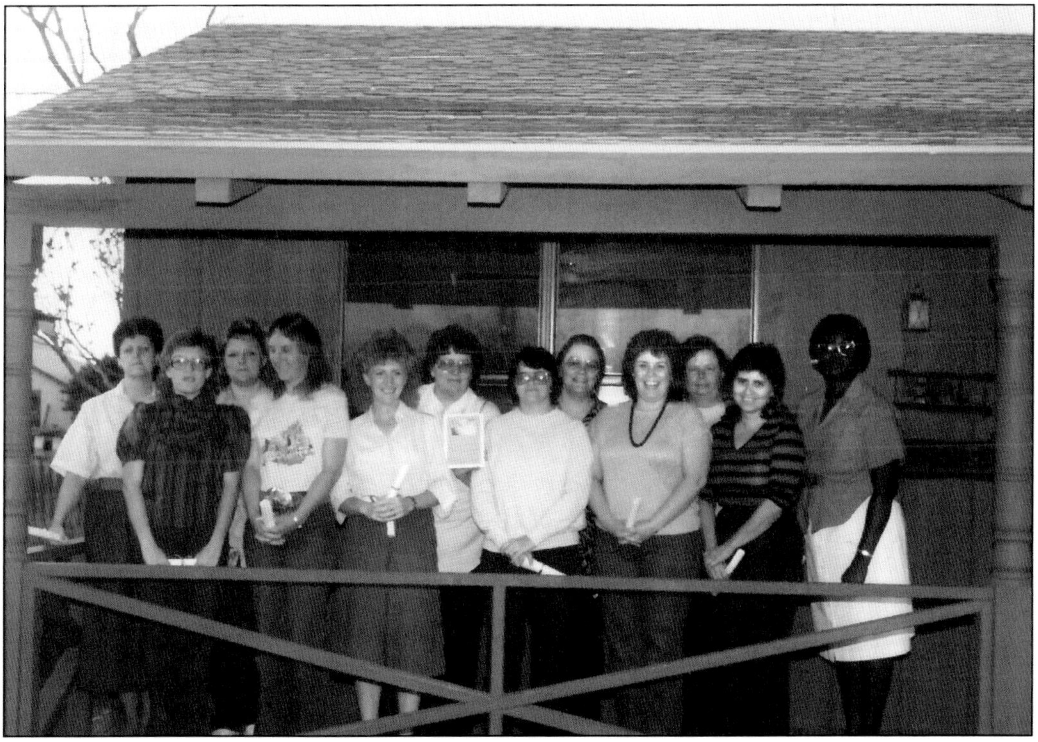

Girls Scout leaders pose at the Girl Scout hut. They are, from left to right, Rebecca Haney, Kathy Hubble, Teressa Scoonover, Billie Fae Littrell, Cynthia Colvin, Nell Morris, Diana Poe, Carol Tobias, Jennie Francis, Barbara VanderValde, Hope Garza, and Pat Cruse.

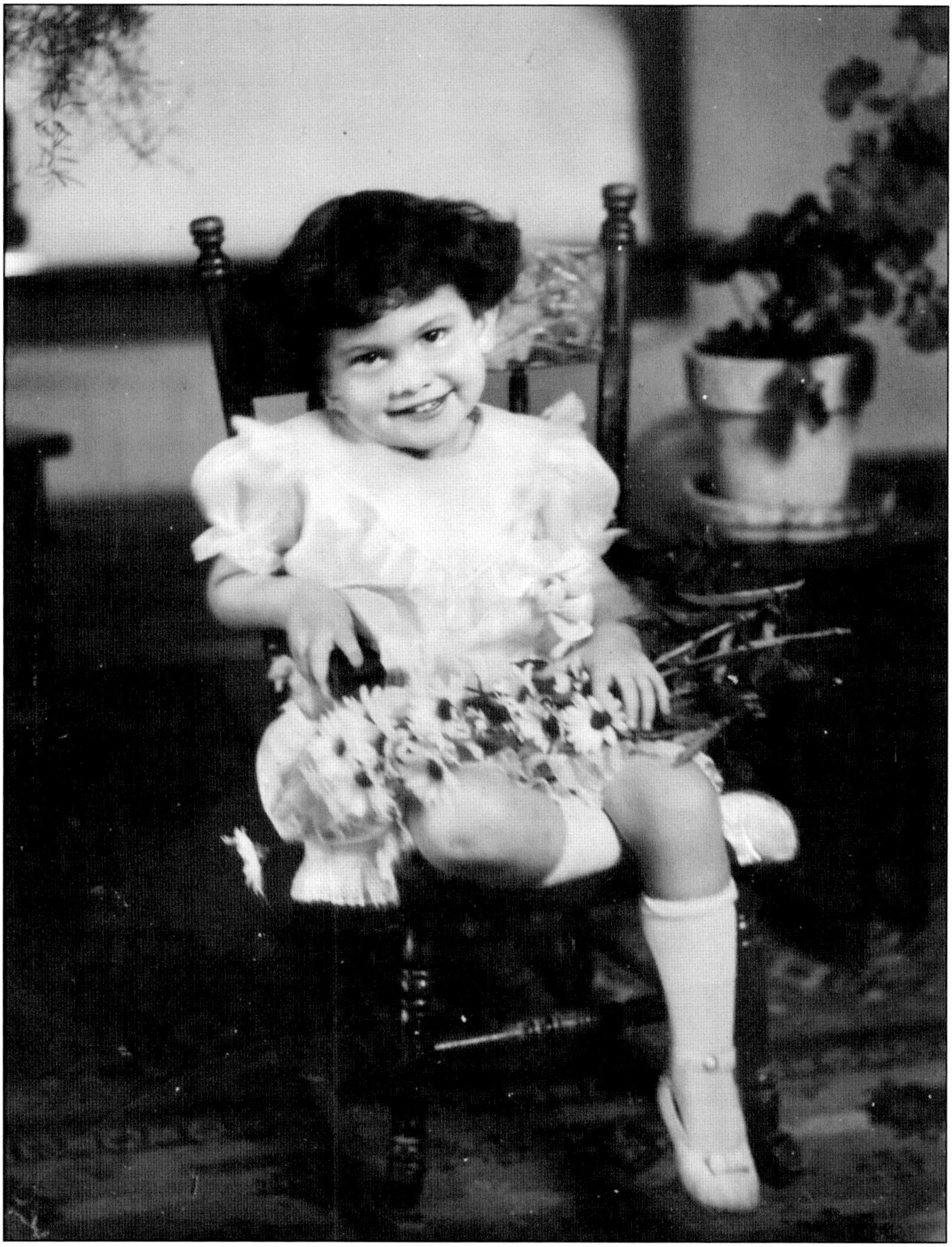

Maxine Durrett poses for the camera around 1923. Maxine's parents were James and Mayme Durrett, who came to Post in 1913. James Durrett worked as a bookkeeper for the Double U Company. Maxine grew up to be a lovely person who never met a stranger. She earned a teaching degree from the University of Texas and taught in Post public schools for many years. Always involved in cultural and community development, she spent her life promoting Post.

Six

GETTIN' AROUND GARZA COUNTY

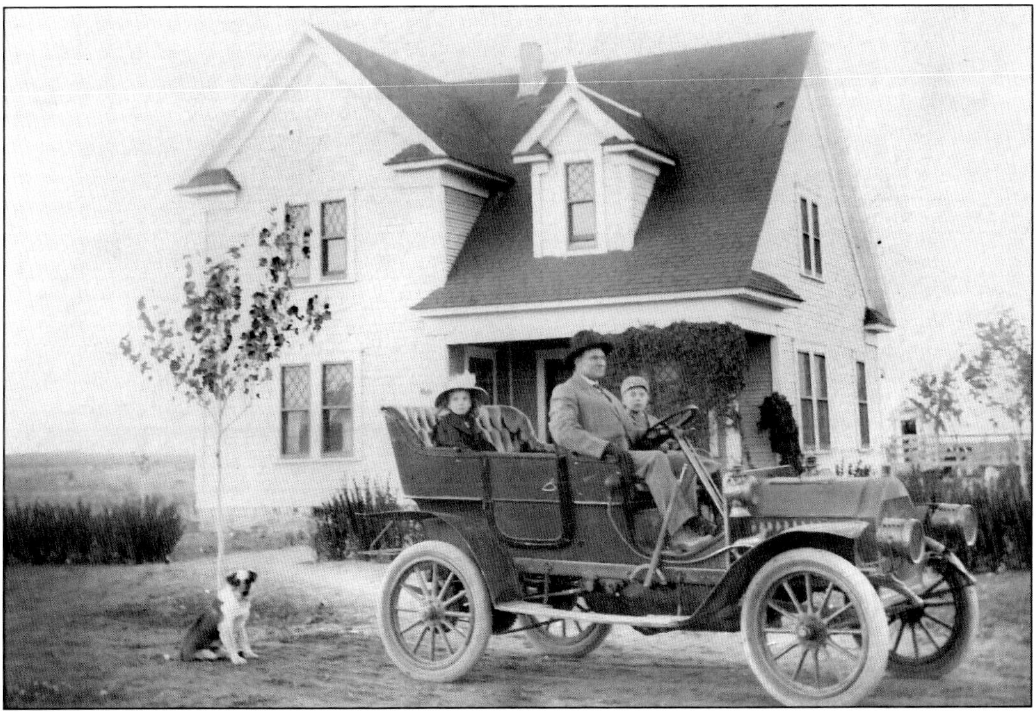

Judge James M. Boren is at the wheel, with son, Walter, beside him and daughter, Mildred, seated in back. Their dog is also posing for the camera. This great automobile must have been the envy of the neighborhood. Built in 1908, the Boren home in the background has been occupied by family members for more than 100 years. It was awarded a Texas Historical Marker in 1967. (Courtesy Mildred Boren Sentell.)

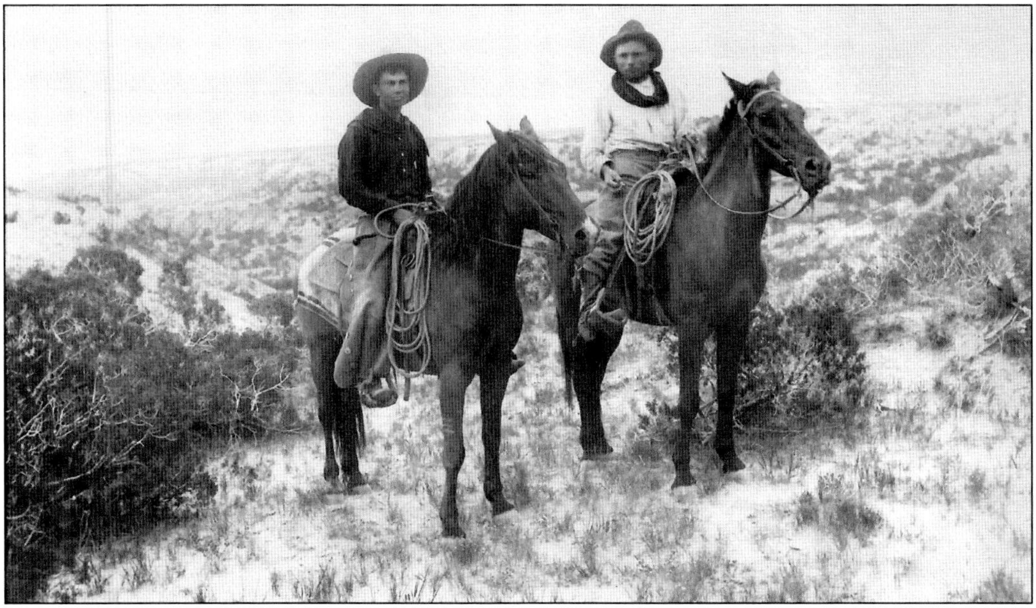

In this 1914 photograph, Elton Nance (left) and Perry Graham (right) are working cowboys for John B. Slaughter, owner of the U Lazy S Ranch. Graham was known as "Horse Fly." Seeing these guys mounted and ready to ride lends new meaning to the term horsepower. (Courtesy Marie Neff.)

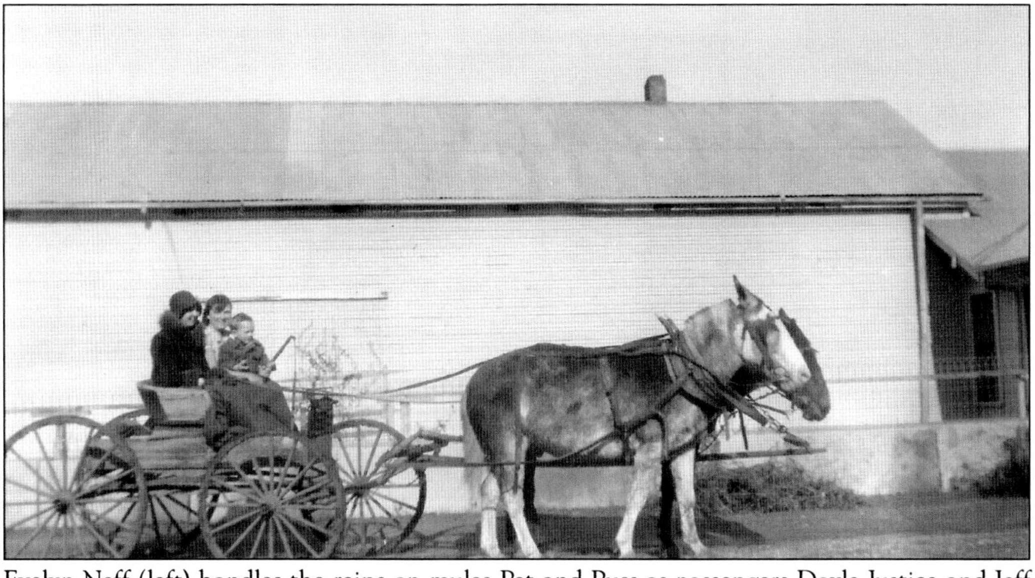

Evelyn Neff (left) handles the reins on mules Pet and Puss as passengers Doyle Justice and Jeff Justice (baby) ride along in 1928. They are at Elizabeth Pirtle's store in Justiceburg. (Courtesy Marie Neff.)

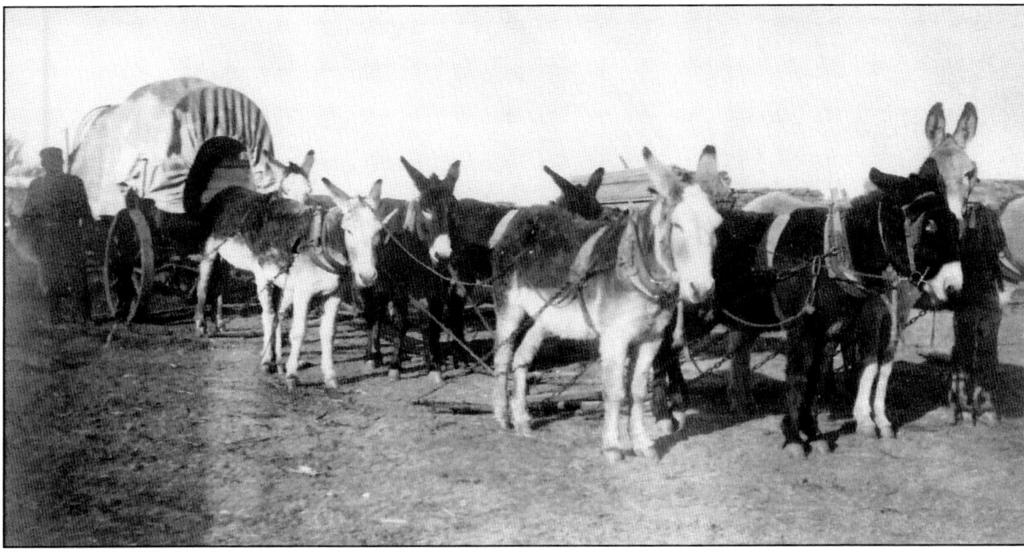

A mule train brings supplies to Post City from Big Springs in 1907. It was a long trip at a snail's pace by today's standard, plus the drover had stock to contend with. By 1911, C. W. Post's promise to bring the railroad would be fulfilled, to the great relief of both men and mules.

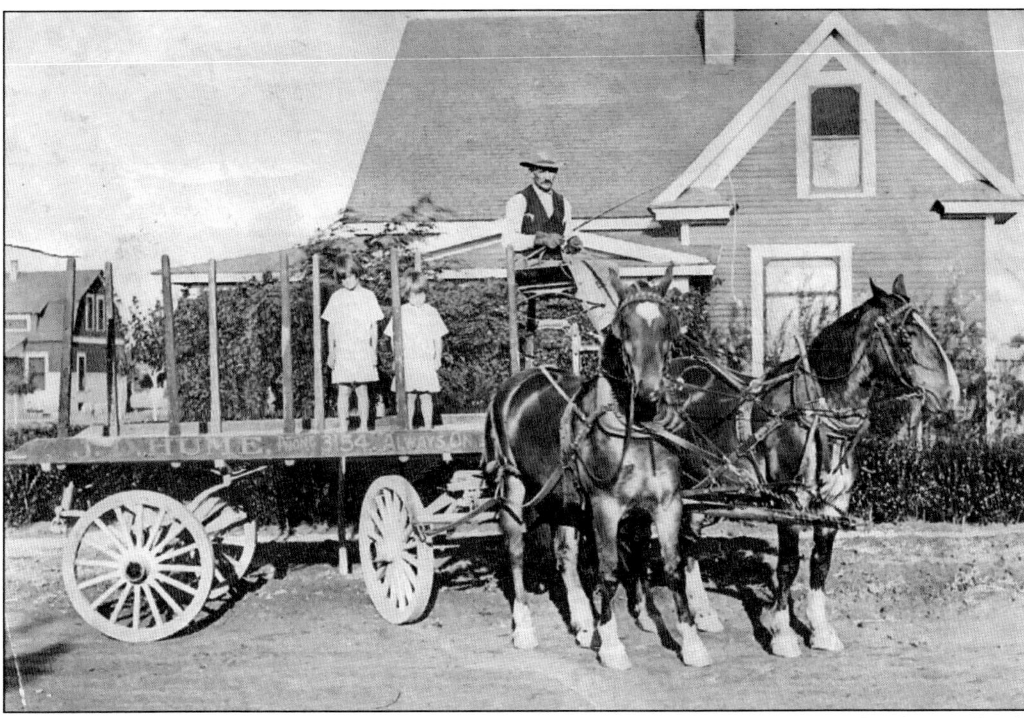

J. D. Hume drives his dray wagon with Helen Mack (left) and Leita Pat (Tootsee) riding in back. The pioneer Hume family came from Fulton, Missouri. J. D. hauled freight from Snyder by mule train. A Mrs. Hume gave birth to the first child born in Post in 1907, a little girl named Postie. Sadly, Postie passed away at age seven.

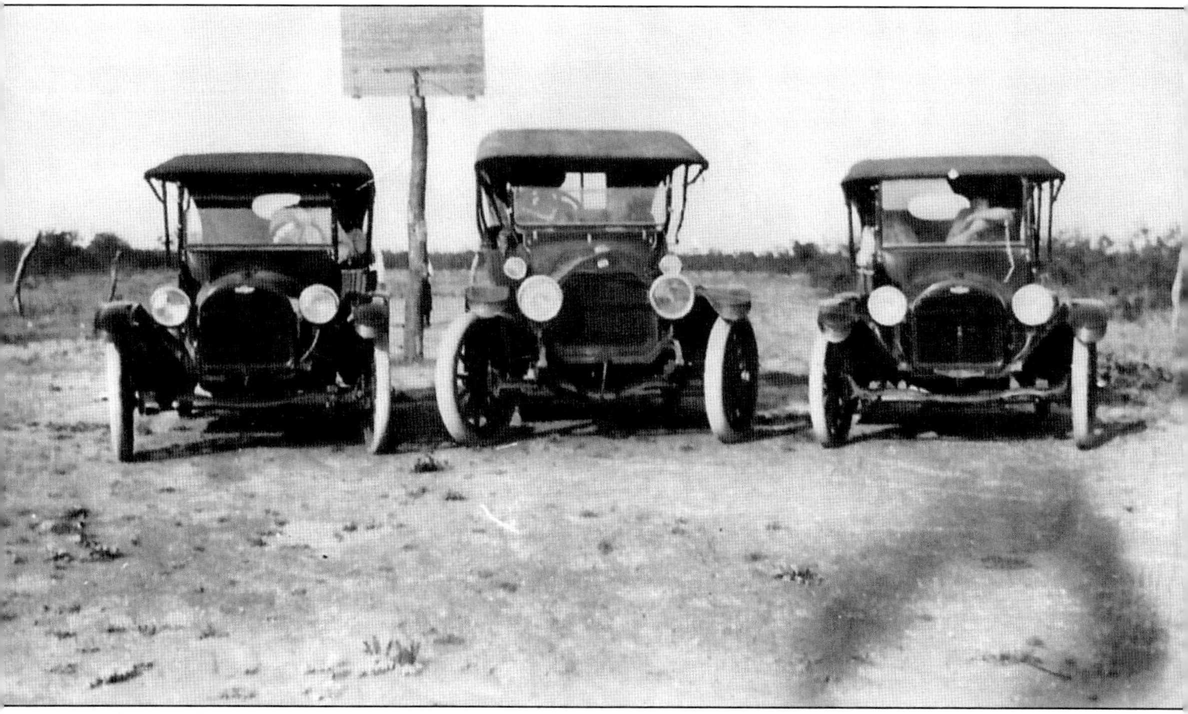

These old automobiles have character and are certainly a step up from riding in a buggy. The one in the center has its steering wheel on the opposite side. Managers of the Double U Company found it difficult to oversee all of C. W. Post's property in a buggy, so Post shipped them two Reo automobiles to Big Spring in June 1907. It took some doing to find someone to drive them to Post. As they chugged along the roadway, people heard them coming and came from miles away to see what the commotion was about. The Reo had a two-cylinder motor that could speed down the Caprock at a top speed of 15 to 20 miles per hour, though going up was another matter. One time, a doctor from Fluvanna was traveling to Post in his automobile and met a mule train on the way. The wagon boss pulled a gun and ordered him off the road for scaring the mules.

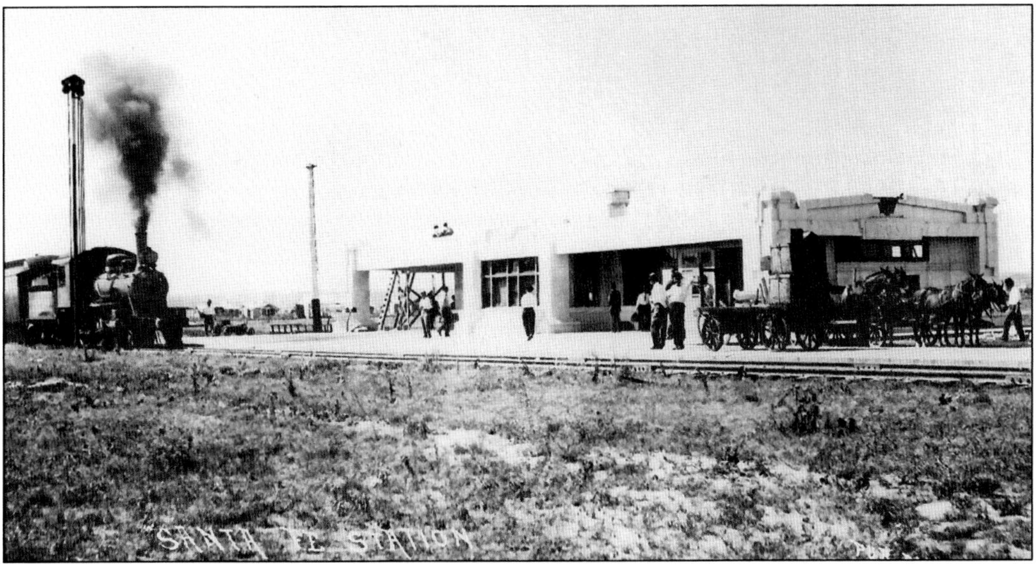

On January 15, 1911, the train rolled into Post, or actually backed in since the engineer wanted a forward pull when climbing the cap. Daily trains arrived with loads of surfacing gravel from the pit in Lubbock and a combination baggage-coach car was at the rear to handle Post City freight and passengers. By the end of the month, a station, a freight depot, and a railroad yard had been built.

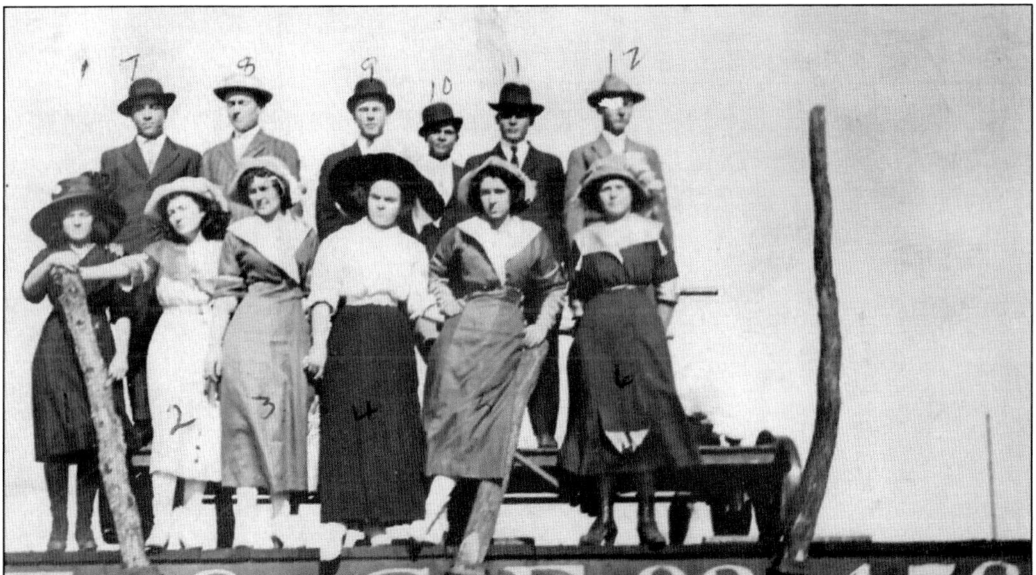

This 1911 photograph was taken when the first train came to town. Everyone in Post and the surrounding area came to see. Those standing on the flat car are, from left to right, (first row) Maude Nalor, Florra Farmer, Anice White, Mrs. George Dent, Edna Hume, and Maude Mason; (second row) Gus Sowell, unidentified, George Dent, two unidentified, and Lonnie Farmer.

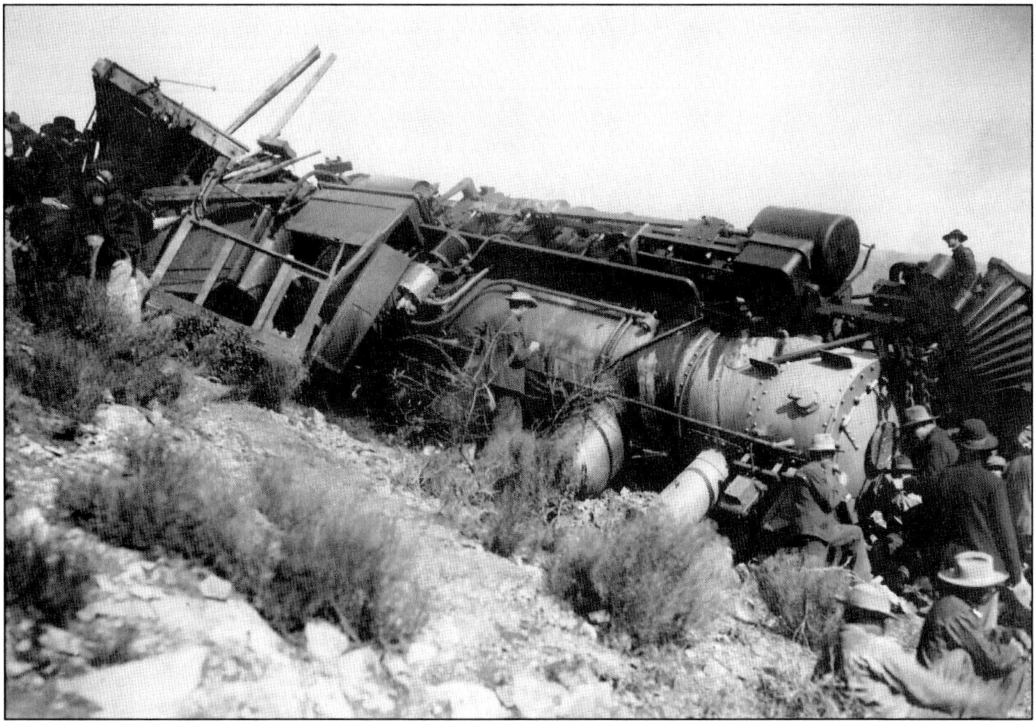

The 1920 photograph above shows the aftermath of a major train wreck that occurred near Post on July 8, 1920. There is no documentation regarding the cause of the derailment, which caused catastrophic damage to the engine and freight cars. The cost of laying 14 miles of track over the Caprock to Post was $800,000, a great deal of money in 1910. Below are the cars that tumbled off the track.

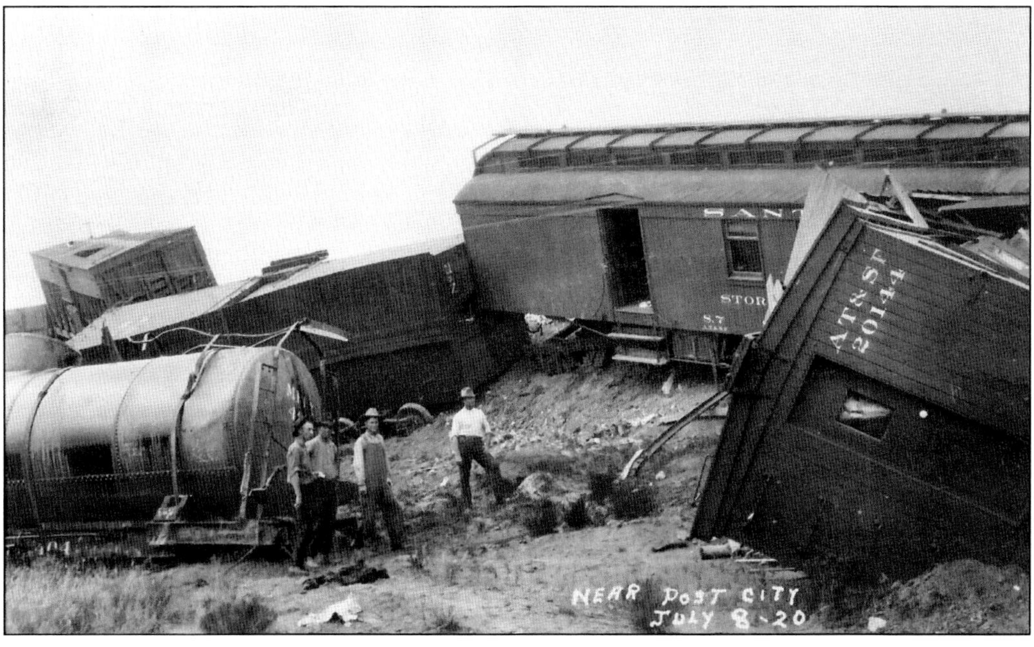

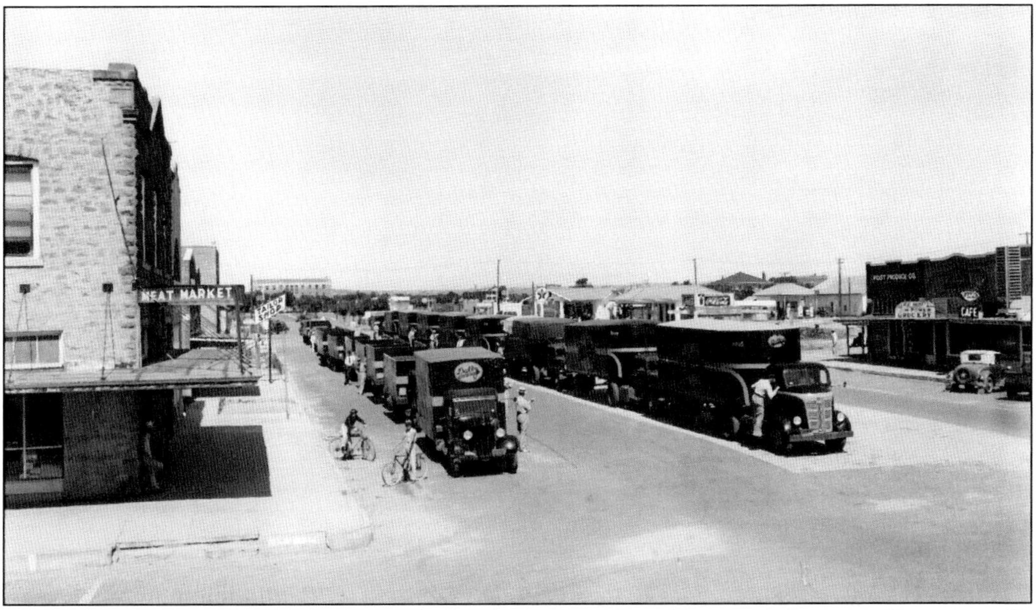

In the image above, Dalby Motor Freight trucks are lined up along Main Street in Post. Arno R. Dalby was a self-made man with a purpose. When his family moved to Garza County in 1916 to grow grain and cotton, he was eight years old. Arno became bound and determined to get off the farm. After completing school at Close City and a bookkeeping course at Abilene Business College, he returned home. His father had arranged a job for him at a motor company, making $175 per month, a large amount of money for an 18-year-old in 1926. Arno declined the offer and persuaded his father to back him in a $200 loan at the bank for a first payment on a Model T truck. Dalby Trucking would evolve into TIME-DC, the nation's fifth largest motor freight company. Arno Dalby stands in the photograph below.

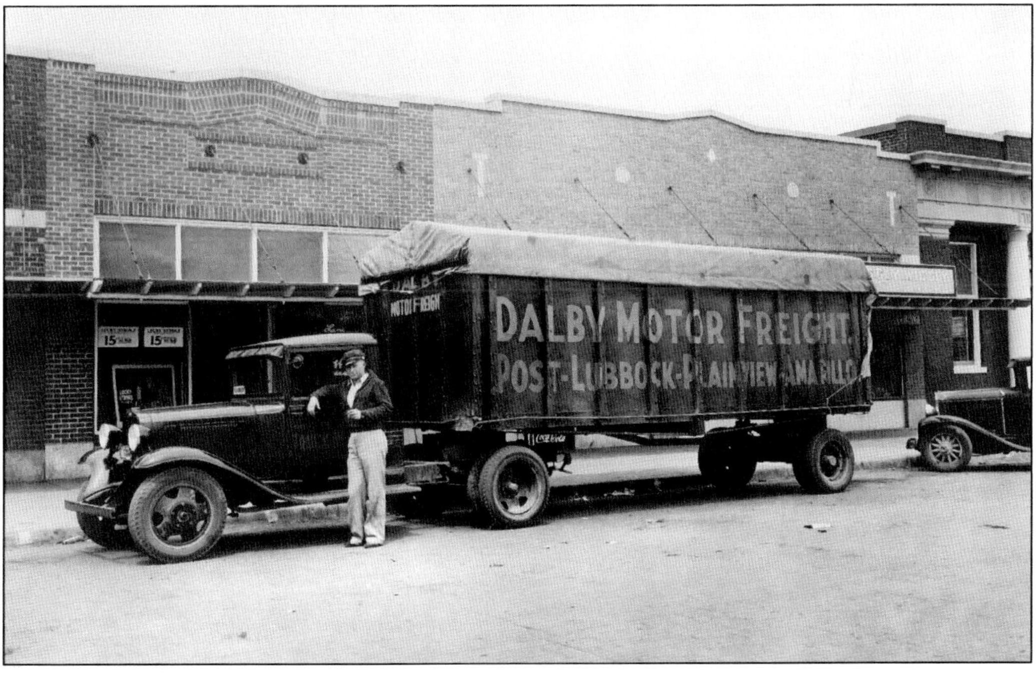

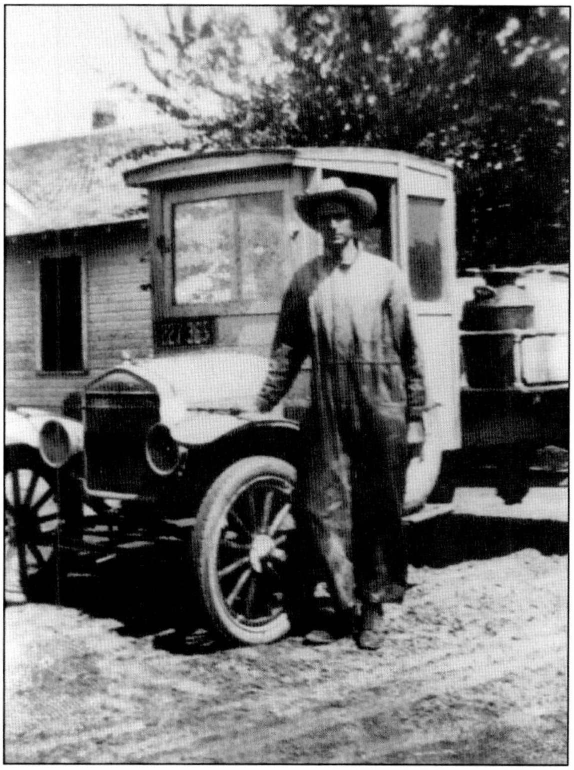

Shown here in 1928 standing by the delivery truck, James Arthur Taylor worked for City Service. James and his wife, Pearl, had one child, a daughter named Marie. Marie was a real daddy's girl and loved to ride along with her father on the delivery truck or just hang around the business.

Bob Macy and young daughter Charlotte pose by his helicopter in 1970. For a rancher like Bob, this Hughes 300 helicopter was probably a multipurpose tool—whether it be for herding cattle out of the brush or just flying around for fun.

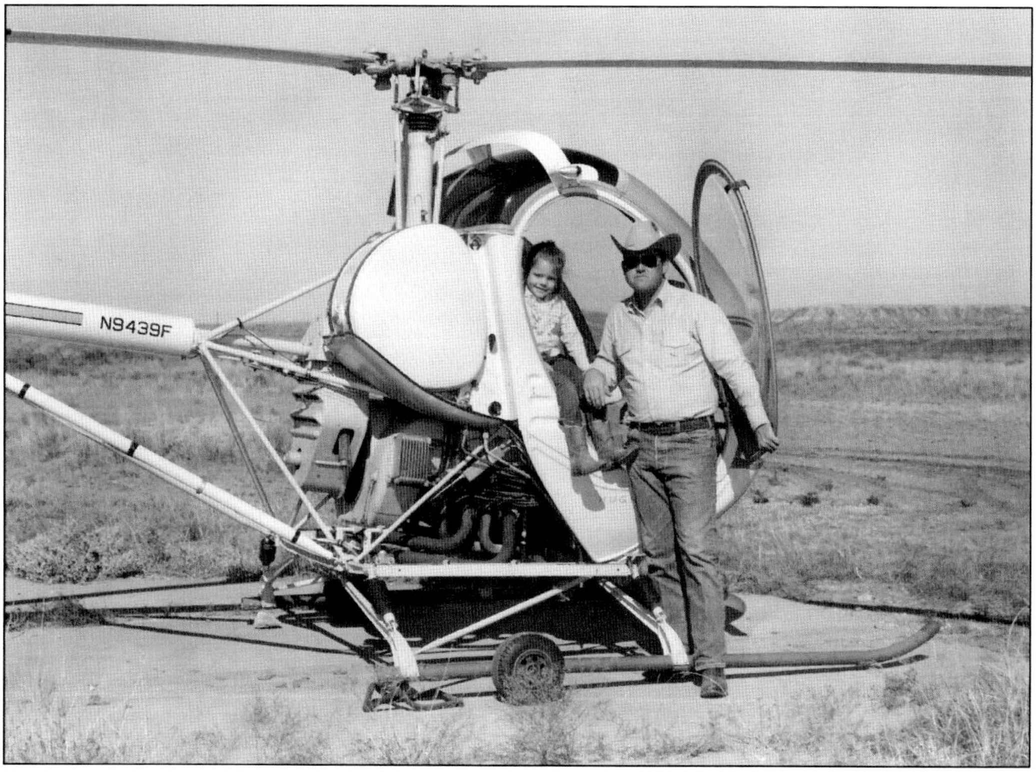

Seven

Body and Spirit

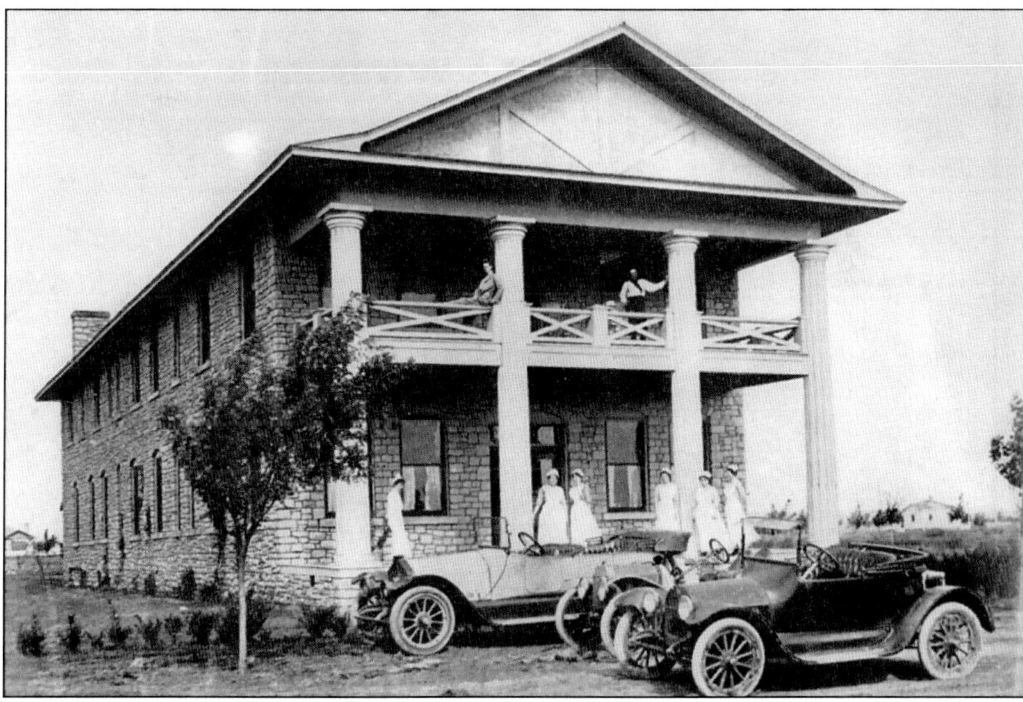

The Post Sanitarium was said to be the finest facility this side of Fort Worth, Texas. A young physician named A. R. Ponton came to Post in 1910. He was formerly affiliated with the Santa Fe Railroad. The Double U Board was favorably impressed with Ponton and wrote C. W. Post about his ideas on socialized medicine. By the spring of 1913, a building was completed, and Ponton was performing operations.

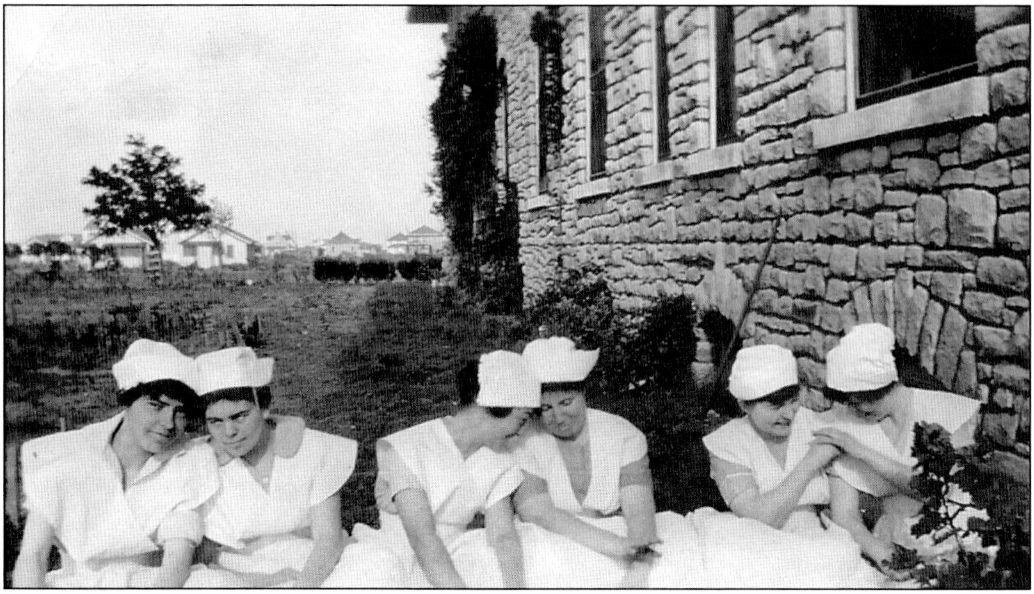

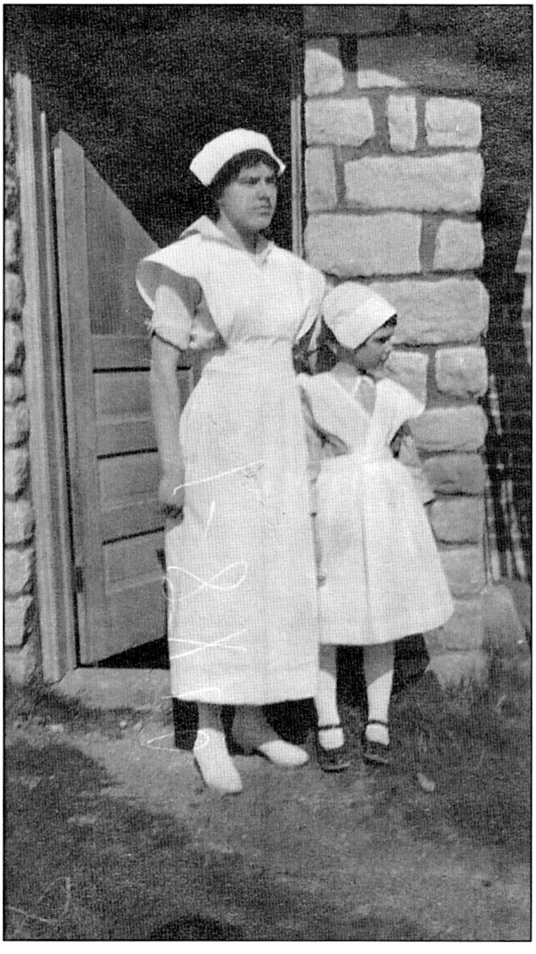

These young nurses are in training at the Post Sanitarium in 1917. On the back of the photograph is written, "To Ervin: Thought you might use these to scare the animals off when you go to the trenches." This was during World War I. The Post Sanitarium Training School for Nurses was a three-year program. Upon graduation, nurses passing the final examination received a diploma, signed by the officials of the school. A dormitory was built next door to the sanitarium for the doctors and nurses. The photograph at left was taken at the basement door of a Miss Gaines (left) and Jewel Self in 1916. Jewel is a little too young to be a student, but she is certainly cute in her little uniform.

The nurses standing on the front porch of the dormitory are unidentified. They may well have been the last class of the school. As the war progressed, Dr. Arnold C. Surman and Dr. David C. Williams were called into service, and Dr. A. R. Ponton moved to Lubbock and built the Lubbock Sanitarium.

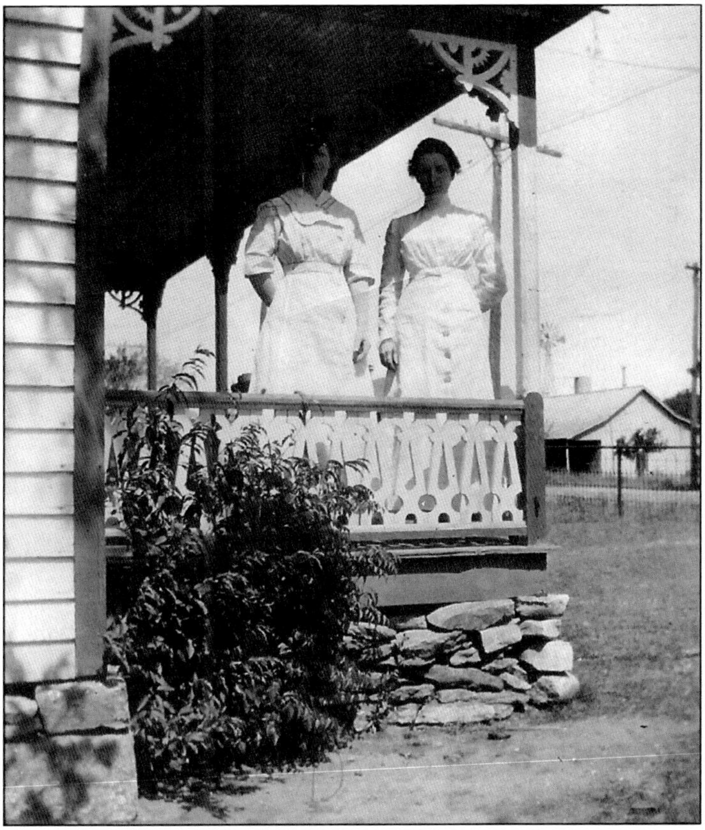

Pictured below, this structure was the actual dormitory for the doctors and nurses. After the closing of the nursing program, the building became the residence of the Graeber family, shown standing in the front yard in 1939. Minnie Graeber named the home Pleasant Lodge.

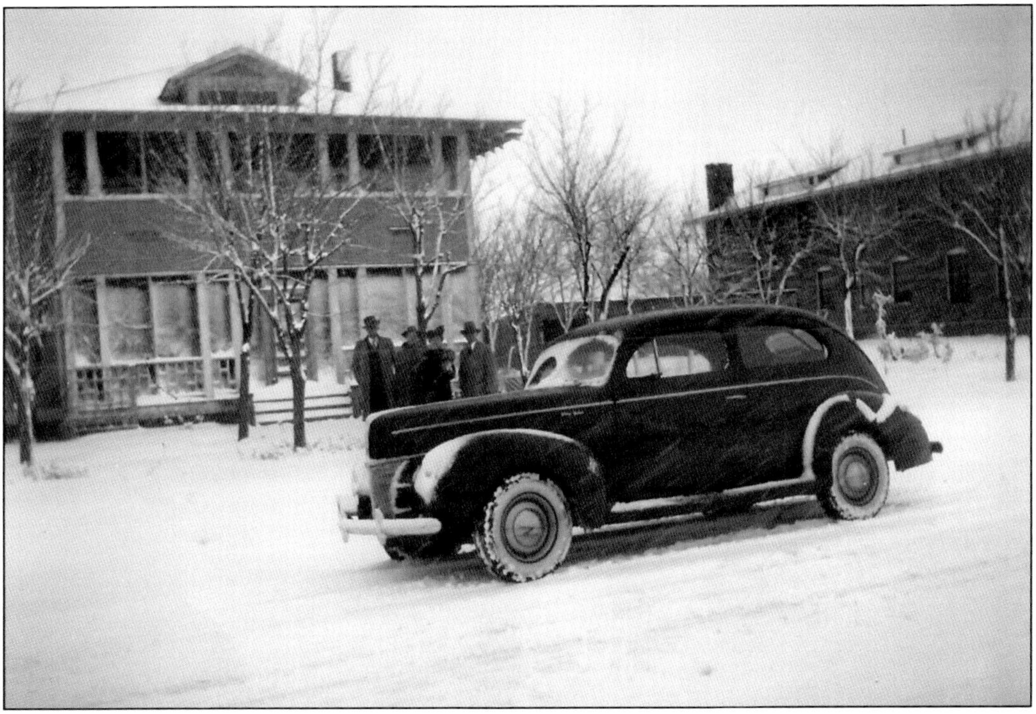

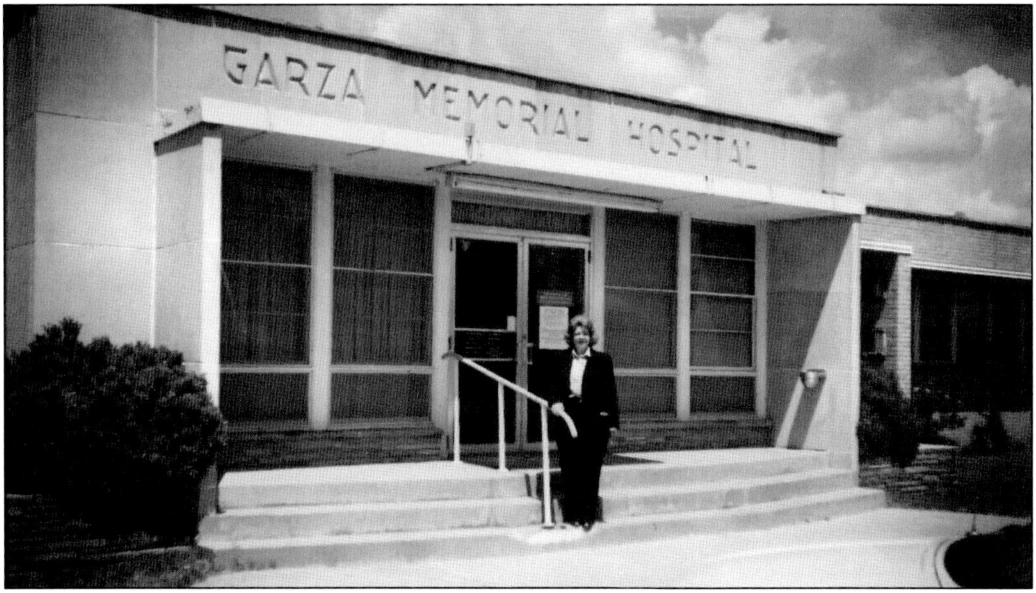

Garza Memorial Hospital was built in 1952 and served the people of Garza County and the surrounding area for 44 years. Marietta Reed is standing on the steps. She served as administrator for more than 25 years and continued serving on the hospital board until 1999.

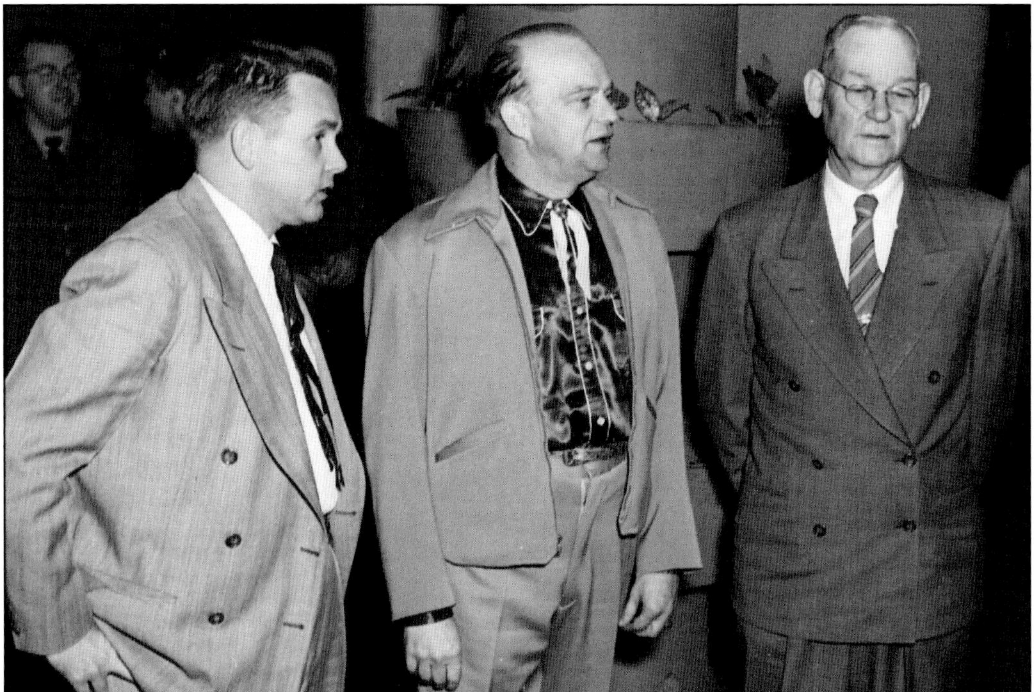

A fund-raising event was held to build a hospital in Post. A stage was put up, and celebrity ventriloquist Edgar Bergen and his sidekick, Charlie McCarthy, entertained at the gala. Bergen (center) stands with T. L. Jones (right) and an unidentified man at the event, which generated the revenue needed, and hospital construction soon followed.

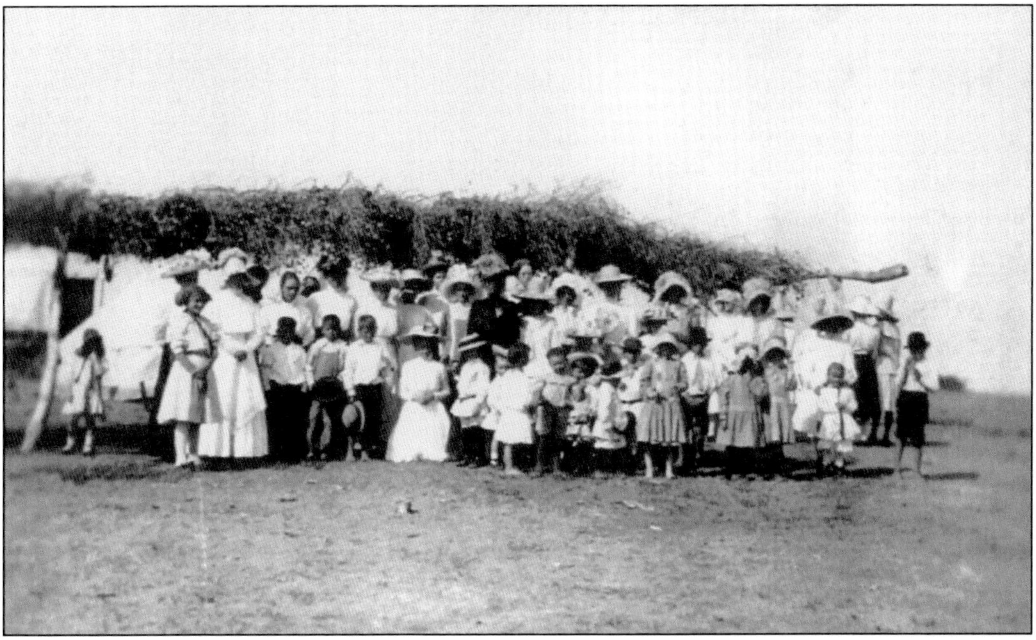

Rural churches often were wherever people gathered to worship, whether a schoolhouse, a barn, a tent, or a picnic in a brush arbor. This was the case in Verbena and other communities around the county. The image above may be Easter Sunday in 1910. Everyone is dressed in their Sunday best. Some boys in the first row have their hats in hand. The photograph below was taken at Verbena on Sunday, July 13, 1913. Only one person is identified, Henrietta Nickols.

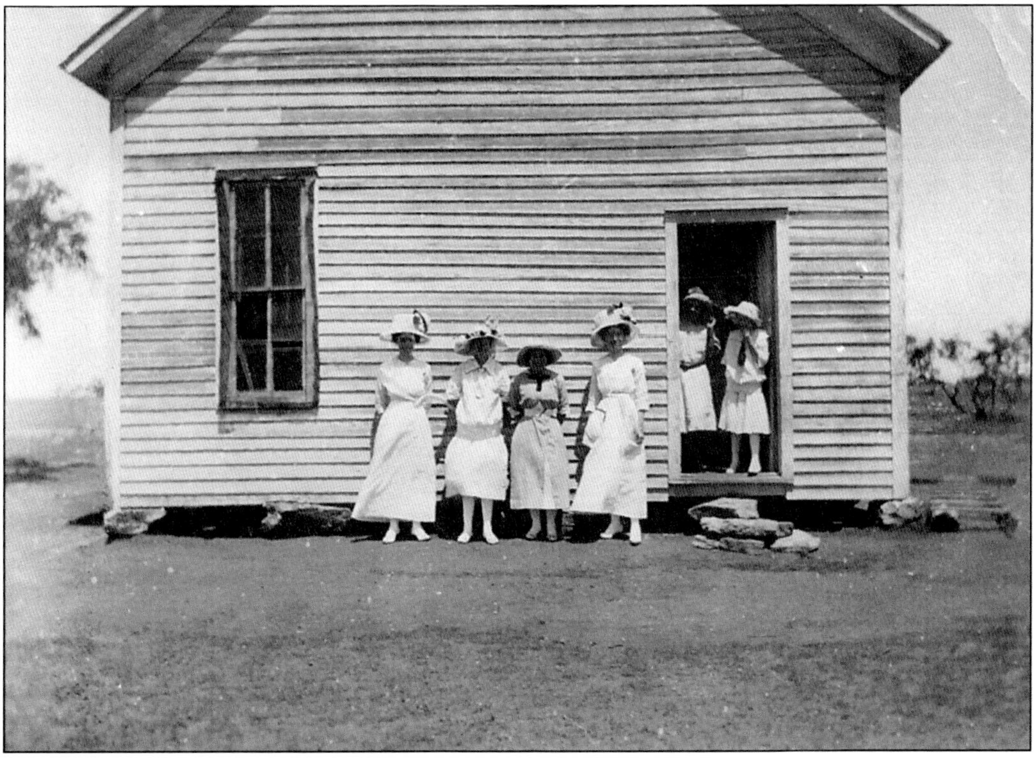

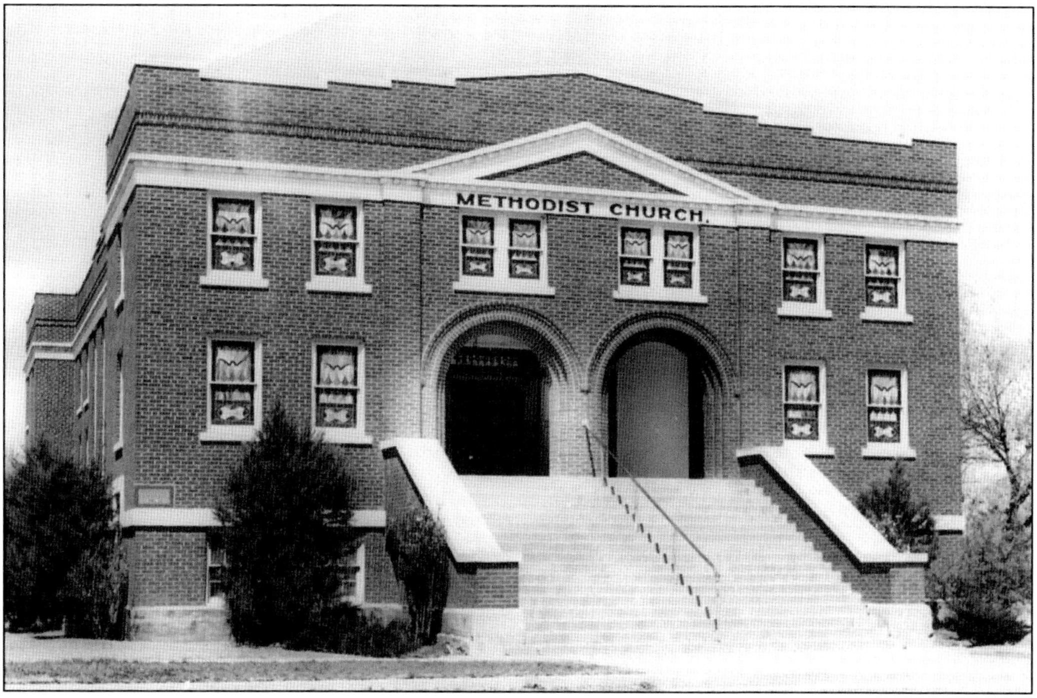

The First Methodist Church was organized in September 1908. The first church building was constructed in February 1909 on a lot donated by C. W. Post, who provided a carpet as well.

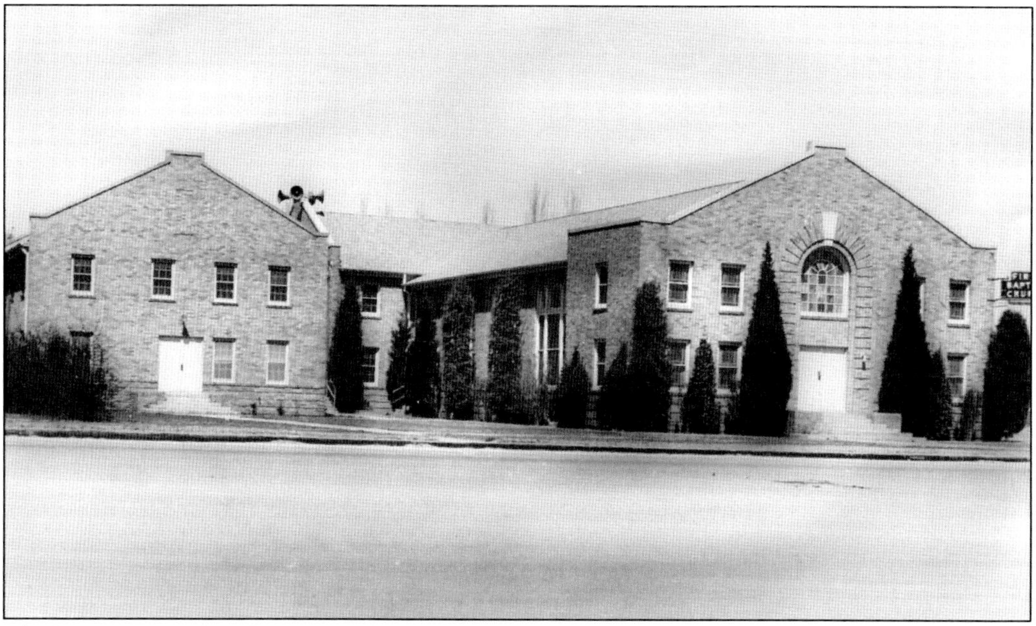
The First Baptist Church, organized in 1907, was also given a lot by C. W. Post on which to build a church. By July 1908, the structure was complete, and Post provided a carpet he had commissioned to be made in Battle Creek, Michigan.

Eight

Cultural Warriors of the Plains

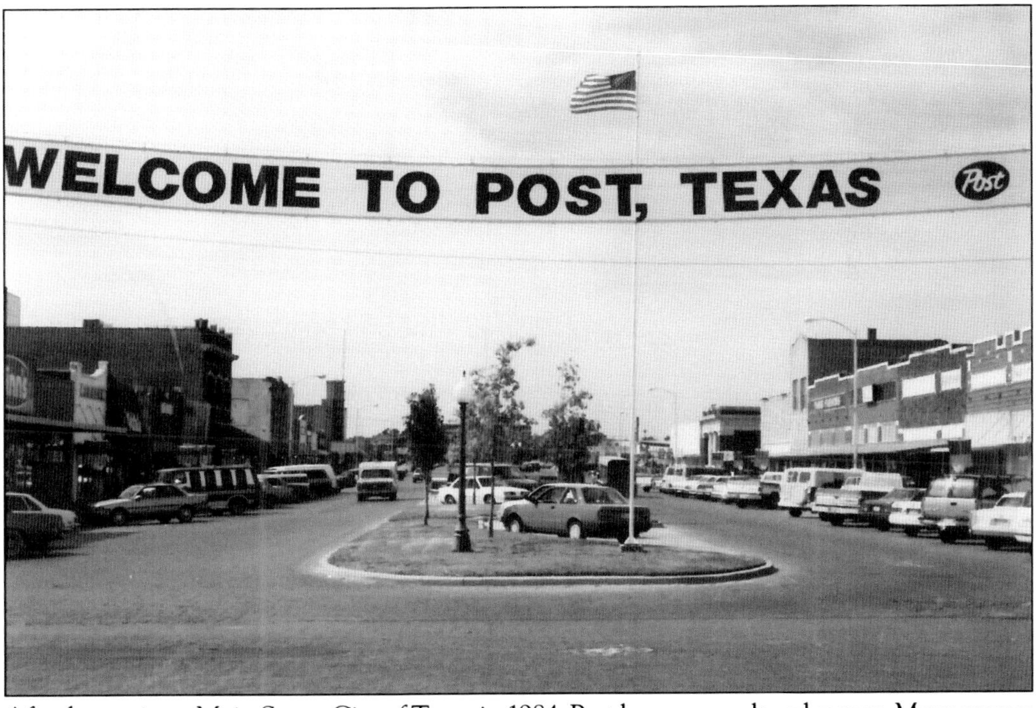

After becoming a Main Street City of Texas in 1984, Post became a cultural mecca. Many venues were already in place: the OS Ranch Art Show, which attracted hundreds of tourists and art buyers; the Post Art Guild annual show at the Algerita Art Center; two museums, the Garza County Historical Museum and the OS Ranch Museum; and two live theaters, Ragtown Gospel Theater and the Garza Theatre.

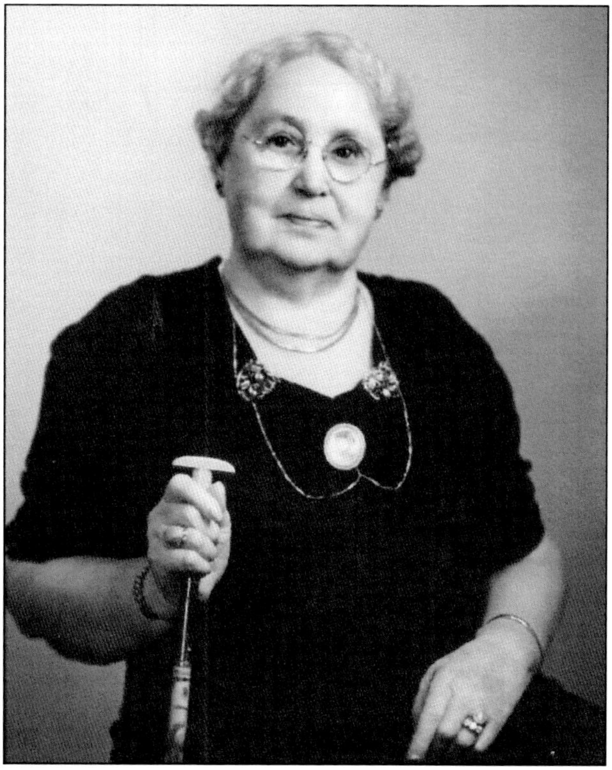

Isabella Slaughter organized the Novelty Luncheon Club in 1920. The club had a membership of 12 prominent ladies, each committed to putting on an elaborate luncheon one month of the year. Some recalled how they farmed out husbands and children to make room for their luncheon, sometimes spending their entire food budgets for the month. This organization later became the Women's Culture Club.

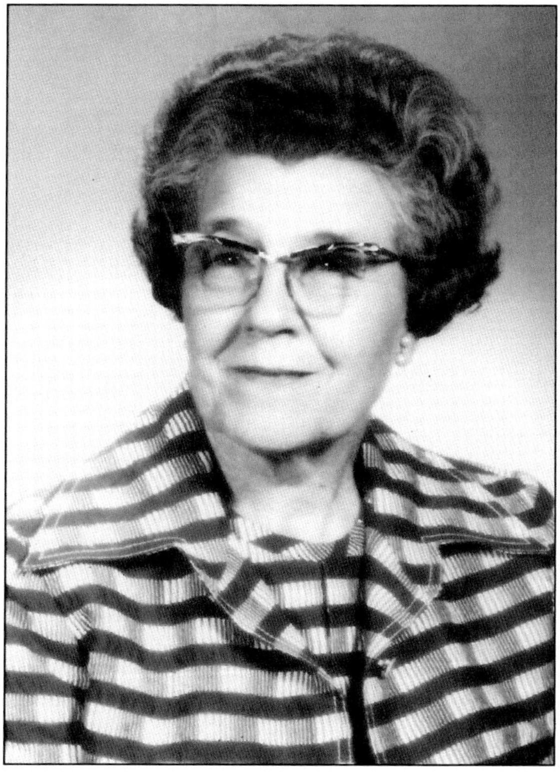

Ruby Kirkpatrick moved to Post with her new husband in 1923. She was a graduate of Texas Christian University (TCU) in 1927. Kirkpatrick received an honorary doctorate from TCU in 1977 for her continued support of ministerial students. Pres. Ronald Reagan later honored Dr. Kirkpatrick in a ceremony in Washington, D.C., for her generosity to TCU. A devout Christian during here 101 years, she participated in many cultural organizations in the community. Kirkpatrick became the first female member of the Post Rotary Club and was named Citizen of the Year in 1955.

Wanda Mitchell, with her hands on her hips, prepares for the Black Tie and Boots party at the Macy Ranch. Mitchell is a great promoter, who served as the Main Street manager for many years. She may be retired, but she is a real shaker and doer, always involved in some project.

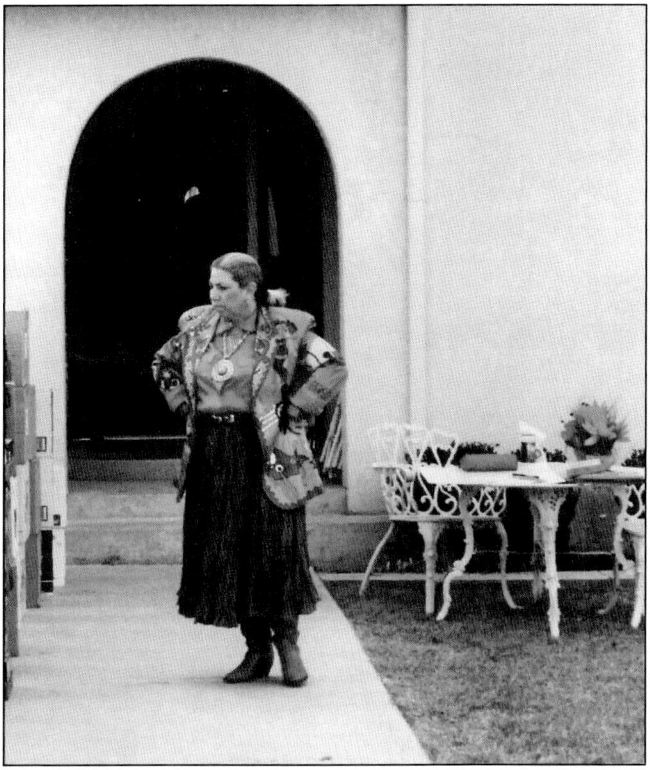

The OS Ranch Museum houses a wonderful collection from all over the world. In the image below, Delores and Jimmie Redman admire a sculpture in the gallery.

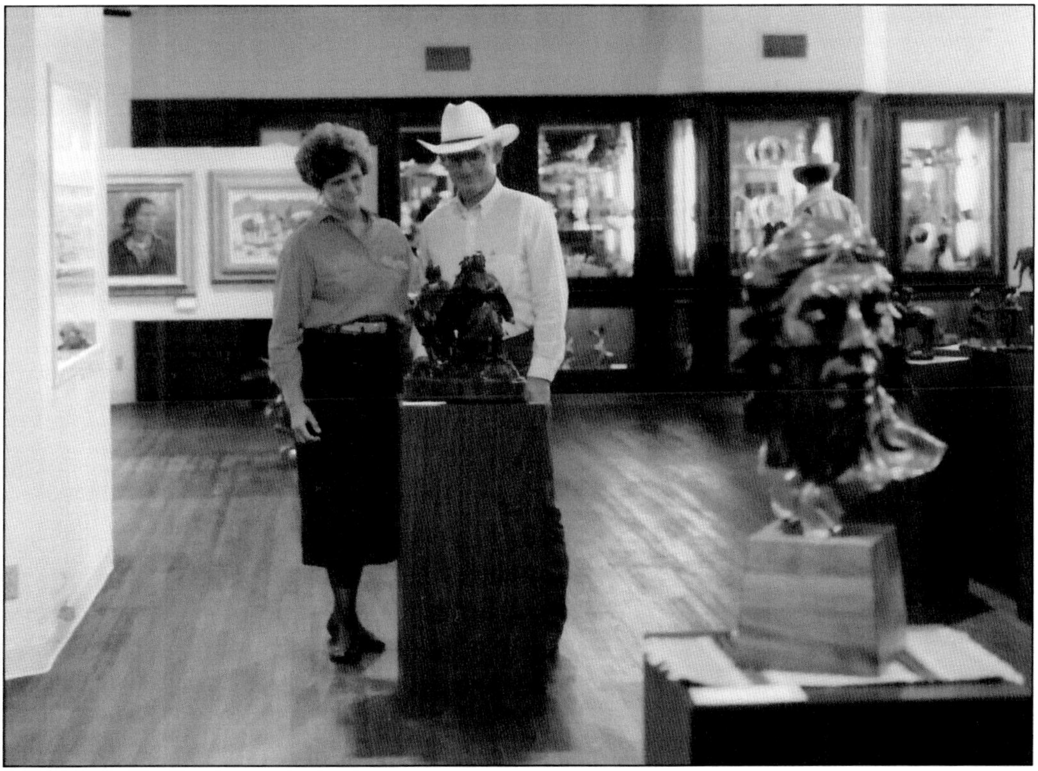

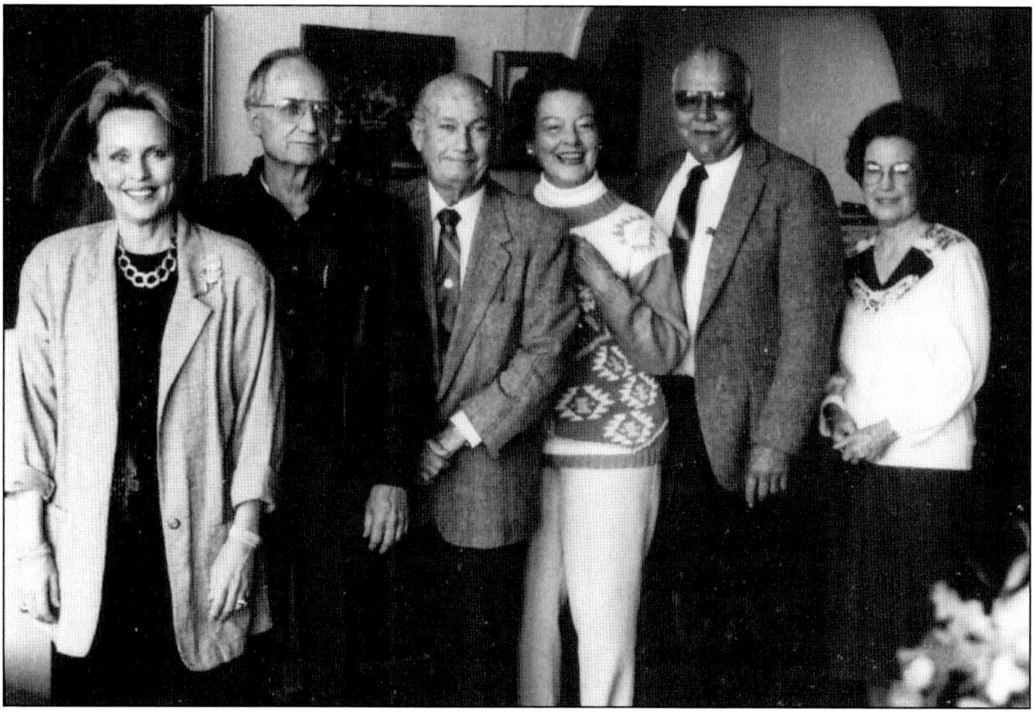

Pictured above is a group of cultural advocates at the Algerita Art Center. They are, from left to right, Patty Kirkpatrick, Carroll Bowen, Giles McCrary, Maxine Durrett Earl, Mayor Jim Jackson, and Geraldine Butler.

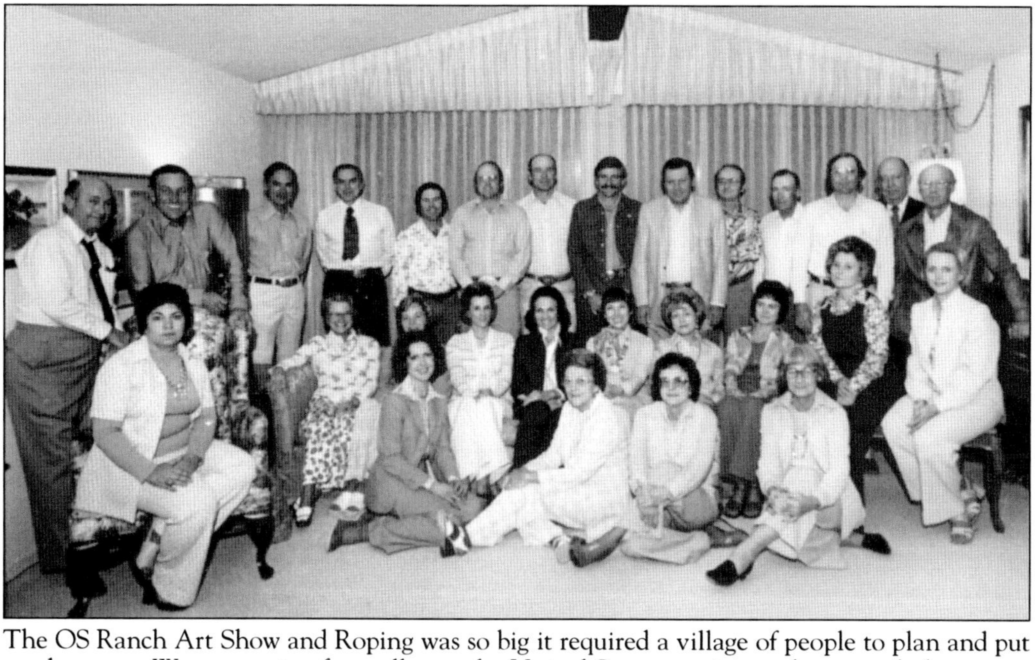

The OS Ranch Art Show and Roping was so big it required a village of people to plan and put on the event. Western artists from all over the United States participated, many of whom were houseguests of those pictured. Proceeds from the event went to the Texas Boys Ranch. Giles McCrary (standing at the far left) is the owner of the historic OS Ranch.

Will McCrary, a New York actor, came home to Post to start the Garza Theatre. McCrary wore many hats as an actor, director, visual artist, and set designer. He could be difficult and demanded excellence but could easily ad lib if one of the performers forgot a line. He was a true showman who knew his craft.

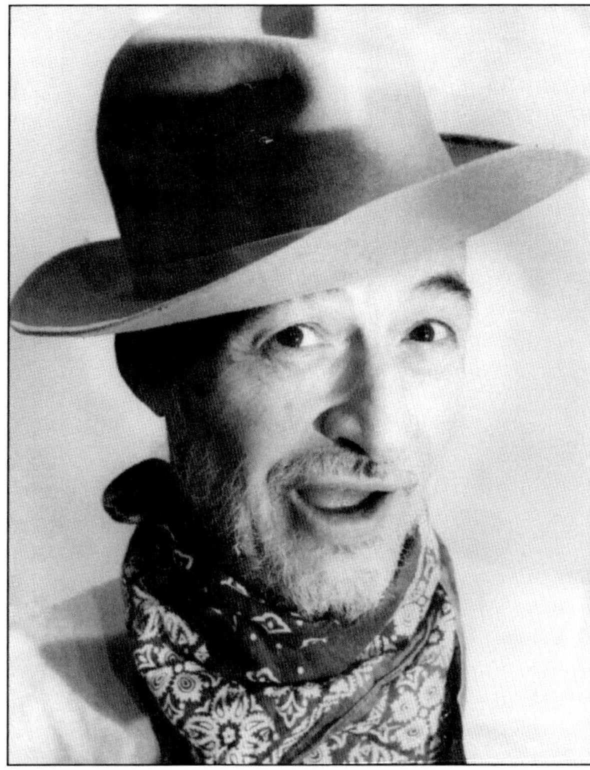

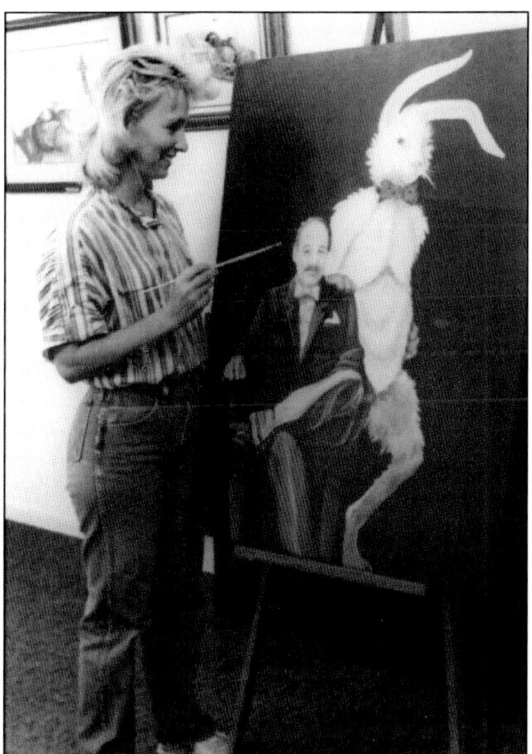

Vicki Diggs, an accomplished artist, captures Will McCray in the play *Harvey*. The original painting hangs in the Garza Theatre lobby. Diggs is also a wonderful Western artist.

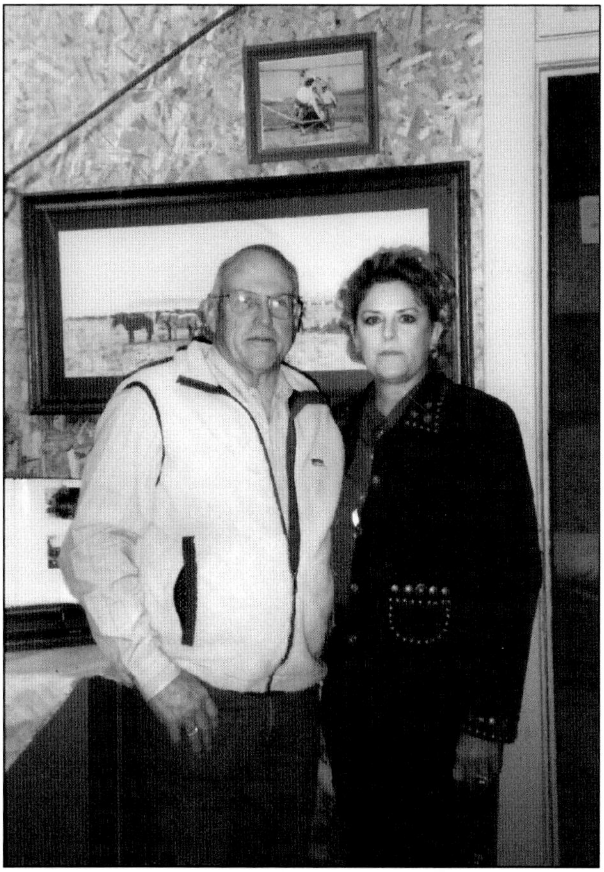

Bob and Debbie Macy own the Macy–Flying M Ranch. They have been great supporters of many events over the years, hosting a Black Tie and Boots party and much more. When the rains come and a football game is scheduled, Bob's helicopter can sometimes be seen hovering above the field, attempting to dry it out.

The Ragtown Gospel Theater is a real asset to Post, transporting audiences to the streets of Jerusalem. From left to right, co-owners/performers are Chip and Robin Polk, Nancy and Ronald Thuett, and Ray and Earline Bagby. Robin Polk is an architectural designer who did a wonderful job creating the theater.

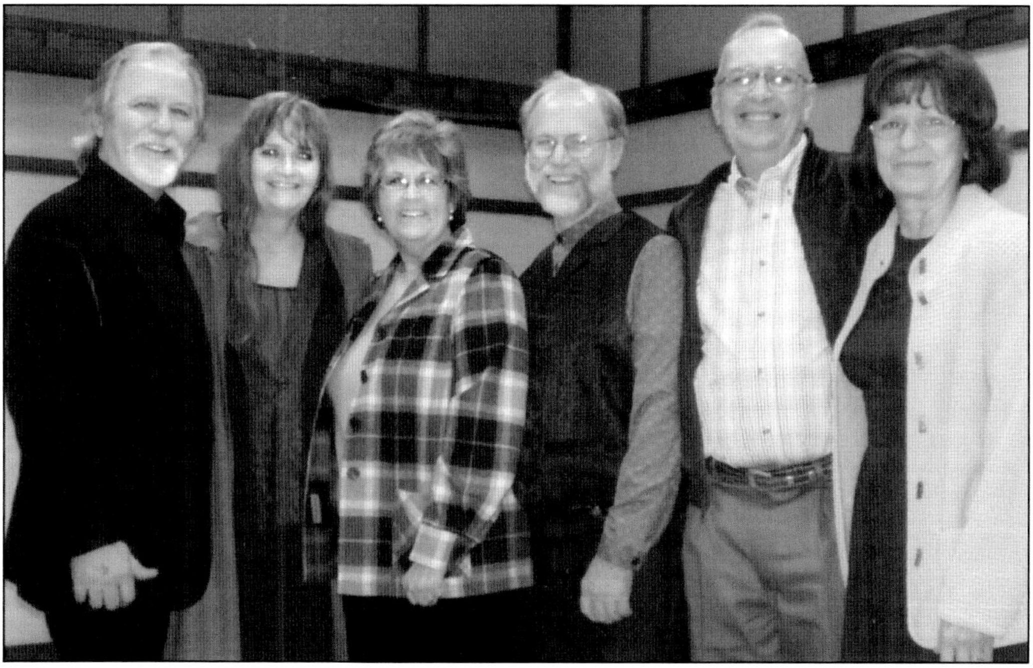

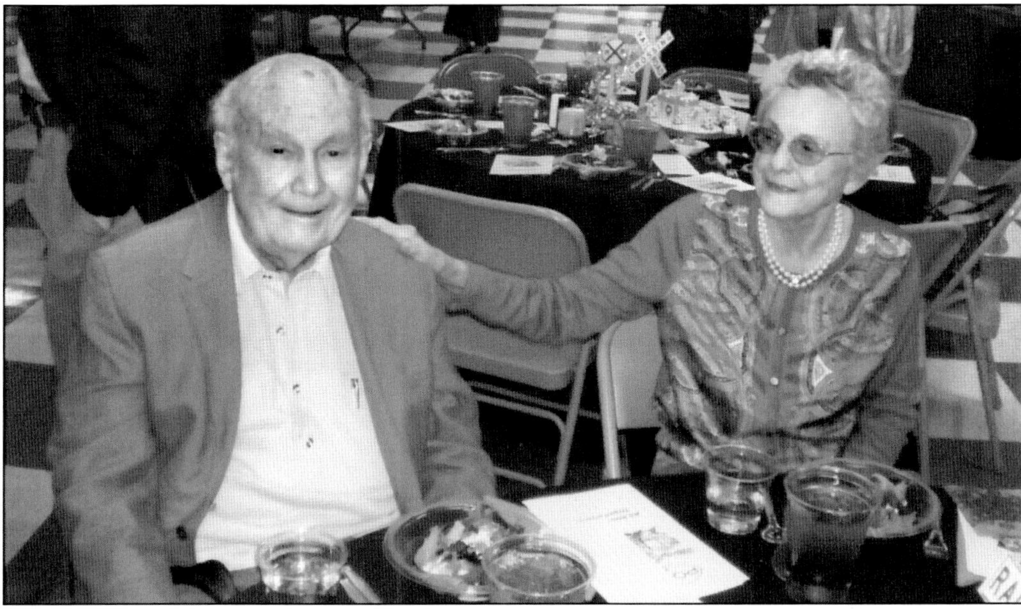

Giles and Louise McCrary have made untold contributions to this community. They once met with Pope John Paul II at the Vatican, and Giles and Fr. Malcolm Neyland were responsible for bringing the Vatican Exhibit to Lubbock. Giles served as mayor of the city for 24 years and still found time to travel the world. His opinion is often sought regarding projects of merit, and he gives his support as well.

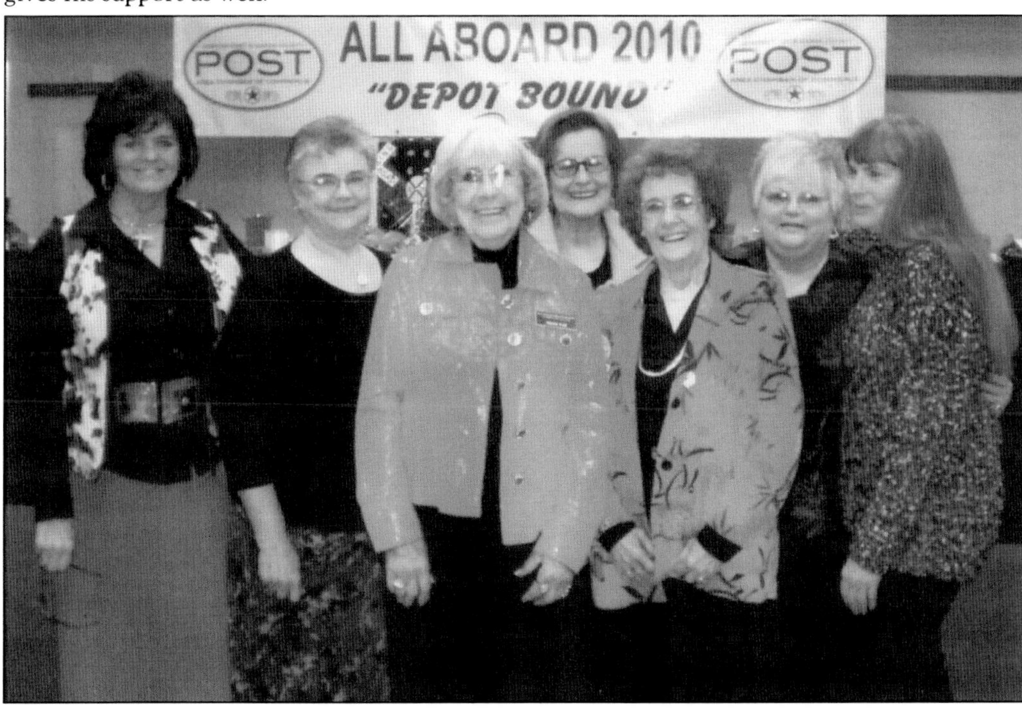

The Women's Division of the Post Area Chamber of Commerce is a community service organization that contributes to or sponsors many worthy causes in Post. Members are, from left to right, Linda Puckett, Naomi Matsler, Marie Neff, Anne Sims, Betty Posey, JoAnn Stelzer, and Sue Davis.

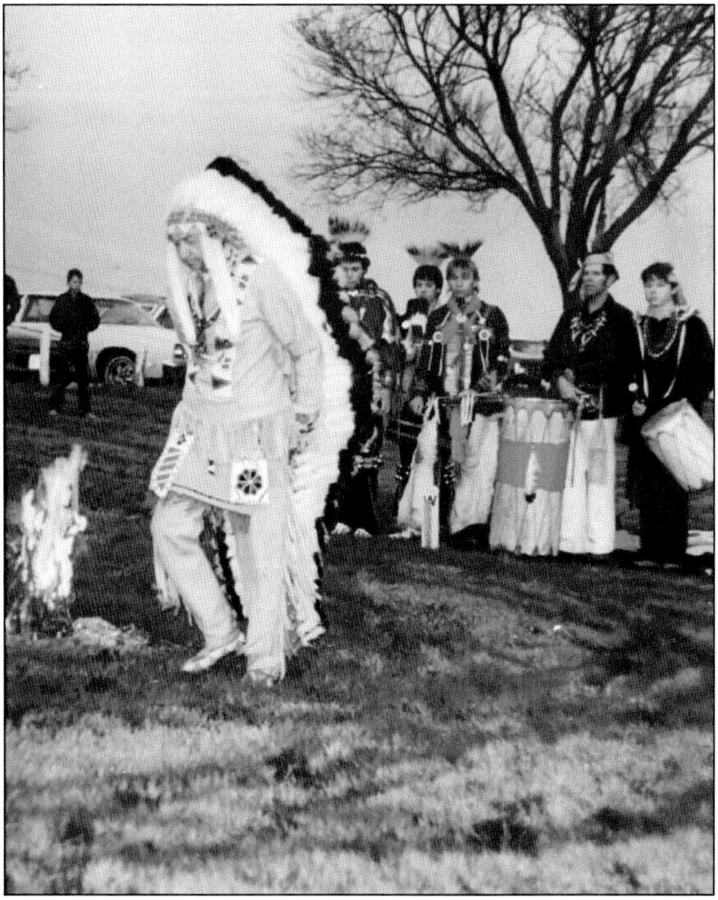

Chief Frank Runkles dances at the Tabana Yuane Sunrise Wind Ceremony in 1986. The Quahadi Dancers attended that year. Jack Ramey is at the drum (second from right). This event takes place at sunrise every March 22.

This photograph is of the Tabana Yuane participants, known as the Clan, at the annual meeting. They are, from left to right, (first row) Zoe Kirkpatrick, Shirley LeBlanc, and Linda Puckett; (second row) Jack Ramey, Linda Ramey, Pearl Cory, John Cory, Ken LeBlanc, Christy Morris, Mike Cory, and Charla Lee.

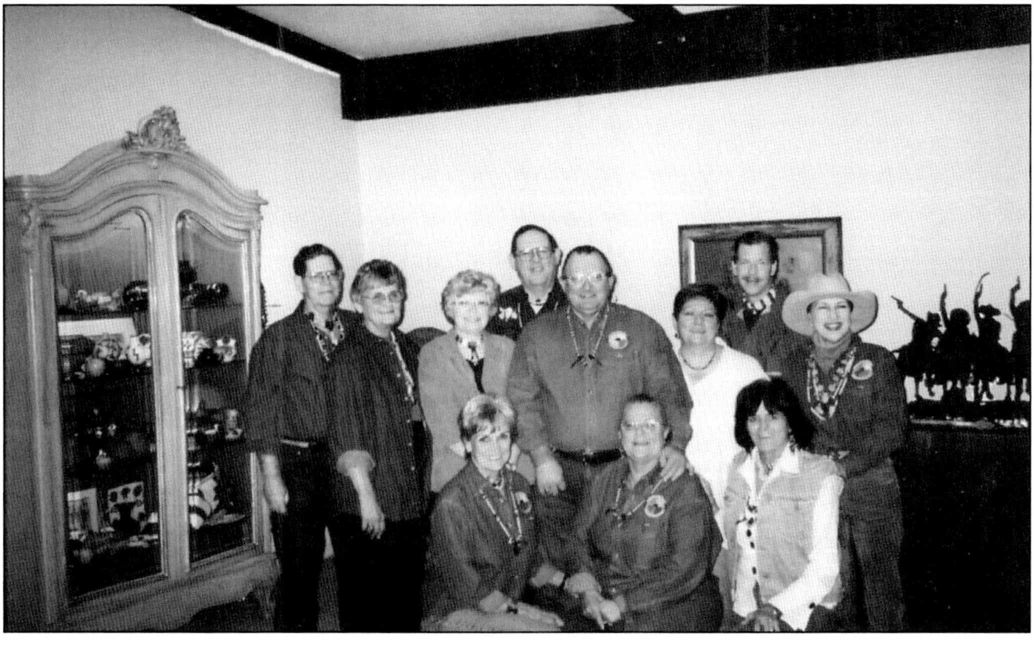

Theresa Harp is the mayor of Post. If she is not involved in a local project, it has not been thought up yet. Harp is willing and committed to achieving great things in Post. She was awarded the Citizen of the Year title for 2007.

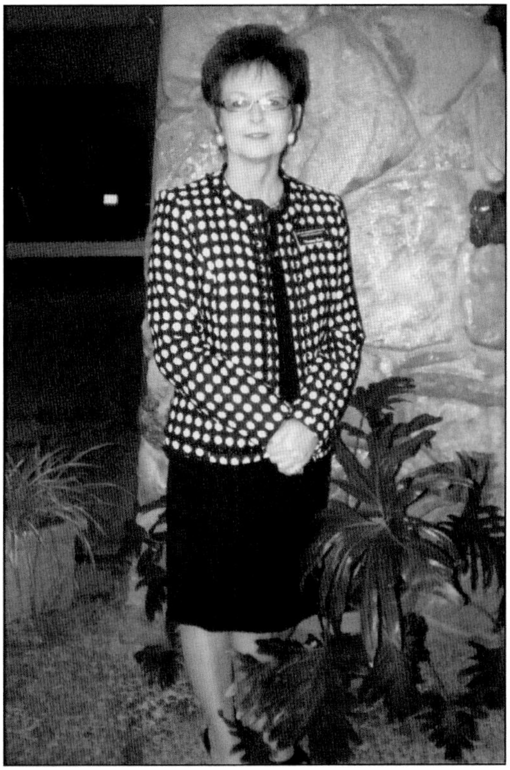

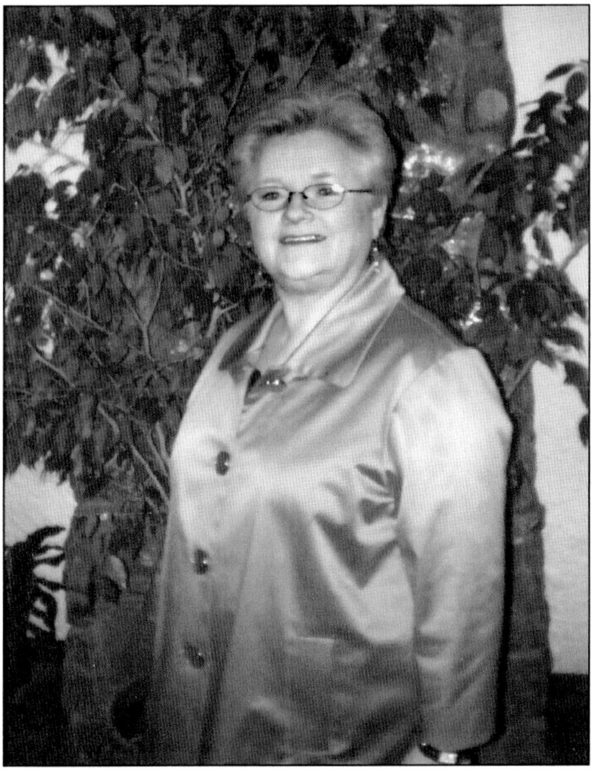

Rosa Latimer Bell is the owner of Ruby Lane Books and editor of the *Post Dispatch*. Bell is an accomplished writer and playwright, and serves on the Post Area Chamber of Commerce.

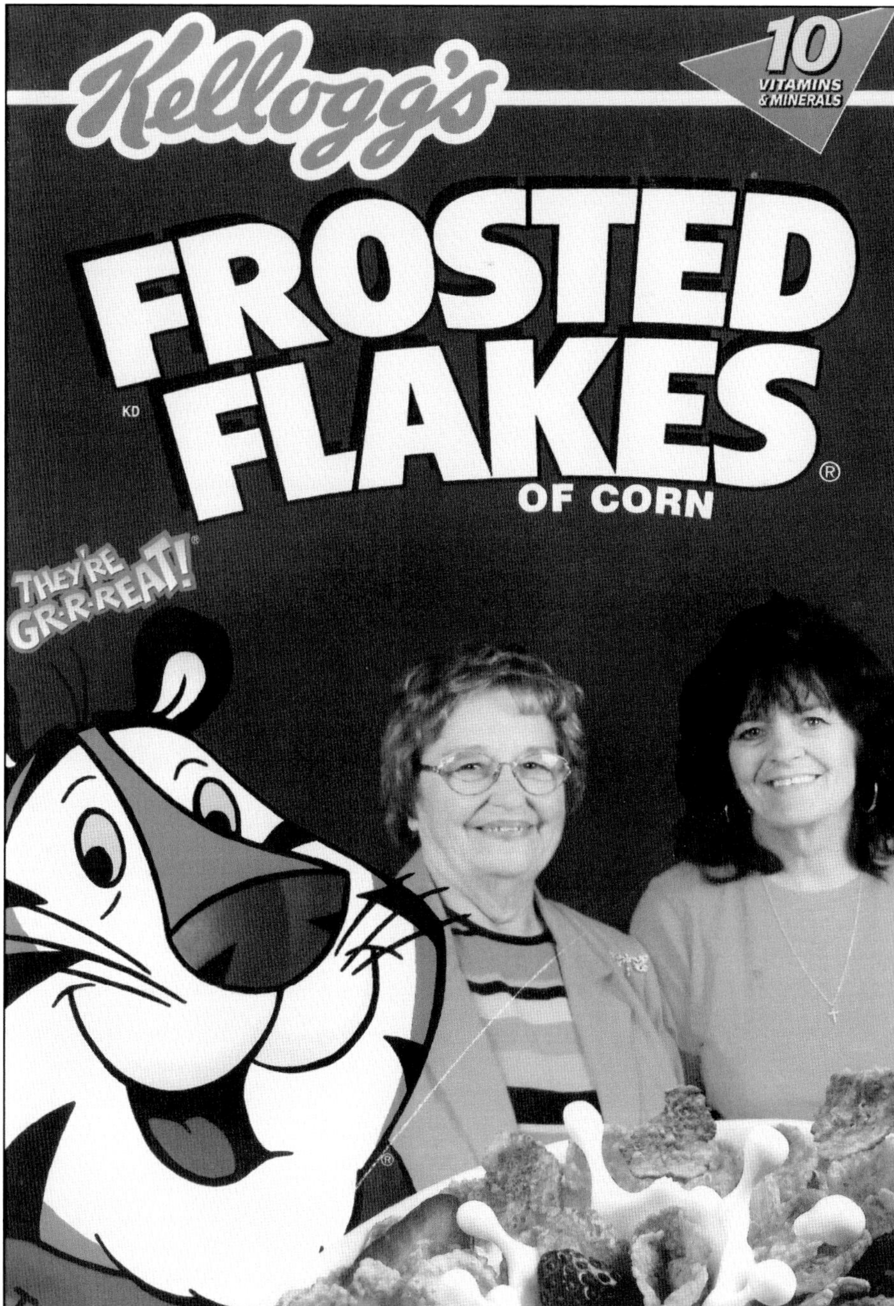

JoAnn Mock (left) and Linda Puckett pose for a Kellogg's cereal box photograph with Tony the Tiger in Battle Creek, Michigan. Their 10-day, connect-the-dots trip started in Springfield, Illinois, birthplace of C. W. Post. On the second leg of the trip, they spent three days in the "cereal capital of the world," Battle Creek, Michigan, with wonderful tour guides who became good friends. According to Puckett, "We couldn't take a tour of Post Cereal factory, but the Kellogg folks were most gracious and even putting us on a cereal box." The third stop was Hillwood Museum in Washington, D.C., the home of Marjorie Merriweather Post.

Nine

A Family Tradition

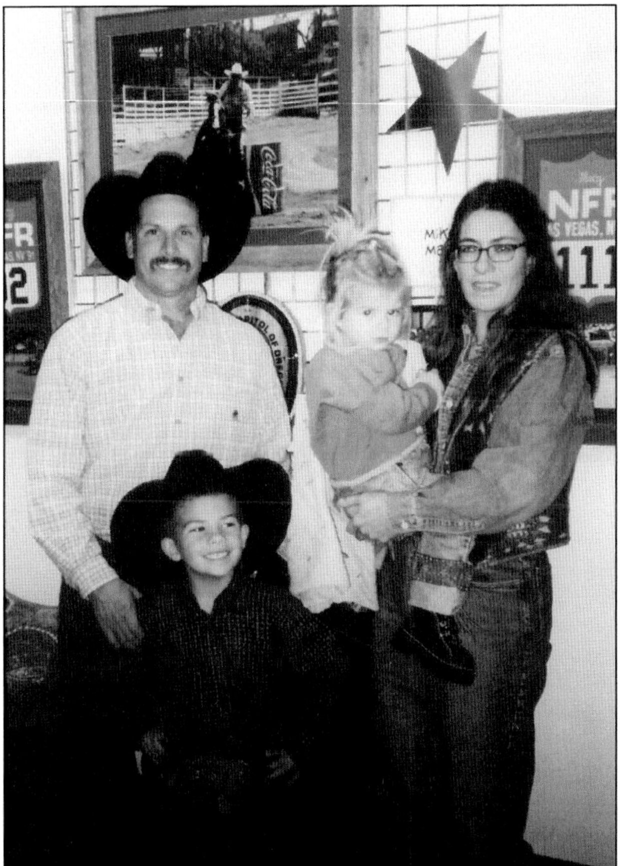

Rodeo is an amazing sport. It is not for everybody, but those who know no fear except the stopwatch enjoy it. Rodeo events draw millions of spectators and fans. From the cradle to the PRCA (Professional Rodeo Cowboys Association) best describes the Macy family. A family of champions, father Mike Macy is a roper-header; his wife, Kellie, a barrel racer; son Aaron, a roper-header; and daughter Brogan, a barrel racer.

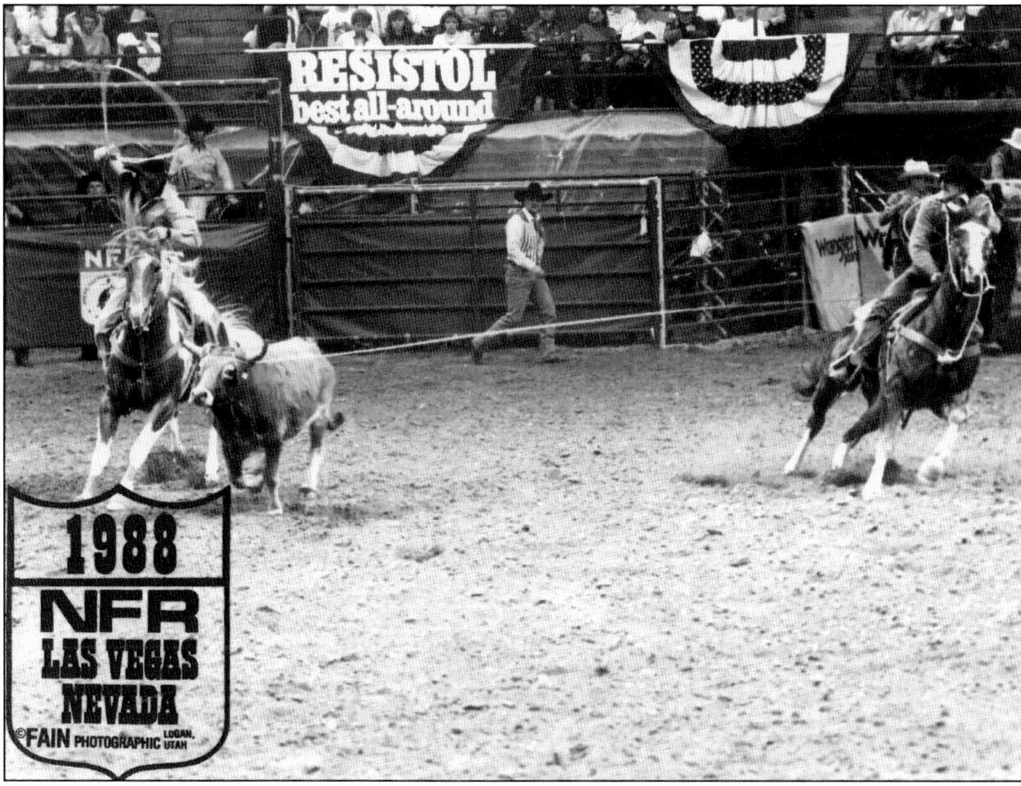

Pictured above are Mike Macy (right) heading and Flynn Farris (left) heeler in the sixth round of the National Finals Rodeo in Las Vegas in 1988. The photograph below shows Aaron Macy (right) competing in the Junior High National Finals at Gallup, New Mexico, in 2009. (Both, courtesy Kellie Macy.)

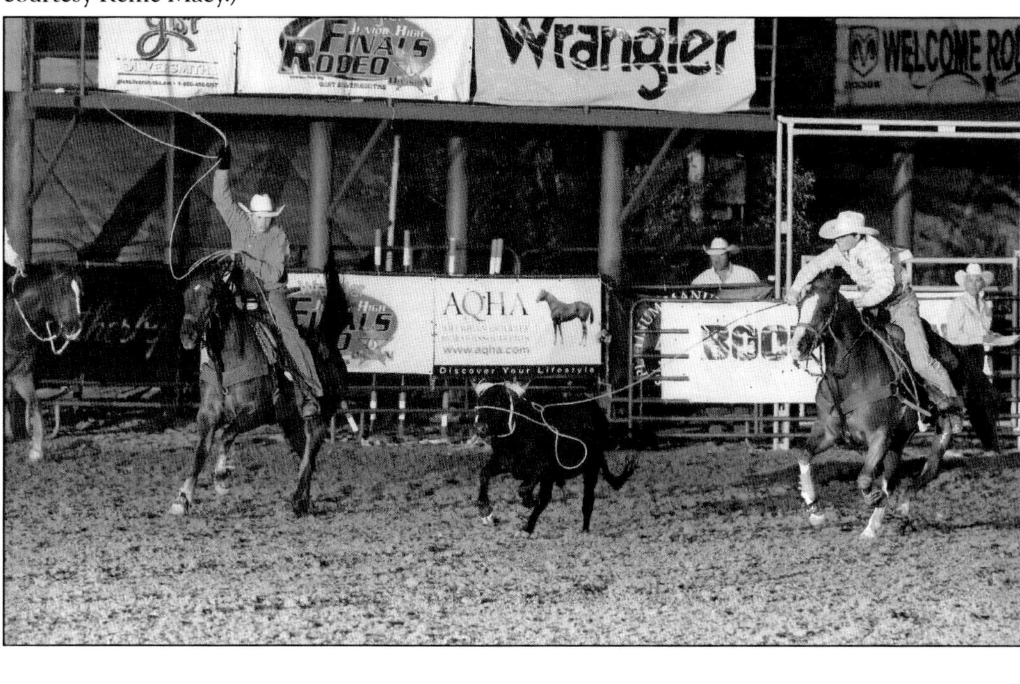

Brogan Macy won the Ogden's Eight and Under World Junior Champion Barrel Race in Abilene in 2006. Pictured at right, Brogan is riding Buck. (Courtesy Kellie Macy.)

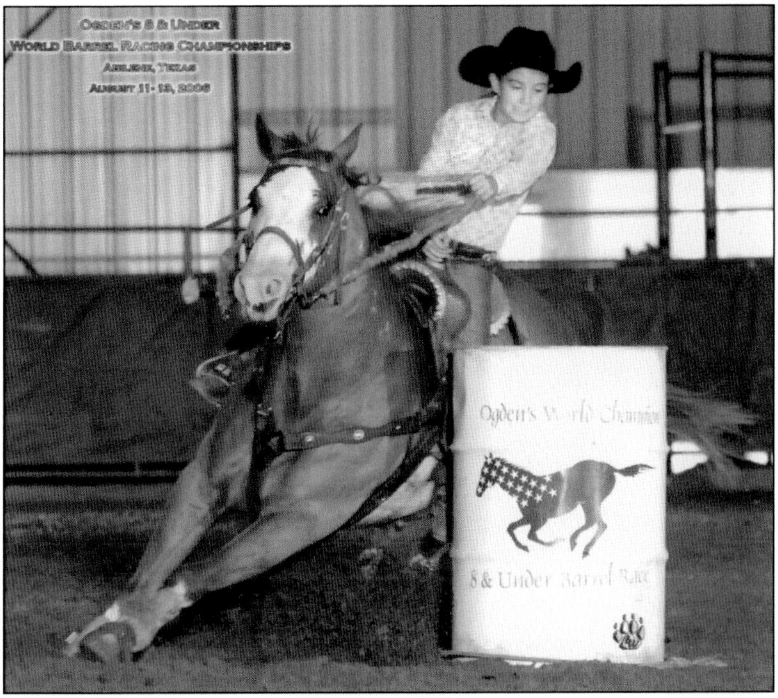

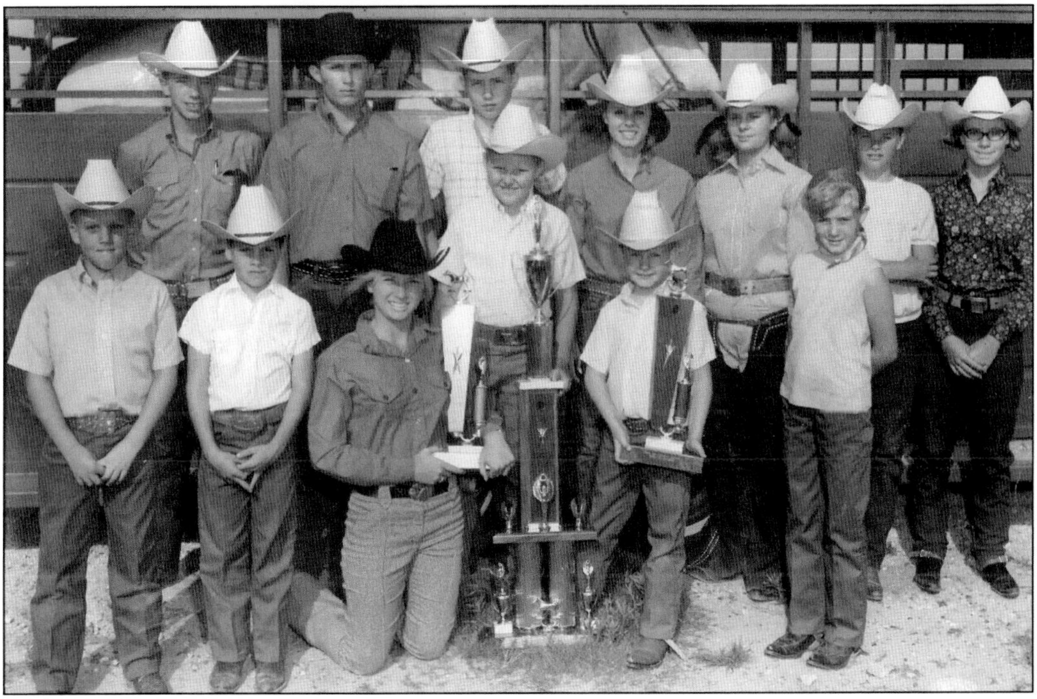

The 1969 Graham Chapel 4-H Club won several events at the Brownfield horse show. Members posing with trophies are, from left to right, (first row) Bobby Macy, Mike Macy, Melvena Stewart, Steve White, John Bill Hedrick, and Jarita Norman; (second row) John Johnson, Karl Bruce Hall, Jimmy Norman, Natha Jo Mears, Cynthia White, Melonie King, and Sherry White. (Courtesy Natha Jo Arnold.)

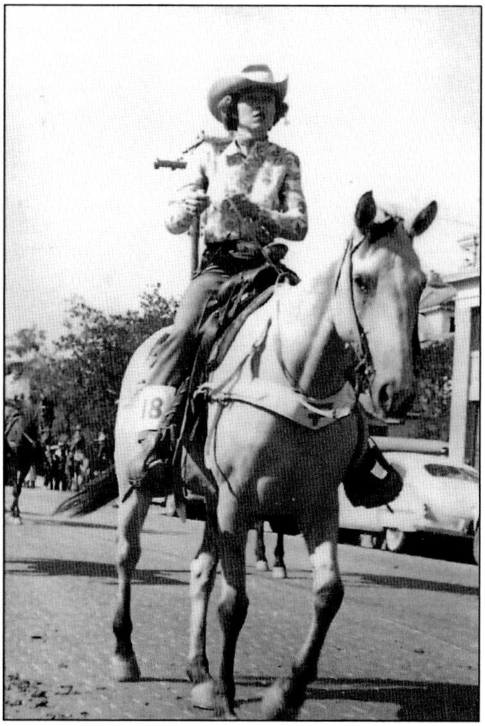

Pictured at left, Bil Kennedy, Texas Tech Rodeo Queen, rides in the parade at Stamford, Texas, in 1947. Her horse sports a breast harness with the school's Double-T logo. The photograph below shows Kennedy at the Post Rodeo Grounds in 1948. This was the site of the Original All Jr. Rodeo, founded by Alvin G. Davis, later named the American Junior Rodeo Association. The association's office was located in Post. (Both, courtesy Natha Jo Arnold.)

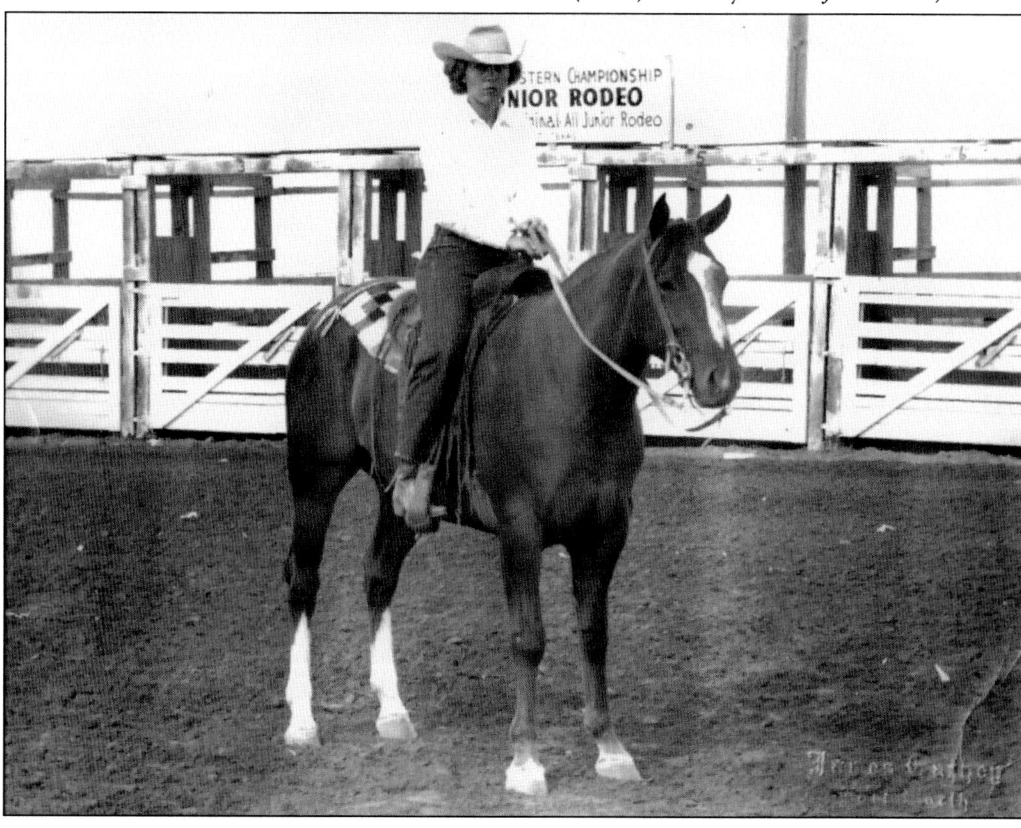

Lori Hudman Marsh started barrel racing at an early age, competing in junior and then high school rodeos. She won fourth in the state finals in Abilene on her horse, Fancy. This win earned her a spot on the Howard County College rodeo team. She later transferred to Tarleton University. (Courtesy Julie Hudman.)

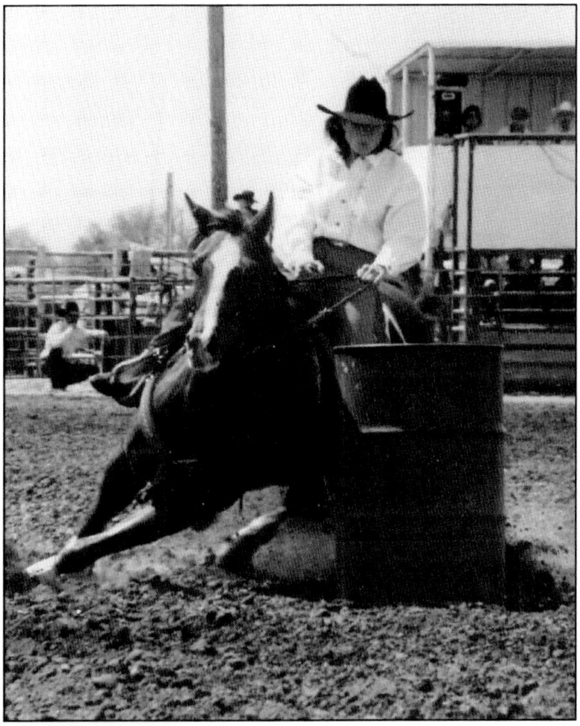

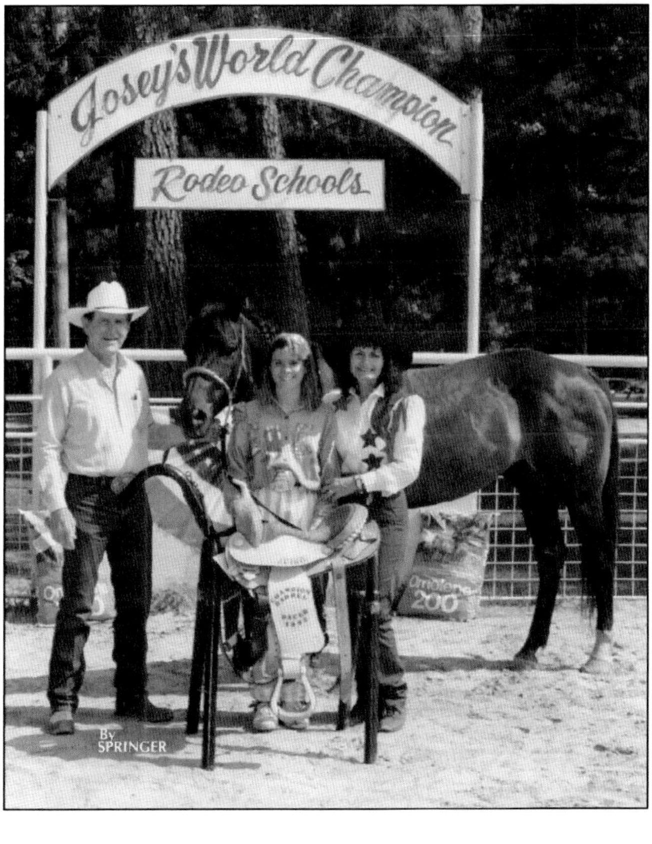

Lori Hudman Marsh (center) won the Josey Summer Barrel Racing Clinic Champion saddle at Josey's World Champion Rodeo School in 1992. With Lori are R. E. Josey (left) and Martha Josey. R. E. was former a pro roper and Martha a barrel racer who went to the National Finals Rodeo (NFR) for six decades. Both have enriched the abilities of countless students who continue to attend the Josey Clinics at the ranch in Karnack, Texas. (Courtesy Julie Hudman.)

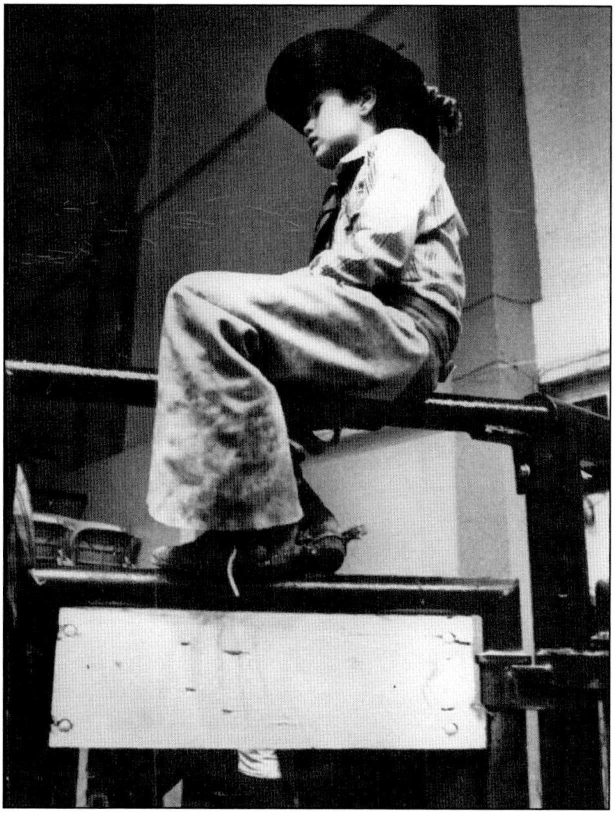

Gary Puckett rode a steer at his first rodeo, in El Paso, Texas, in 1979. This photograph made the front page of the *El Paso Times*. While his mother was thinking in the short term—to get through the night without injury—this little boy sitting on the chutes was on a mission that would encompass the next 20 years. (Courtesy Linda Puckett.)

A cowboy's best friend is the bullfighter. Photographer Robert W. Mello captured this shot of Gary Puckett fighting bulls at a rodeo in Lubbock. Mello's photograph won a contest and was published in a national magazine. (Courtesy Linda Puckett.)

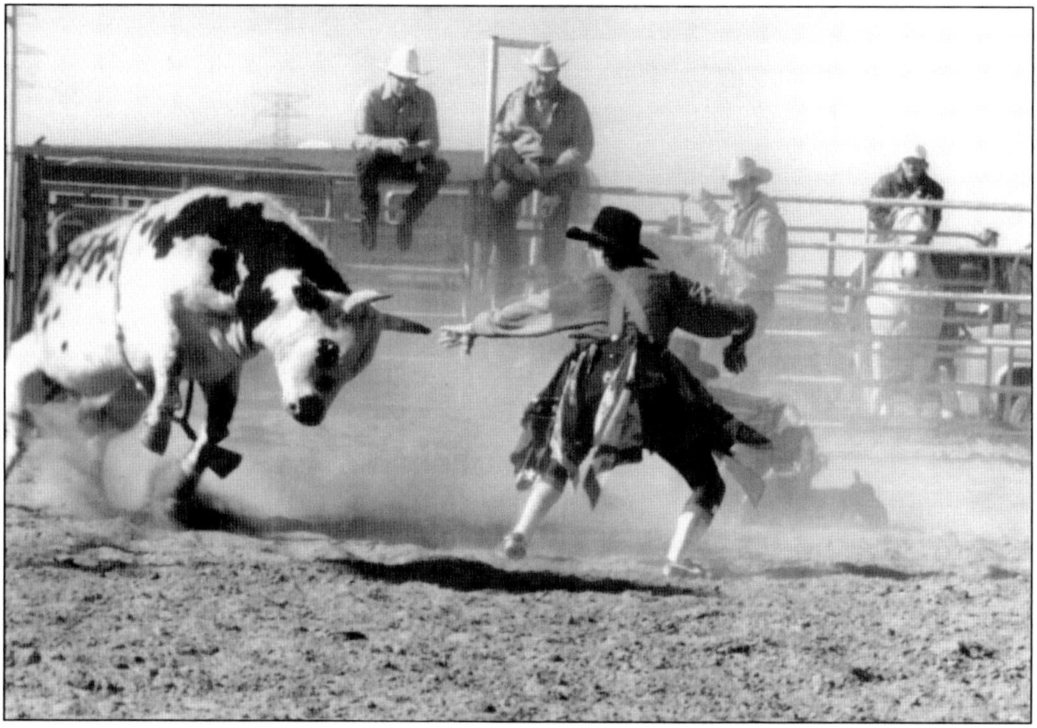

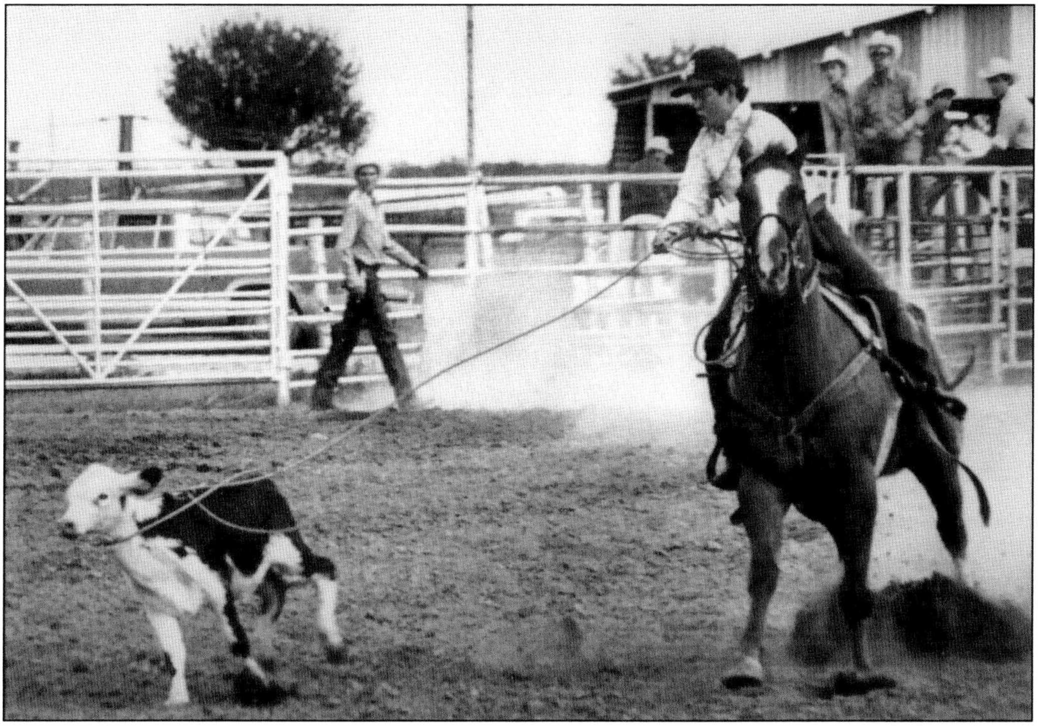

Pictured above, John Bill Hedrick ropes at Uvalde, Texas, in 1975. The photograph below shows Hedrick riding a saddle bronc at Sul Ross College Rodeo. Henrick was a member of the Western Texas College Rodeo Team. (Both, courtesy Natha Jo Arnold.)

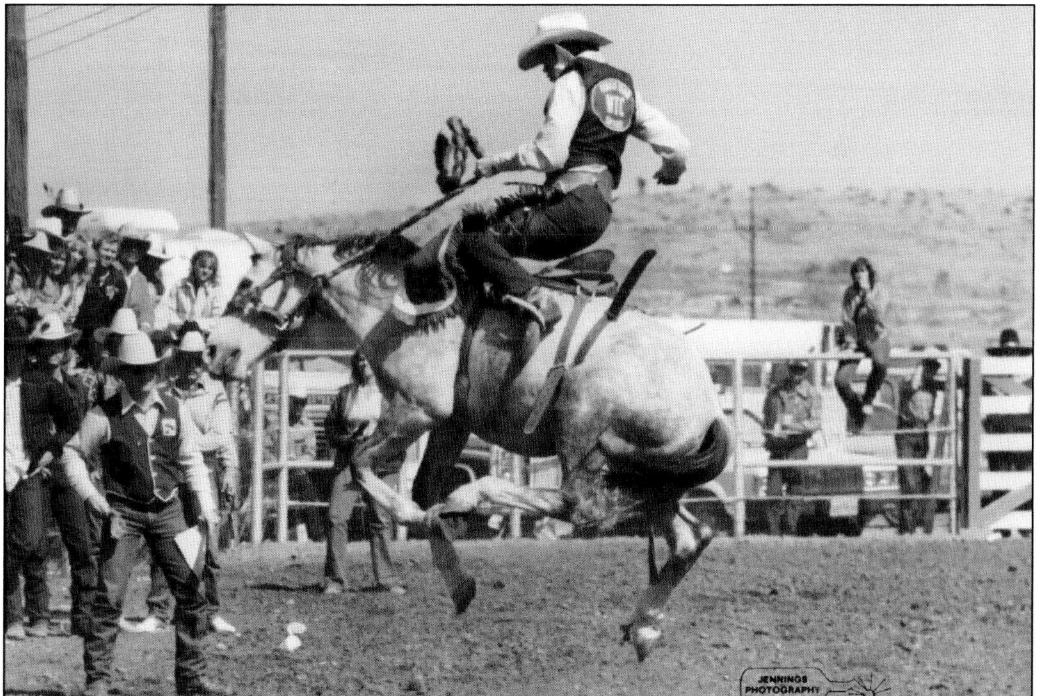

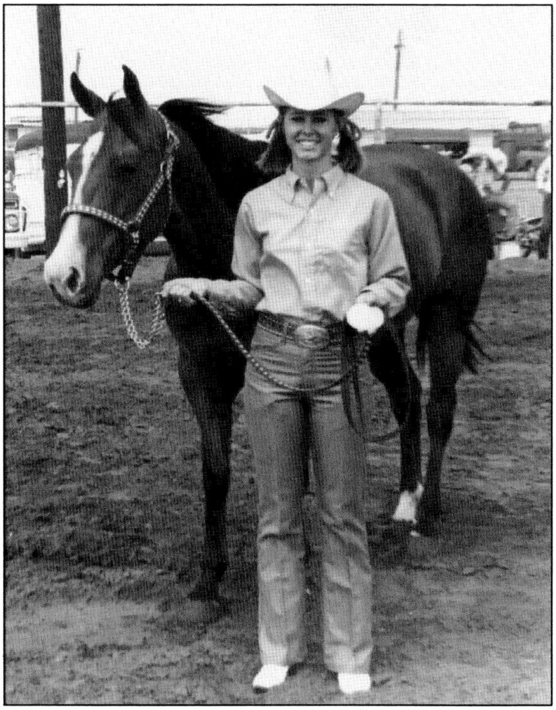

Natha Jo Mears stands with her horse, Contessa, at Stamford, Texas, in 1970. She had just won another buckle to add to her collection.

Jo Arnold of Post rides her great-looking horse, Prime Example. Arnold won the breakaway at Odessa and was fourth in the world on this same horse in American Paint Horse Association (APHA) pole bending.

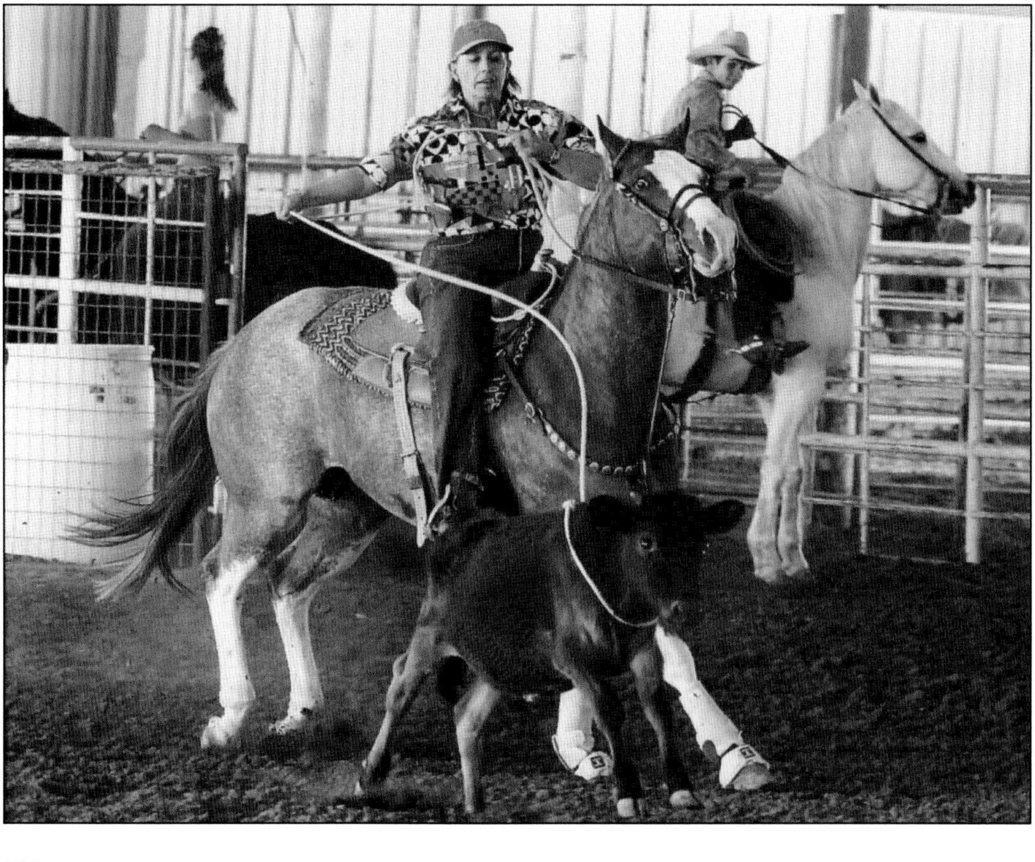

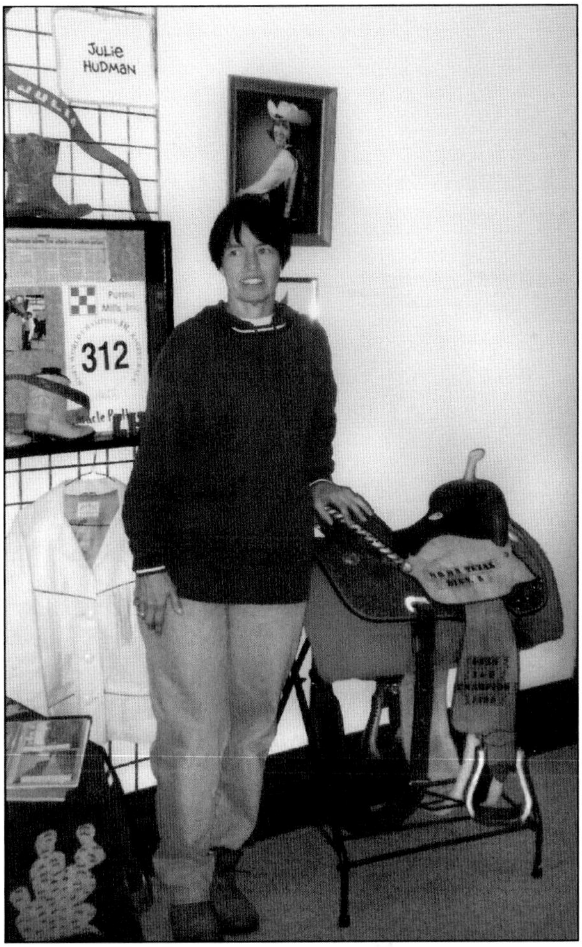

Julie Landers Hudman (right) poses with her collection, part of the Cowboy Christmas display at the Garza County Historical Museum. Hudman was born to be a cowgirl. She loved horses and boots. Her mother had to tell her not to wear boots to church. Looking at a cowboy standing next to them in the sanctuary, she would ask, "Why not? He is wearing boots." After her third child left for college, Hudman went back to barrel racing on Zipper, winning buckles and three saddles. She won the state senior 4-D division in 2003. Below, Hudman and Zipper show their trophy saddles. (Right, courtesy Brent Armstrong; below, courtesy Johnny Davenport.)

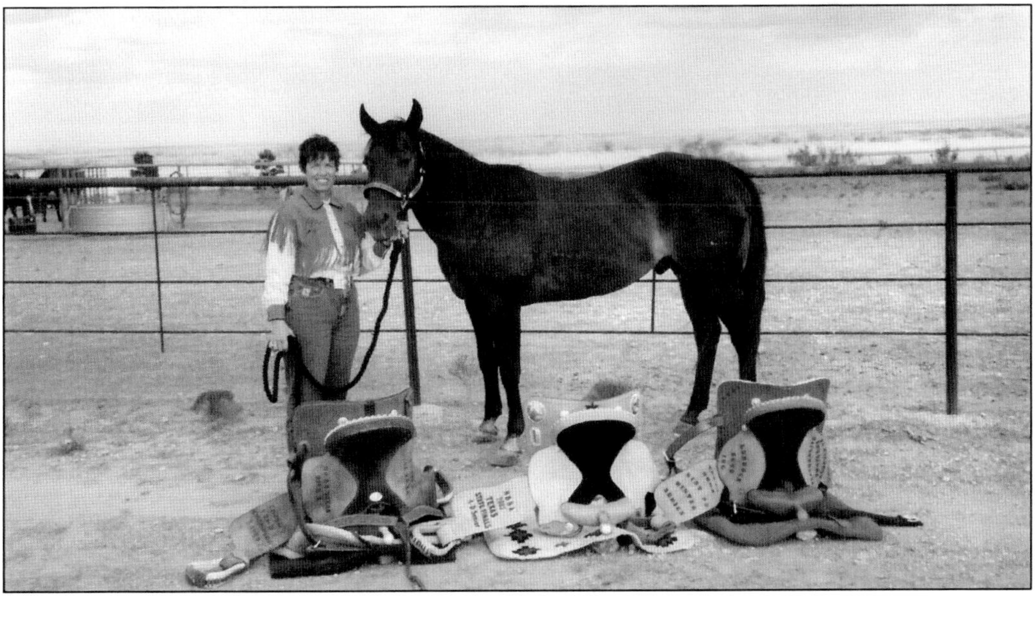

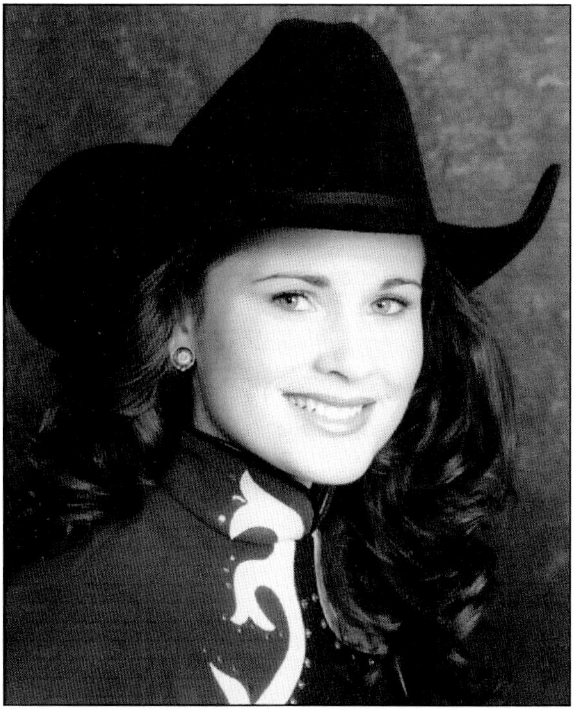

Texas Tech senior Amanda Puckett was Top O' Texas Rodeo Queen for 2004. She has won numerous awards in barrel racing and pageant, including the 2000 American Association of Sheriff Posses and Riding Clubs District Two Queen and the 2005 Miss Rodeo Texas second runner-up.

Eight-year-old Jay Bird comes out of chute No. 2 on a mean-looking bronc. This was his first rodeo in Post, Texas, in 1960. Post cowboys will remember these old wooden bucking chutes. (Courtesy Ada Lou Bird.)

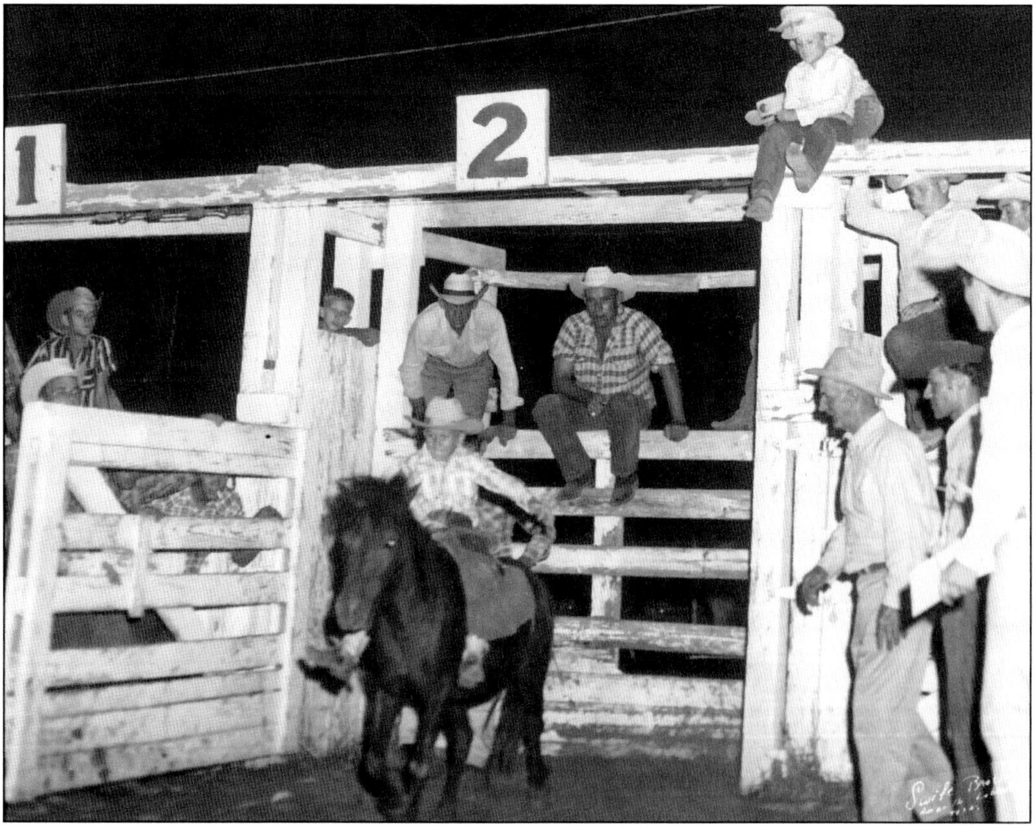

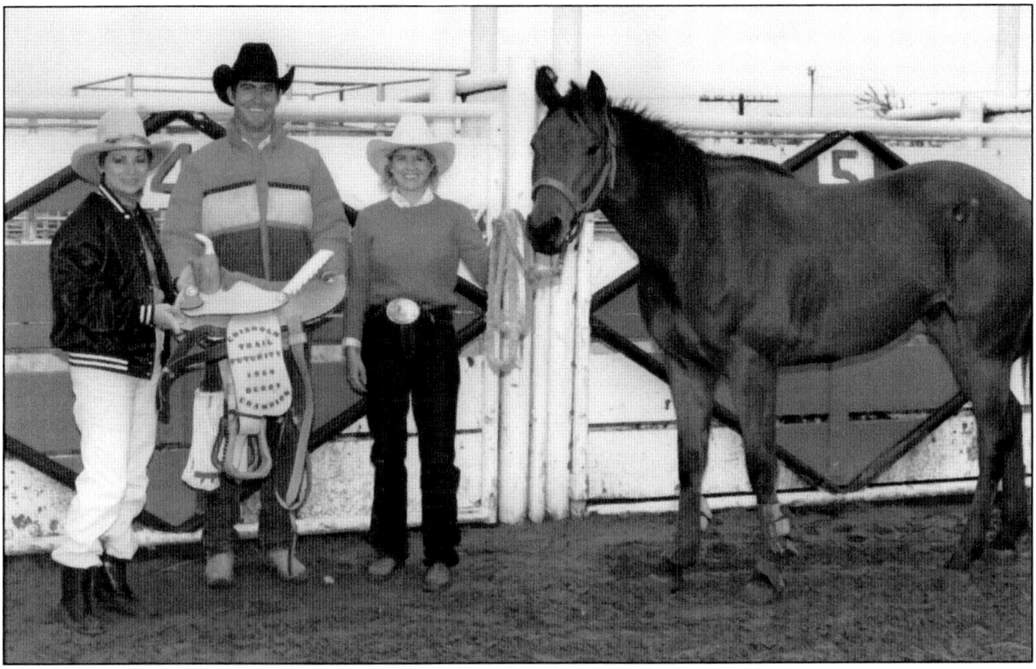

Cindy Bird DeMere (pictured above, far right) poses after winning the Derby Champion Saddle–Chisholm Trail Futurity in 1984. DeMere has won six saddles and numerous buckles in her barrel-racing career. She won the barrel racing and a saddle at the 1984 Stamford Cowboy Reunion Rodeo. At the Stamford Rodeo in 1946, her father, Jimmy Bird, won calf roping and a saddle. He is seen calf roping in the image below. (Both, courtesy Ada Lou Bird.)

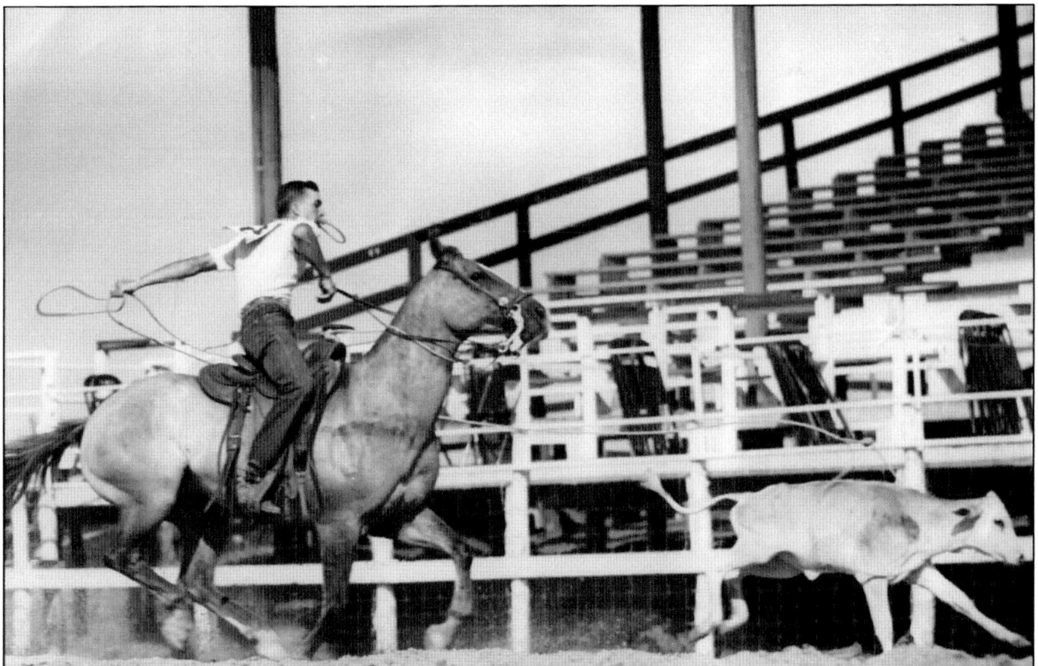

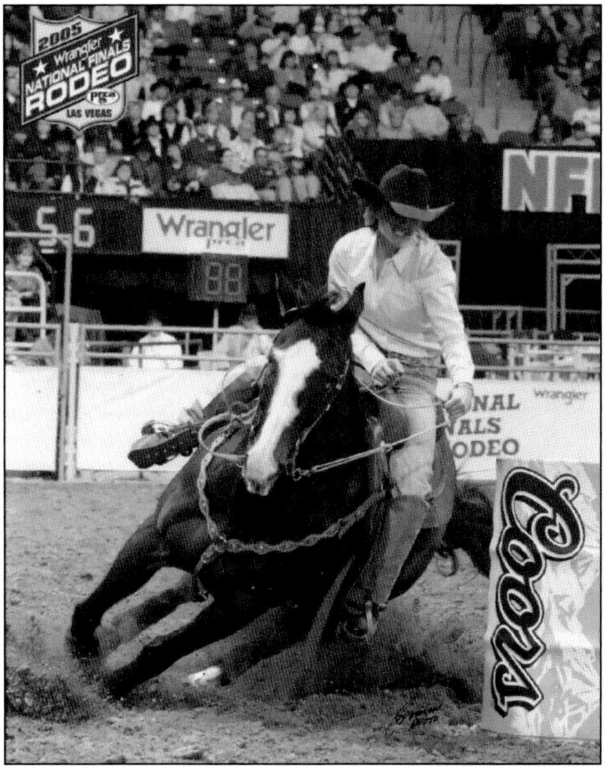

Barrel racer Talina Bird competes in the 2005 National Finals Rodeo in Las Vegas. She was 11th in the world and 6th in the average. Bird has been competing in rodeo events since age eight. Her grandfather Jimmy Bird hauled her many miles during those early years.

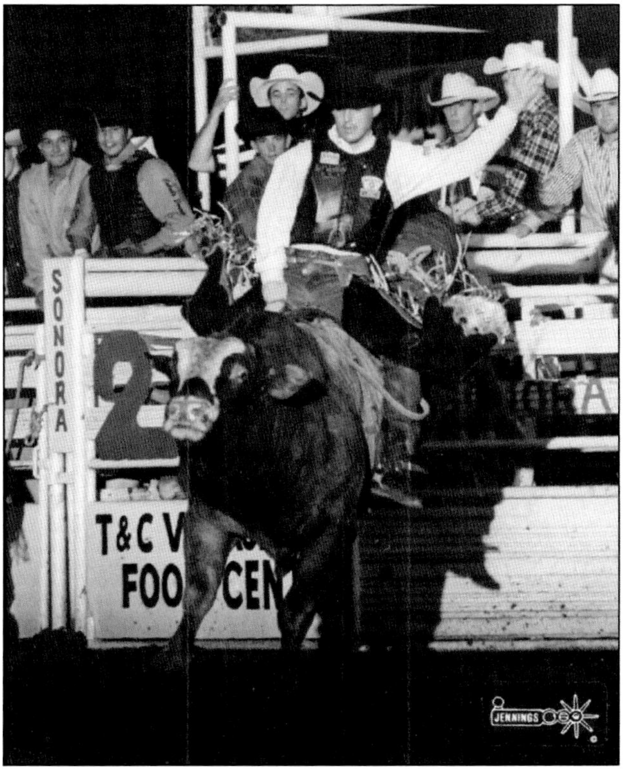

PRCA bull rider Gary Puckett (right) qualified for the Texas Finals in Waco in 1999, featuring the top 15 bull riders in Texas. Puckett also competed in the bareback and bullfighting events. Rodeo can be a tough go, and competitors must love it, travel thousands of miles, and stay healthy.

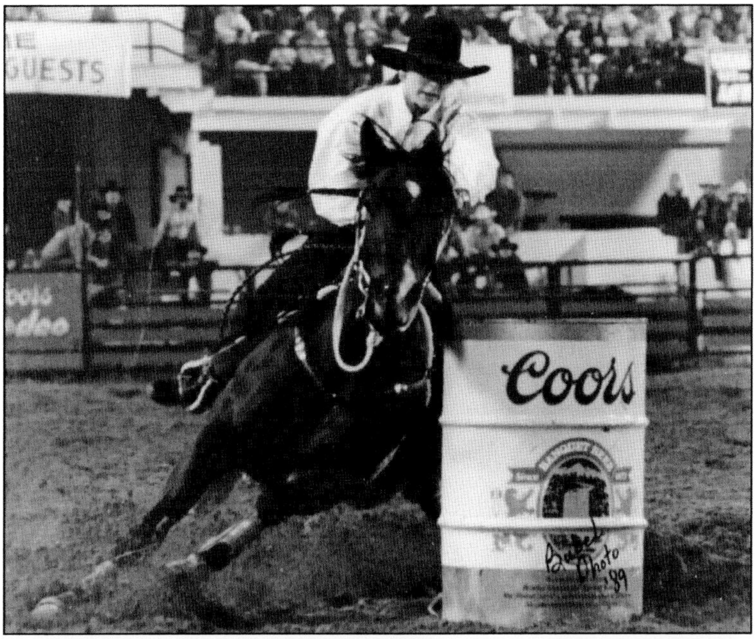

Joy McDaniels rides her seven-year-old bay mare, Charmin Cherokee, called C. C. McDaniels won events in Clovis, Sonora, and Prescott in 1990 and made the top 15 in the Texas circuit standing that same year. She won Rookie of the Year on the Texas circuit in 1990.

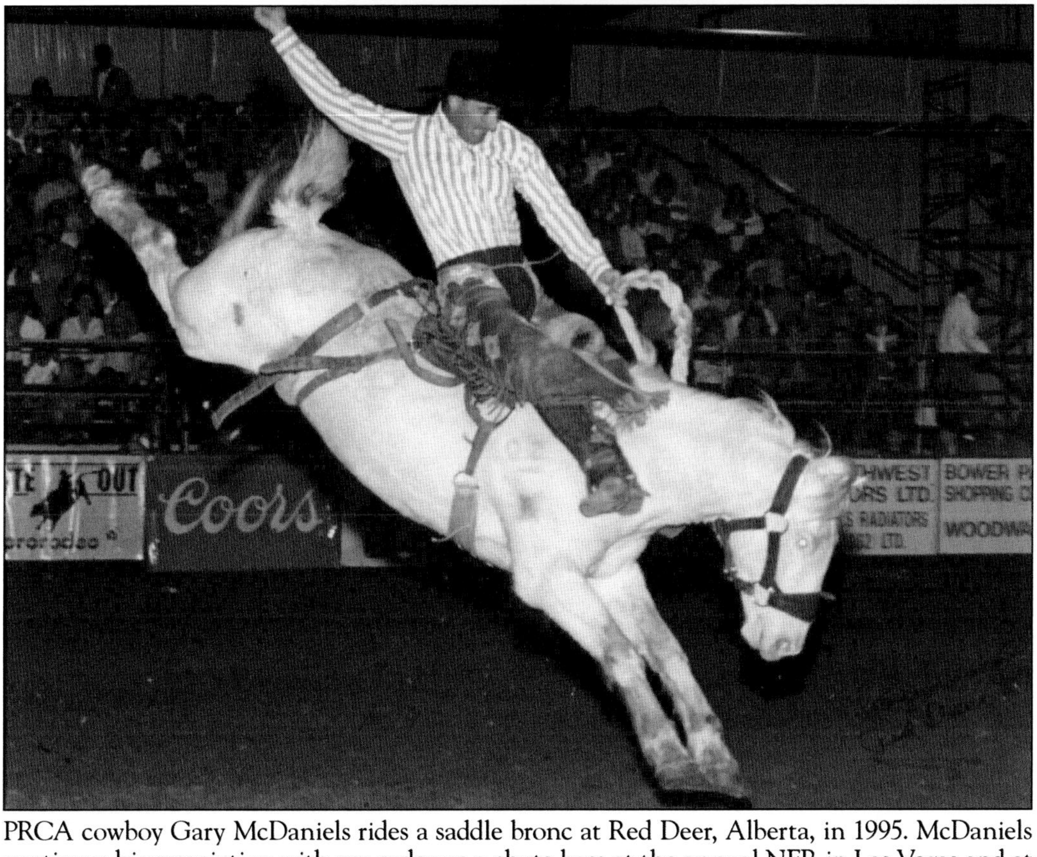

PRCA cowboy Gary McDaniels rides a saddle bronc at Red Deer, Alberta, in 1995. McDaniels continues his association with pro rodeo as a chute boss at the annual NFR in Las Vegas and at other major rodeos. He is a rancher and Garza County commissioner.

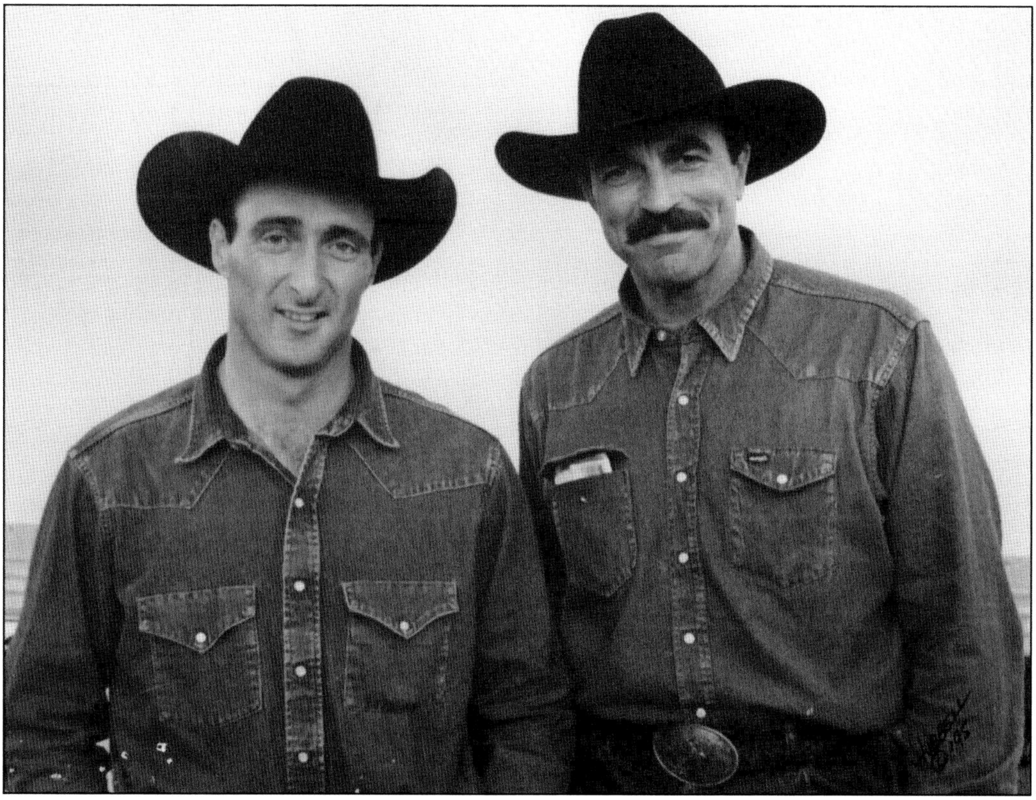

Pictured above, Gary McDaniels (left) poses with Tom Selleck in 1996. McDaniels was Selleck's stunt double for the bronc riding scenes in the movie *Ruby Jean and Joe*. Selleck played fading rodeo performer Joe Wade, and costar Rebekah Johnson was a young hitchhiker named Ruby Jean.

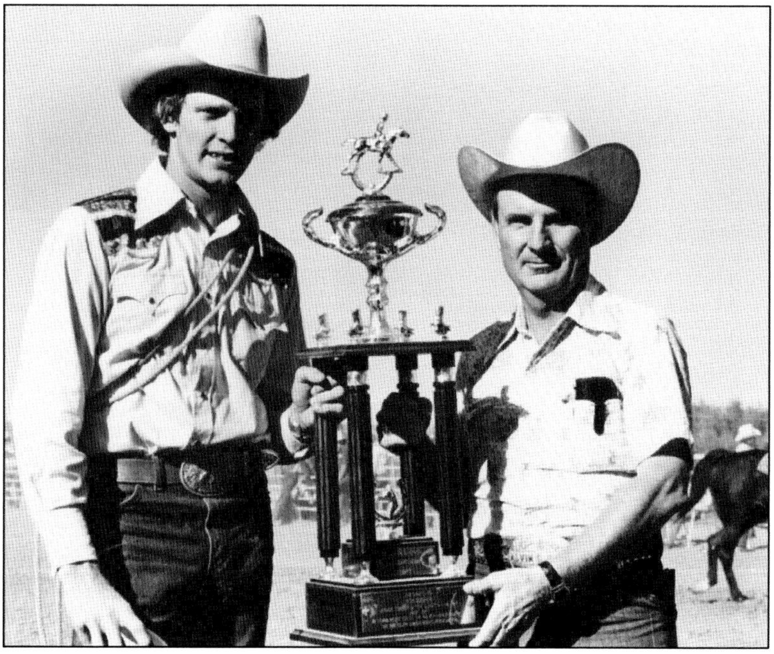

Roper Roy Cooper (left) receives the Silver Award from the American Junior Rodeo Association (AJRA) from AJRA founder, Alvin G. Davis. The presentation was made during the OS Ranch Roping and Art Show. Cooper went on to win eight world championships. Davis has spent a lifetime promoting and preserving the life of the American cowboy. Both gentlemen are true living legends.

Ten

One Hundred Years and Counting

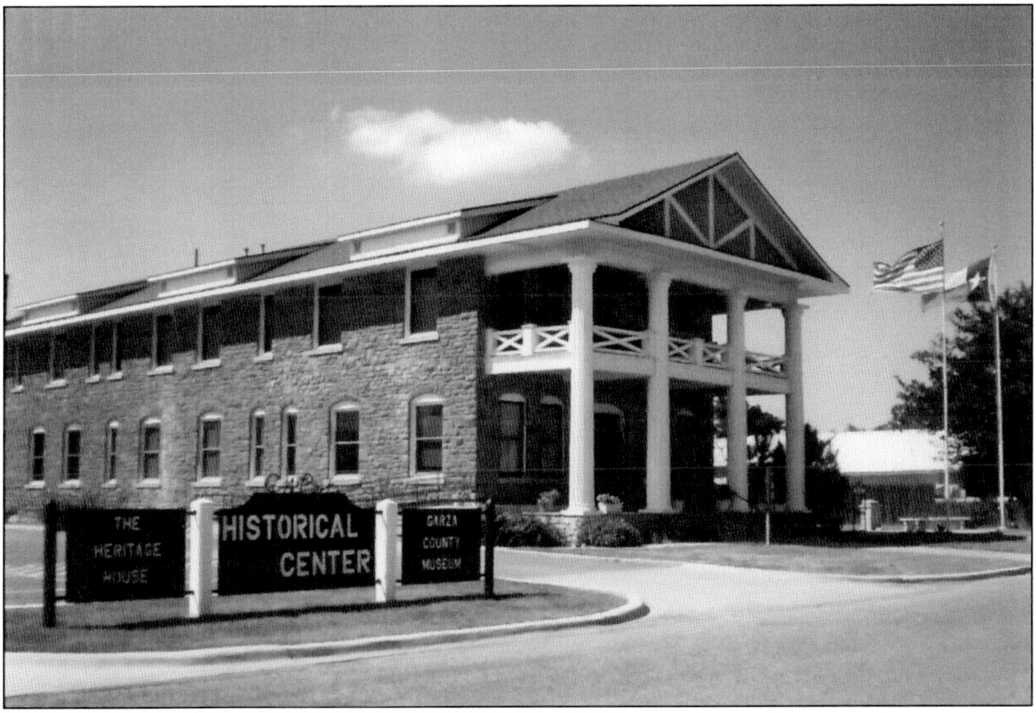

The Garza County Historical Museum collection, a conservatory for the history of Garza County, is housed in this historic 1912 property, donated by the Mason families to Garza County for use as a museum. The facility and the Heritage House next door, formerly the Post Sanitarium dormitory for doctors and nurses, are located in the recently designated C. W. Post Historical Center, at 119 North Avenue N in Post.

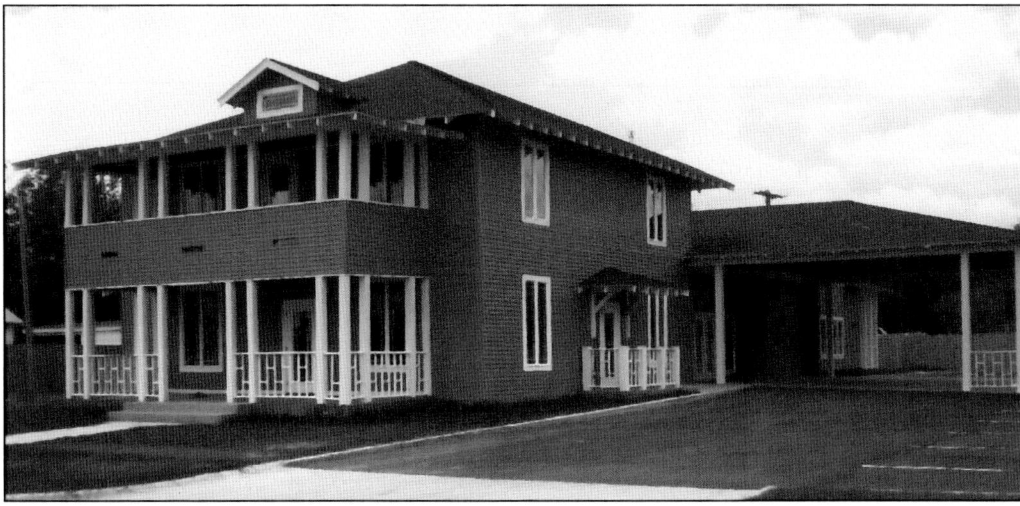

The Heritage House is the new incarnation of the old Post Sanitarium dormitory. A Post native son, Don Collier, an architectural design professor, raised about $750,000 to remodel and completely outfit the old building with period furnishings. A beautiful place, it is now used for social events, weddings, and meetings.

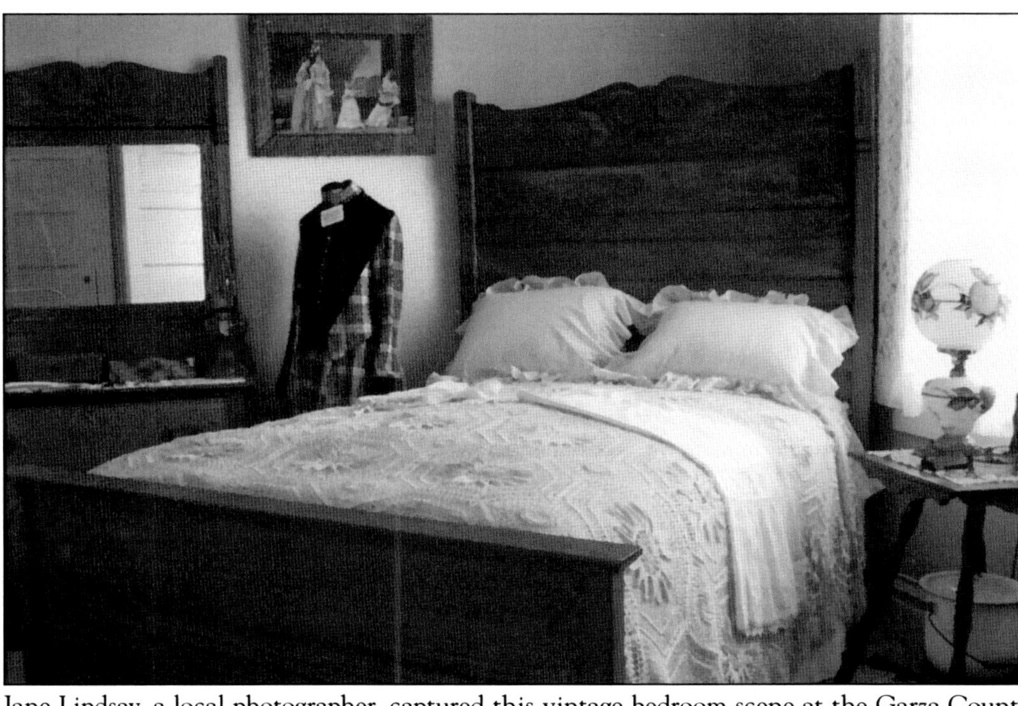

Jane Lindsay, a local photographer, captured this vintage bedroom scene at the Garza County Historical Museum. A chamber pot rests on the nightstand shelf, and a beautiful crocheted spread covers the 1890s bed. (Courtesy Jane Lindsay.)

Alvin G. Davis was born in Post, Texas, in 1927. He founded the American Junior Rodeo Association in 1952 and the National Cowboy Symposium in Lubbock in 1989. Davis was inducted into the Rodeo Hall of Fame in 2009. Davis has received many honors over the years, but his finest is his wife, Barbara, the 1953 Texas Tech Rodeo Queen. On the old door behind Davis are the earliest photographs of the American Junior Rodeo Association.

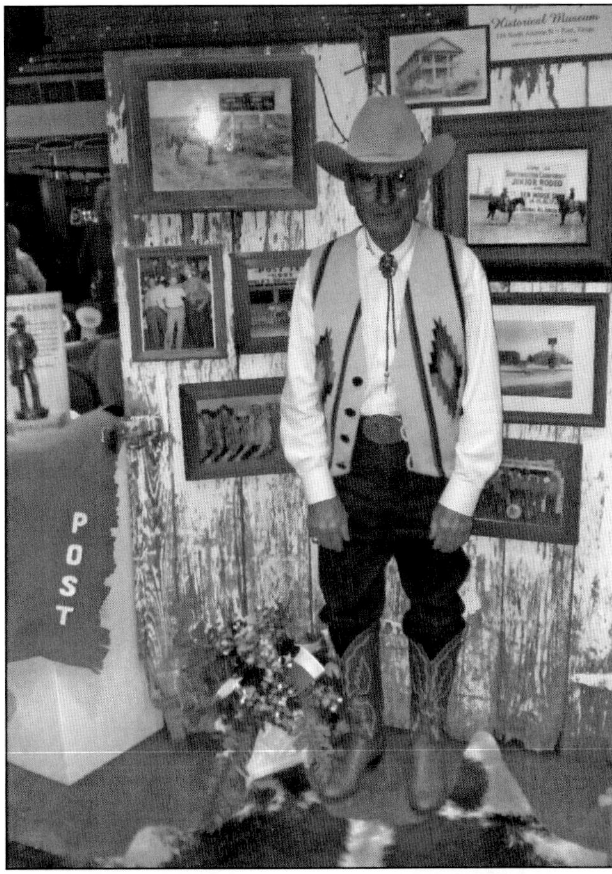

Pat Cruse, assistant director of the Garza County Historical Museum, stands by the exhibit she created for Black History Month. A baptismal scene print hangs against a handwoven African rug. Cruse is a collector of All God's Children® figurines. On the tabletop are figures of Harriett Tubman (left) and Sojourner Truth. Truth is buried in Battle Creek, Michigan, near the tomb of C. W. Post.

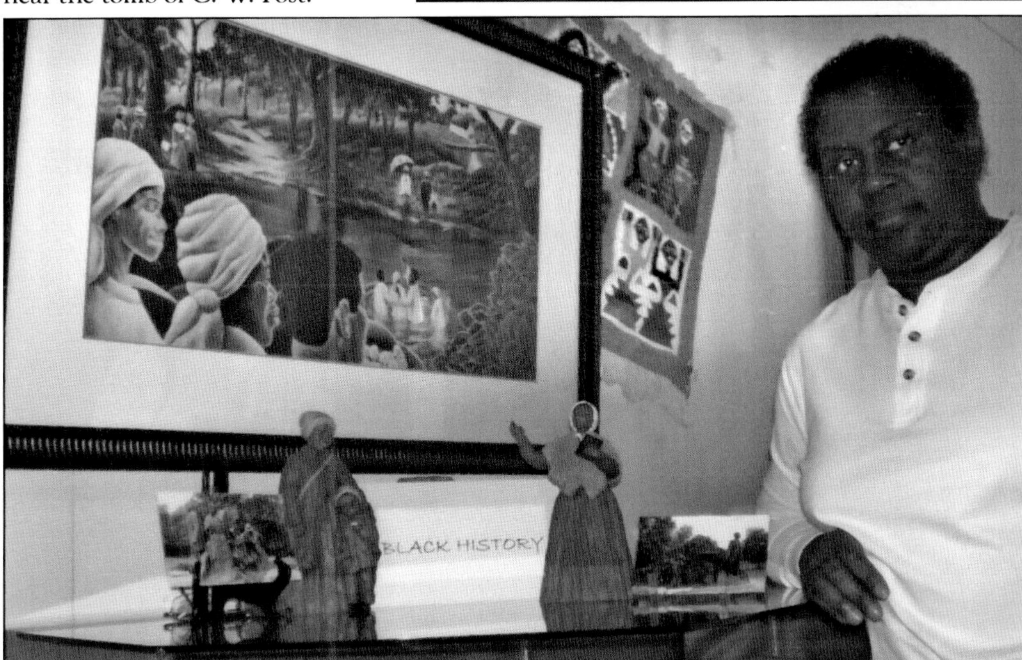

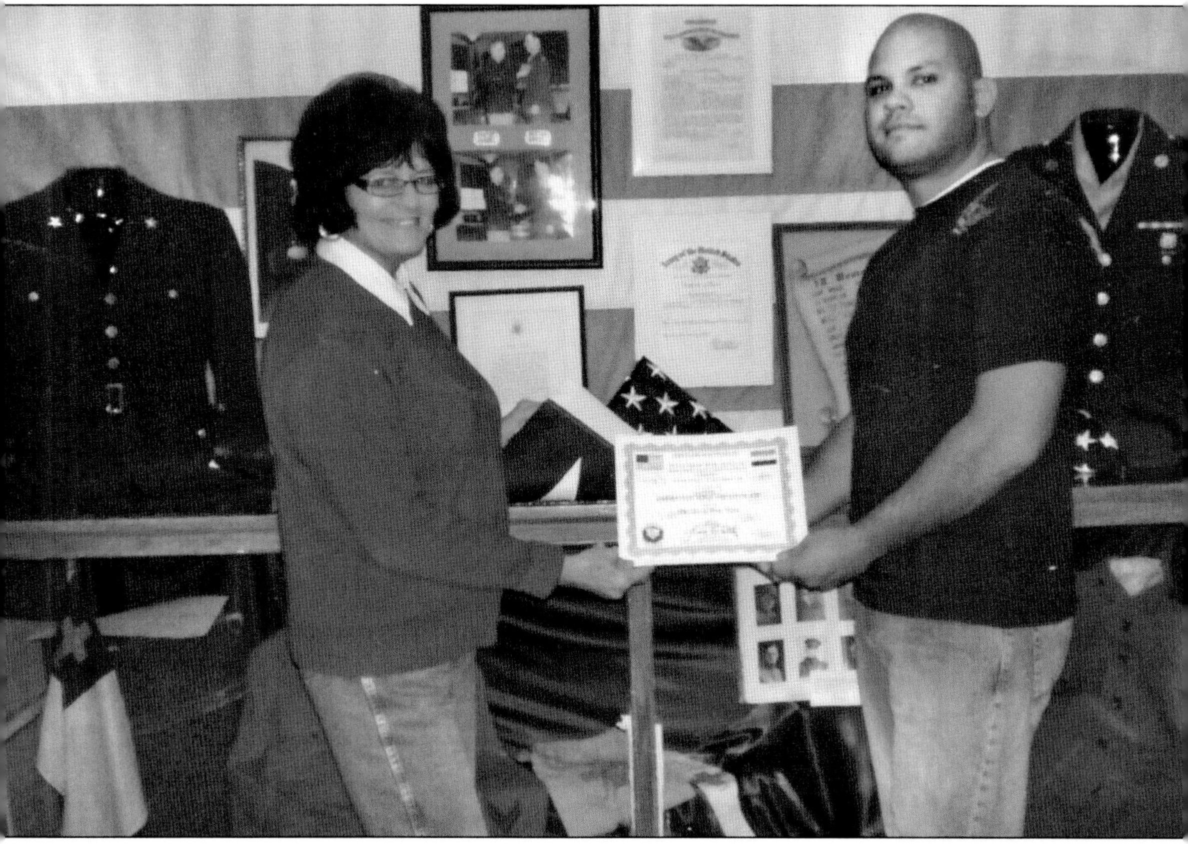

Linda Puckett (left) and U.S. Marine staff sergeant Orlando Castillo, home on leave, present the museum with a Texas state flag and an American flag that flew over Al Asad Airbase in Iraq during Operation Iraqi Freedom. Castillo was to redeploy to Afghanistan in February 2010. He was born in Post and still remembers his Kids N Art teacher. Puckett is honored to have served as director of the Garza County Historical Museum since 1995. On behalf of Garza County, she invites history buffs to visit the museum, consisting of 26 exhibit rooms that tell many stories of life of the pioneer families, military, ranching, farming, oil, archeology, and more. The museum welcomes those doing research and is always willing to assist. Business hours are Tuesday through Saturday from 10:00 a.m. to 5:00 p.m. The museum can be reached by telephone at (806) 495-2207 or by e-mail at garzamuseum@yahoo.com.

Bibliography

Didway, Charles, ed. *Wagon Wheels: A History of Garza County*. Seagraves, TX: Pioneer, 1973.

Dudley, Charles and C. A. Eaves Hutchinson. *Post City, Texas: C. W. Post's Colonizing Activities in West Texas*. Denton, TX: Texas State Historical Association, 1952.

"Garza County Historical Courthouse Master Plan." Parkhill, Smith, and Cooper, Inc., 2000.

Women's Division of Post Chamber of Commerce. *Foot Prints: A History of Garza County and Its People*. Post, TX: Taylor, 1976.